THE ILLUSTRATED HISTORY OF

MAGIC
& WITCHCRAFT

THE ILLUSTRATED HISTORY OF
MAGIC
& WITCHCRAFT

A STUDY OF PAGAN BELIEF AND PRACTICE AROUND THE WORLD, FROM THE FIRST
SHAMANS TO MODERN WITCHES AND WIZARDS, IN 530 EVOCATIVE IMAGES

SUSAN GREENWOOD

LORENZ BOOKS

This edition is published by Lorenz Books,
an imprint of Anness Publishing Ltd,
Blaby Road, Wigston,
Leicestershire LE18 4SE

Email: info@anness.com

Web: www.lorenzbooks.com;
www.annesspublishing.com

Anness Publishing has a new picture
agency outlet for images for publishing,
promotions or advertising. Please visit our
website www.practicalpictures.com for
more information.

Publisher: Joanna Lorenz
Editorial Director: Helen Sudell
Senior Editor: Joanne Rippin
Typesetter: Diane Pullen
Picture Researcher: Veneta Bullen
Designer: Lesley Betts
Editorial Reader: Jonathan Marshall
Production Controller: Steve Lang

ETHICAL TRADING POLICY
Because of our ongoing ecological investment
programme, you, as our customer, can have
the pleasure and reassurance of knowing that
a tree is being cultivated on your behalf to
naturally replace the materials used to make
the book you are holding. For further
information about this scheme, go to
www.annesspublishing.com/trees

A CIP catalogue record for this book is
available from the British Library.

Previously published as
The Encyclopedia of Magic & Witchcraft

PUBLISHER'S NOTE
Although the advice and information in this
book are believed to be accurate and true at
the time of going to press, neither the authors
nor the publisher can accept any legal
responsibility or liability for any errors or
omissions that may have been made.

CONTENTS

INTRODUCTION

Our earliest forebears would have possessed an intimate knowledge of the features of the world around them: the rising and setting of the sun, the movement of the moon through the sky, the changing seasons and minute details about plants and animals. They depended on this knowledge for their survival – as a matter of life or death. We do not know the answers to questions about the early beliefs of humanity. All we can do is examine the evidence left in cultural artifacts, such as cave rock paintings, to imagine what life would have been like, and then make educated guesses. Probably the first forms of spirituality arose through human interaction within the social group and with relationships with the wider surroundings; perhaps rituals were performed to find the whereabouts of animals to hunt or to heal a sick person. We can imagine that rites may have developed out of sharing the wonder at the birth of a child, or expressing grief in the face of death.

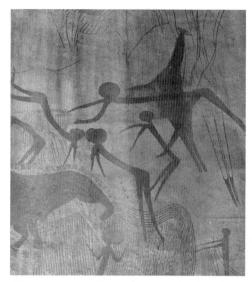

Shamanic or magic trances are depicted in these Palaeolithic rock paintings from Tanzania.

Modern human beings, or *Homo sapiens*, were not the first hominids to have complex social groups: the Neanderthals were also a sophisticated parallel species, which buried their dead with flowers, decorations or grave goods, possibly in readiness for a next life. What we both share is the ability to create order out of our experiences. Our large brains are able to question, experiment and search for answers to essential questions about life and death. The ability to question, to reflect, to represent experiences symbolically – in cave art and in language – is part of a process of creating meaning. Spiritual beliefs, religion and magic all play a part in this process.

Spirituality for early humans was probably associated with keeping a social group or band together, curing the sick and controlling the natural world. It concerned much that we would describe as magical today. Only later did it come to be formalized with sacred texts and called religion. However, magic and religion are categories that are difficult to maintain, and for most of human history, and across the world in varying cultures, there is no absolute separation.

In the following pages we will look at the rich variety of magico-religious beliefs around the world. We will explore how different cultures, varying in both place and time, have created meaning through worlds of spirits. Starting with what has been termed shamanism, humanity's oldest spiritual practice, we will see that although it has occurred in many different places there is an underlying essence that involves specialist communication with spirits.

The earliest human civilizations used magic and religion to explain natural manifestations.

Through undertaking a trance journey to the spirit realms, a shaman attempts to resolve some difficulty or dilemma in the human domain. It can be said that shamanism is the basis of all forms of spirituality.

Belief in a spiritual realm is also the foundation of ideas about witchcraft – witches inhabit a universe in which powers and forces may be directed for good or ill. Definitions of witchcraft, like those of magic and religion, change from society to society and through the passage of time. What is called witchcraft in Africa is very different to that of European societies.

As the chapters of this book unfold, the fascinating variety of differences will become apparent. We will meet the Azande of central Africa to see how life is ordered through ideas about witchcraft and divination, and how oracles are used to determine important events. In Europe we will see how the Christian Church played a central part in the creation of the stereotype of the evil witch, and how ordinary women, and to a lesser extent men, were tried and executed as witches during the period 1450–1750. More recently, witchcraft

Birth, rites of passage, marriage and death have been marked throughout history by all cultures. Here, a funeral ceremony is taking place in the village of Pa Bu, Thailand.

has gained a new following for many people who look back to the past to create a pagan system of beliefs. Magic is currently undergoing a revival in the West, and more and more people are turning to alternative magico-religious traditions such as Druidry, the New Age, Western forms of shamanism, Heathenism, and Chaos Magic as ways of creating meaning and of expressing their spiritual lives. This book aims to act as a guide on a journey through the different ways of seeing and understanding the world.

An Indian priest performs a ceremony to capture spirits, which has its roots in prehistory.

Modern pagans in Europe celebrate rituals that mark the passing of the seasons, with symbolism and practices that they claim go back to the days before Christianity.

MAGIC IN MYTH, RELIGION AND SCIENCE

Throughout the world, human beings have engaged in a multitude of beliefs and practices to express, explain and give meaning to the cosmos. In the past magic and religion and also science, which often overlaps the two, are categories that have been difficult to distinguish between, but today we tend to see magic and religion as entirely different from each other. Although sometimes dismissed as merely fantasy, magic is also sometimes seen as manipulation of the divine, even to the extent of being evil. Religion, on the other hand is regarded as involving the worship of an essentially good diety. Through history, the word magic has been a term of abuse for what is thought to be antisocial and immoral forms of spirituality; it has become a scapegoat for everything that an established religion disapproves of. This chapter will explore the differences and similarities between the way creation mythologies, religious beliefs, scientific endeavour, and magical practices are linked.

WHAT IS MAGIC?

The dictionary definition of magic is that it is the art of using spells to invoke supernatural powers to influence events. This is a very general description and it is important to consider in greater detail what these supernatural powers are and which events are to be influenced. This book advocates that magic is a word that describes the inner nature of the beings that make up the universe – the spiritual part of all things. The spirit forms a hidden dimension to the ordinary, everyday world that we inhabit. Most of the time we are unaware of it (hence magic often being called "the occult" – literally "concealed") and when something uncanny happens, we tend to put it down to coincidence. What we call coincidence today would be interpreted very differently by people of cultures other than our own, or by people from varying times in the past. Unfortunately, magic is often used as a derogatory term used to encompass all that orthodox religion disapproves of or prohibits and is therefore frequently viewed in negative terms.

To many peoples throughout the world there are spirits in nature.

Stop for a moment and imagine what it would be like to live in the world of our ancestors, where everything was perceived as alive and permeated with vibrant force and energy, both good and bad. This included not only mountains, rocks, rivers, oceans, plants, algae, fungi and insects, but also human ailments, such as toothache or the common cold. How differently would we perceive the world around us? Would we feel linked to everything – from the chair we sit in to the trees in the fields, the sun, moon and stars? Spirits were part of everyday life for our ancestors and it is likely that these ancestors performed rituals to create meaning, balance and a feeling of connection between them and the spirit world. These ceremonies would have integrated the group and the cosmos into the world, providing security on physical, psychological and social levels. This spirit world that co-exists with the physical world could be called a "magical" world. Today's focus in the Western world on rationality and the development of a view of science that does not take spirits into account has meant that this magical connection between humankind and the spirit world has been lost.

In many cultures around the world, the everyday world co-exists and overlaps with a spirit dimension. Living in touch with spirits can bring anxiety. The way in which spirits are manipulated can be a constant source of speculation and concern in such societies, and problems such as illness, death or misfortune are frequently put down to witchcraft or sorcery. When people practise magic they attempt to control, communicate or influence spirits. Magical specialists explore, modify or move the borders between the ordinary world and the spirit

The importance of the sun to human life has given it a special place in many belief systems around the world.

The highest mountains were often seen as the kingdom of the gods; their inaccessibility and their nearness to heaven ensured their special status.

world – the known and the unknown. These technicians of magic, who may be called shamans, sorcerers, magicians, witches, witch doctors or medicine men and women, all share a relationship with the spiritual realm.

Magic involves an animistic world-view. Anima means "the soul", the innermost part or essence of a being and its animating principle. Animism is the belief that the world is profoundly alive and that all natural objects and phenomena – the trees and rocks, wind, rain, snow, birds, insects and fish, as well as humans – are alive and have vital essence; everything that exists lives and has consciousness. The consciousness of spirits can merge into human consciousness, and the soul of a living human is believed to become spirit when it dies, dead people becoming either ancestor spirits or part of a larger elemental spirit. For the Native Americans, each wind is the breath of some being that lives in the direction from which the wind blows. The wind talks with the voice of its spirit as it roars, moans, sighs or whistles.

The nineteenth-century anthropologist Edward Tylor (1832–1917) claimed that the origins of religion lay in animism, which he defined as a "belief in spirit beings". Tylor saw the origin of religion in individual psychology. He thought that in primitive humans the idea of religion arose from the notion of a soul which came from dreams. The soul was transformed into a spirit being after death, leading to the development of ancestor and spirit cults.

Tylor was an evolutionary thinker: he reflected the ideas of his time by seeing animism as a lower form of religion than polytheism (a belief in many gods) and monotheism (a belief in one creator god). He saw a natural progression from animism through polytheism to monotheism, with Christianity as a higher revealed religion that is characterized by intercessionary worship and prayer.

SACRED GEOGRAPHY

The ancient native religions of Central and South America – including the Aztecs, the Maya and the Inca – had elaborate rituals that linked the people

and the land in a sacred relationship. The Mayans conceived the earth as a square – flat and four-cornered – with an elaborate colour symbolism that placed red in the east, white in the north, black in the west, yellow in the south, and green in the centre. This pattern formed the back of a monstrous crocodile that lurked in a pool of waterlilies. For the Mayans the sky was multi-tiered, supported on the four corners by gods, and formed a double-headed serpent; the 13 layers of the heavens had their own gods. The underworld had nine layers and the sun and the moon passed through it after they had disappeared below the horizon.

For the Inca a supreme creator called Viracocha, a white-bearded god who created the sun, moon and stars after a flood that destroyed the world, was a controller of the various spheres of the cosmos. Inca religion emphasized harmony with the land and the ceremonial at Cuzco (which means navel in Quechua, the Incan language) integrated the life of the people with the wider cosmos.

SHAMANISM

Human beings have often turned to a spirit world for help and advice in times of trouble. In early groups of people it is likely that a shaman would have undertaken trance journeys to mediate between the human and the spirit worlds; it was the shaman who perhaps helped to resolve problems as to why someone was ill, or to find out why the animals had not returned from a particular migration and there was nothing to hunt. Even today in small-scale societies – from Siberia to the Amazonian region to Africa – shamanism is still practised, albeit under increasingly difficult conditions.

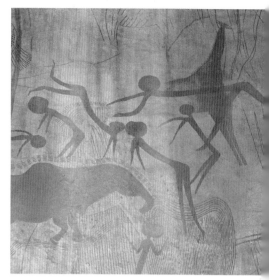

A *Stone Age rock painting that records a shamanic trance, known as simbo, in which dancers somersault above hallucinated animals.*

PREHISTORIC SHAMANS

The discovery of prehistoric cave paintings around the world has led to many speculations that the earliest people to practise magic were shamans. These cave paintings may represent the shaman linking the spirit world to the real world – for example, by painting scenes of certain wounded or dead animals, he was communicating his wish for a successful hunt.

Some cave paintings are 30,000 years old, others may be older, while some are much more recent. Rock art has been found throughout the world – in Africa, Australia, Europe and South America. Made with flint blades and coloured with iron ochre or black manganese dioxide, the paintings are detailed and delicate portrayals of prey animals such as wild cattle, mammoths, deer, horses and bison and, more rarely, predator species such as lion, wolf and bear. Some of these paintings show hunting scenes with animals carrying spear-inflicted wounds or dead carcasses; representations of human beings are much less common.

What did these paintings mean for the people who created them? We will never know for sure, but we do know that the peoples who painted them were culturally sophisticated and that the paintings in all probability contributed to relationships of reciprocity between humans in their everyday social inter-actions, and between humans and animals. What made modern human beings so successful was the ability to create a web of social alliances in kinship links and trading associations, as well as passing on information about animals to hunt. People thought about the animals that they hunted. The visual images of the animals may have involved a form of sympathetic magic whereby a hunter, or a group of hunters, in a state of altered consciousness or trance, would dance the animal that they wanted to capture, creating a powerful link between themselves and their prey.

Art may have had a part in creating and maintaining these links. It seems likely that it had a role to play in rituals to communicate clan or tribal values and important information regarding adulthood – perhaps the secrets of menstruation or hunting techniques.

A *shaman of the Huli tribe from Papua New Guinea stands at an altar in a sacred place that is decorated with painted skulls.*

A LIFE OF SPIRIT

Sometimes it is helpful to look at contemporary modern humans who have gathering and hunting lifestyles to gain some sort of idea about what the spiritual beliefs of our ancestors might have been. Modern hunter-gatherers, such as the !Kung of the Kalahari Desert in southern Africa, practised a semi-nomadic lifestyle until comparatively recently. According to anthropologist Richard Katz, there was much emphasis on sharing, and all resources were circulated among band members, and also between bands. Neither was religion a separate enterprise for the !Kung – the life of the spirit was an inextricable aspect of everyday life. The god Gao Na sent good and bad fortune through the spirits and to Kauha, a lesser god, and Gao Na was human in his follies and pleasures. The gods lived in the sky and were attended by the spirits

A Siberian shaman at a sacred site, wearing clothes that are made from animal hides.

of the dead; they were god-like in their powers but were a part of everyday life as well as being apart from it.

The !Kung practised healing dances, which they performed at night. These dances were an integrating and enhancing force central to group solidarity. The dances may have cured an ill person by "pulling out" a sickness, but the healing was also synergistic – bringing people together and thereby creating a whole society from separate individuals.

!Kung healers are what we might call shamans and they were able to see what was troubling everyone. By getting into a trance they could 'see' inside people's bodies, or travel to the realm where the gods and the spirits of dead ancestors lived. A struggle would ensue between the spirits of the dead and the healer, who would attempt to bring back the soul of a sick person to the realm of the living.

Men and women of the San "Bushman" Tribe from the Kalahari, Botswana, dancing a traditional dance at night.

THE SHAMAN'S ROLE

The historian Mircea Eliade defined a shaman as a man or woman who "journeys" in an ecstatic trance, usually induced by rhythmic drumming or, in some cases, by the use of psychoactive drugs. In its widest sense a shaman is someone who has specialist techniques for communicating with spirits through entering a trance or alternative state of consciousness. It is the shaman's task to make sure that relationships between the human world and the spirit world are kept harmonious.

A shaman is often "called" by the spirits. He or she is one who is set apart from others by a special sign such as being born with a caul (the membrane that encloses the fetus in the womb), a deformity or a tendency to be dreamy, or through some life crisis such as serious disease or mental breakdown. A shaman's initiation usually takes the form of a psycho-spiritual disintegration, which leads to a death of the former self and a rebirth into a shamanic life with the spirits.

Shamanic initiation involves visiting the underworld, a place where the initiate shaman has to undergo dismemberment. The initiate has to "die" in everyday reality and enter a special relationship with spirit beings, a process whereby knowledge and teachings about the spirit world are communicated.

Petroglyphs on a sandstone slab in Johns Canyon, Cedar Mesa. The triangular figure is thought to be a bird shaman, illustrating the belief that a shaman could take on the characteristics of a chosen animal.

Eliade tells of how each Yakut Siberian shaman has a Bird-of-Prey Mother with an iron beak, hooked claws and a long tail. This mythical bird, which shows itself only at the shaman's spiritual birth and death, takes his soul and carries it to the underworld, where it is left to ripen on a branch of pitch pine. When the soul has reached maturity the bird carries it back to earth, cuts the candidate's body into bits and distributes them among the evil spirits of disease and death. Each spirit devours the part of the body that is his share, and this is seen to give the future shaman power to cure corresponding diseases. After devouring the whole body, the evil spirits depart, the Bird Mother restores the bones to their places, and the candidate wakes as from a deep sleep.

JOURNEYING BETWEEN WORLDS

Shamanic cosmologies are frequently formed from three regions: a middle world corresponding to the everyday world on earth, an upper world related to the sky and celestial realms, and a lower or underworld, which reaches deep down into the earth. These three regions are often connected by a central axis – an opening through which the shaman travels on his

An Inuit carving showing a shaman in a trance, helped by two animal spirits and a drum.

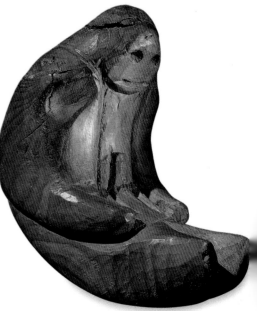

An Inuit carving representing a shaman associated with a spirit called Taqhisim.

or her journey, which may be represented as a tree. The tree connects the three regions – the branches touch the sky, while the roots go into the underworld. The axis may also be likened to a pillar or a mountain, but all the variations of shamanic cosmologies function like spiritual road maps.

When a shaman journeys to spiritual realms, she or he seeks to understand the relationships between different realities and to mediate any breakdown in communications that affect the social group. Knud Rasmussen, an authority on Inuit (Eskimo) shamans, describes how the shaman makes a journey to the bottom of the sea to find out why the sea spirit is withholding animals for the Inuit people to hunt. As the shaman journeys, the household sits waiting and singing songs to help the shaman as he descends on his perilous journey. After overcoming many obstacles, he enters the house of the sea spirit. She sits with her back to the seals, walrus and whales, who are puffing and blowing. The sea spirit is angry with humans because they have broken taboos. Her hair hangs down in a tangled, untidy mess hiding her eyes so she cannot see. Human

An important element of shamanic belief was the link that the shaman had with the animal world. It was thought that while in a trance, a shaman could become one with the spirit of an animal such as a wolf, and benefit from its wisdom.

misdeeds and offenses gather as dirt and impurity over her body. The shaman must turn the sea spirit's face to the animals and comb her hair to appease her anger so that she will clear the way for the animals and rich hunting will return. When the shaman returns to the community the breaches of taboo must be confessed so that harmony between the human and spirit worlds can return. In this way the shaman heals discord within the social group.

A Tibetan shaman wearing a special "ringer" hat, which for centuries has been worn for aiding trances.

A modern day shaman from Kenya, wearing a ceremonial headress.

MAGIC AND RELIGION

Although most religions differentiate themselves clearly from magic, what is meant by "magic" and "religion" changes over time. When we look at spiritual beliefs and behaviour cross-culturally and at different periods in time, it is almost impossible to make clear demarcations between what is magic and what is religion. It is likely that our earliest human ancestors practised what we would now call magic, and only later did spiritual beliefs and practices become more formalized and written down to found the basis of what we refer to as religion today, such as Hinduism, Buddhism, Judaism, Christianity and Islam. In the pages that follow we will look at the cultures of antiquity: those of the Egyptians, Greeks, Romans, Celts and North European peoples. We will also study the ideas of India, Africa and Australia, and then explore the relationship between science and magic, and the role that astrology and alchemy have played in the development of Western thought.

A bronze portal in San Zeno Cathedral, Verona, showing a magical battle between Israel and Egypt. Aaron's staff is being transformed into a serpent and is attacking an Egyptian.

Most cultures have, or have had in their past, some form of magical tradition that recognizes a shamanistic interconnectedness of spirit. This may have been long ago, as a folk tradition that died out with the establishment of a major world religion, such as Judaism, Christianity, Islam or Buddhism, or it may still co-exist with that world religion. Some small societies still retain the remnants of shamanistic practices, such as in Siberia, India or Africa, although because of the pressures of the modern world they are becoming fewer. Many, such as the Native Americans and Native Australians, have been persecuted by European settlers, who have taken their land and annihilated their people. For these peoples, "magic" is an integral aspect of their culture, and one that has survived persecution, and it cannot be neatly separated from religion. However, magic to Westerners became associated with "primitive" peoples who were represented as uncivilized natives with exotic and strange customs.

CONTROLLING HIDDEN FORCES

Magic is similar to religion in its focus on the spiritual dimension and the worship of a supernatural authority, but it differs in its attempt to control hidden forces. It may include an aspect of worship but it is also associated with the coercion and command of hidden (occult) or spiritual forces. This control may be achieved through divination, spells or the making of amulets.

Divination is the art and practice of discovering the past or the future by spirit communication. Spells are all-powerful spoken formulae, words or phrases, which provoke a desired chain of events: these may be destructive, protective or medicinal, or may be used to break other spells or to obtain something, such as love or money. Amulets are protective charms that are worn to ward off evil.

This nineteenth-cenury picture of a medicine mask dance shows how native peoples have been portrayed as an "exotic other", having more to do with Westerner's ideas about Indians rather than the actual reality of their lives.

THE ORIGINS OF MAGIC

The word "magic" comes from the Greek *mageia*, which derives from *magoi*. The *magoi* were a Persian caste of priests who studied astrology and divination. During the Hellenistic period the new words *mageuein* and *magikos* took on a negative meaning. This negative view of magic was adopted by the Romans. Their officials and intellectuals pointed to its fraudulent character, seeing it as a mixture of medicine, astrology and religion. Practitioners of magic during this period made a distinction between lower (*goetia*) and higher (*theourgia*) forms. In practice, the division between lower and higher magic is flexible and, like the distinction between magic and religion, it tends to vary from place to place and from society to society. There are no hard and fast rules, and what may be termed bad and associated with the manipulation of spirits in one setting may be deemed positively beneficial in another.

Divination is the art of discovering the past or the future. Here, in a fresco painting from Pompeii, a Roman traveller consults a sorceress.

FROM SHAMAN TO PRIEST

Originally, in the earliest human societies, it was the shaman who took on the specific role of mediator between the everyday world and the spiritual dimensions, although the rest of the community was also involved in the process. Increasingly, as societies became larger and more complex, religious specialists took over this task. This created a more distinct specialist area, which later came to be governed by the interpretation of religious texts such as the Bible or the *Koran*. Spontaneous trance or possession by spirits began to be viewed as unorthodox practice and was relegated to marginal cults.

THE USE OF RITUAL

Both magic and religion often depend on ritual to maintain cosmic order, either through communication with a variety of sentient beings or through the worship of a divine creator god. Ritual creates a "space between the worlds" for communication with otherworldly beings or supernatural powers.

Rituals demarcate the ordinary from the extraordinary; they focus attention on cosmic processes, and thus often help maintain social solidarity and identity. This helps to define common values and affiliations and marks out those who contravene social rules. So the distinction between magic and religion often depends on the approval and disapproval of different kinds of spiritual practice. Magical elements exist in most religions, and most religions have their roots in some form of shamanic practice.

Fresco from Tepantitla Teotihuacan, Mexico, of an Aztec priest praying.

Three Nepalese shamans, known as Jhankaris, wear traditional clothes and perform an all-night ceremony for a boy with abdominal pains.

Egyptian Magic

Both magic and religion depend on ritual to maintain cosmic order. The power of magico-religious names, spells, pictures, figures, amulets and the performance of rituals, which were seen to produce supernatural results, formed an important part of early Egyptian life. What ancient Egyptians believed to be their religion is today more commonly referred to as magical practice. Egyptian magic dates from a time when the predynastic and prehistoric inhabitants of Egypt believed that the earth, the underworld, the air and the sky were populated by countless beings, some of whom affirmed life and were friendly, while others caused death and destruction. The magical basis of early Egyptian thought is shown through its creation myths.

For early Egyptians, all life orginated from the waters of the Nile. Egyptian myth tells how a hill called Atum, "the Complete One", rose up out of the primordial waters of the abyss at the first

The River Nile in the mystical evening light.

The air god Shu is here depicted separating the sky goddess Nut from the earth god Geb. Detail from the coffin of Nespawershepi, chief scribe of the Temple of Amun c.984 BC.

time of light. Every day this was repeated in the birth of the sun from the abyss of the night, and also every year when the waters of the Nile flooded the surrounding land, bringing it to life. Atum, the risen land and light, generated the male Shu and the female Tefnut who gave birth to Nut (the sky goddess who gave birth to the stars) and to Geb (the earth god).

ISIS AND OSIRIS

Nut and Geb gave birth to Osiris and to Isis, and their brother Seth and sister, Nephthys. Osiris became the first king of Egypt and the creator of civilization, and his sister-wife Isis ruled in his absence. However, their brother Seth was jealous and conspired to kill Osiris. He constructed a chest and tricked Osiris into lying inside it, whereupon the lid was nailed shut and it was thrown into the Nile. The chest floated to the coast of Byblos and lodged itself in the branches of a tree, which grew up around it and enclosed it. The tree was so beautiful that the king and queen of Byblos had it made into a pillar for their palace.

Isis was stricken with grief and started to search for the chest. Disguising her divinity, she waited by a well in the city of Byblos. She befriended some of Queen Astarte's maidens and braided and perfumed their hair. When the maidens returned to the palace the queen sent for the person who had created such a wonderful fragrance, and made her the nurse to her child. Isis gave the child her finger to suck instead of her breast, and each night placed him in a fire to remove all his mortality. Meanwhile, she transformed herself into a swallow and flew around the pillar. One night the queen entered the room and was horrified to see her son lying in the fire. At this, Isis revealed her true identity and asked to be given the pillar. The king and queen agreed.

Taking the chest containing the body of Osiris, Isis set out for Egypt. While she was in the boat she took the form of a kite, hovered over her husband, and conceived their son Horus. Then she hid the chest and went to Buto to raise her child. However, Seth discovered the chest one night while he was out hunting; he tore the body into 14 pieces and scattered them around the country. When Isis discovered what Seth had done she searched for the pieces, aided by their sister Nephthys and her son, the jackal-headed Anubis. Isis found every part of Osiris's body except his penis, for which she made a replica. When she fanned the reassembled body with her wings Osiris came to life again, to become the ruler of Eternity judging the souls of the dead.

COSMIC UNITY

This myth shows the interconnections between the human world, the realm of the gods and nature. Osiris dies with the parched land, the withering grain, the waning moon and all that is destructive. He returns to life in the rising waters of the Nile, the growing grain, the waxing moon and the affirmative nature of human beings. Osiris is brought to life by Isis. The creative force of Osiris, as the flooding of the Nile, and Isis, as the earth, is interrupted by the necessary element of death and destruction, represented by Seth: from death comes life, and in life there is death. Both are part of the same cosmic unity. This primal Egyptian myth demonstrates the human connection with both the natural world and the spiritual realm of the gods; all are interlinked in the magical processes of life and death.

A wall painting of Osiris c.1300 BC from Sennutem's tomb, Thebes.

The cyclical nature of Egyptian mythology is shown here by the goddess Nut swallowing the sun at night to give birth to it again the following morning. The wall painting is from the ceiling of the tomb of Ramses VI in the Valley of the Kings.

GRAECO-ROMAN MAGIC

Greek religion originally consisted of simple rituals, later developing into complex systems of science and philosophy. It shifted from the veneration of local deities, in the forms of satyrs, shades, furies, nymphs, sibyls and muses, to the worship of an Olympian pantheon, headed by the god Zeus and his consort, the goddess Hera. Magic was a central part of this early Graeco-Roman culture.

ORACULAR MAGIC

Within the Graeco-Roman world, magic formed a common tradition and although each cultural region had its own specialization, there was an enormous amount of overlap and similarity; an abundance of material on magic was brought together and combined in

A detail from a vase painting of Aegeus, King of Athens, consulting the Delphic Oracle.

varying ways. Magic was a common theme in literary works, and Homer's *Iliad* and *Odyssey* contained many descriptions of it. The *Odyssey* in particular was recognized primarily as a book of magic, and Homeric verses were used as magical formulas. Magicians wrote handbooks that brought together spells, ritual procedures, instructions for using and making amulets, curse tablets and magical tools.

The Greeks were polytheists: they believed in many gods. Unpopulated areas of the country were dedicated to the gods, and oracular temples for divination and prophecy were frequently built near volcanic chasms or caverns, where misty vapours arose from underground waters. The oracles were a means by which humans could commune with gods. The best known of these was the Delphic oracle on Mount Parnassus, where people journeyed to learn about the future from the Pythia or priestess of Apollo who would pronounce their fate in an intoxicated frenzy. Attendant priests and priestesses assisted questioners by interpreting the Pythia's speech and sometimes by asking questions about the supplicants' dreams.

CLASSICAL WITCHES AND GODDESSES

Three witches were prominent in Graeco-Roman myth and literature and all presided over the mysteries of darkness: they were Circe, the enchantress visited by Odysseus; Medea, the niece of Circe, who helped Jason achieve his quest for the Golden Fleece; and Hecate, who was a goddess of the underworld.

The Greeks practised a form of rites called "Mysteries", which were known only to those who had been initiated. The most famous were the Eleusinian Mysteries. After a preparatory purifying stage that led the neophyte to a state of readiness, sacred objects were shown and it is thought likely that the myth of

Demeter, the goddess who represents life, welcomes her daughter Persephone, the goddess of the dead, back from the land of Hades.

A nineteenth-century portrayal of Circe, one of the three witches of the Graeco-Roman tradition.

Medea mixing one of her infamous potions.

Demeter and Persephone was performed as a form of initiation into the process of life and death. Demeter is the great mother of life and death and she contains within herself the upper and lower worlds. Demeter and her daughter Persephone are two aspects of the goddess and represent the living and the dead, the upperworld and the lower. Demeter searches for Persephone who has been abducted by Hades the ruler of the underworld. Because she has eaten the food of the dead, in the form of pomegranate seeds, she must spend one third of the year underground with him and two thirds above the ground with her mother. Upper and lower worlds are separated and reunited in a continuous regeneration as Demeter repeatedly loses and finds Persephone.

The practice of magic was seen to bring power, but it also had its pitfalls, as told in *The Golden Ass*, written by a Roman citizen, Lucius Apuleius in the second century AD. In the story, Apuleius is a naive young man who is accidentally transformed into an ass while trying to imitate a witch who is able to change herself into an owl at night. As an ass, Apuleius undergoes many trials and is mistreated by various masters. After a series of exuberant acts of seduction and apparent murders, he escapes in desperation to a beach in the moonlight and prays to the goddess Ceres. She tells Apuleius that the next day there will be a festival in her honour, and that if he eats a garland of roses carried by a high priest he will be transformed back into his human form. Apuleius follows her instructions and in gratitude becomes an initiate.

ROMAN RELIGION

This was very eclectic and adopted the Greek pantheon, albeit with Romanized names. In addition, several cults taken from other traditions arose during the period: of particular note were those of Isis, Mithras (the Persian god of mediation beteen light and dark), and Christianity, which eventually became the state religion of the Roman Empire.

Hecate, goddess of the dark phase of the moon sits facing outwards, Artemis and Selene sit on either side of her, representing the new and full moon respectively.

CELTIC MAGIC

The word "Celtic" has become a convenient label for the indigenous peoples of north-west Europe, who occupied a vast territory from the Pyrenees to the Rhine, and from Ireland to Romania. By about 600BC, most of western Europe was occupied by tribes that were thought to be culturally one people. The Greeks named these peoples of central Europe *Keltoi*. The Celts were despised by the Greeks and Romans, who thought them barbarians, viewing their nomadic lifestyle as lacking the arts of civilization.

Who were the Celts? They left no written records and so no direct information is known about them. All that we have found out comes from archaeological discoveries or through the writings of classical Mediterranean authors such as Caesar, Pliny, Tacitus and Lucian. These accounts are probably biased but they are useful when their descriptions match archaeological evidence. We do not know what the magico-religious beliefs of these peoples were, but classical accounts and archaeological descriptions demonstrate the existence of human sacrifice and head-collection.

CELTIC SPIRITUAL BELIEFS

Archaeologists have excavated a number of sites where votive deposits – including axes, swords, daggers, corn grinding stones and coins – show evidence of ritual activity, and many interpretations have been made, but we have no definite answers to questions about Celtic spiritual beliefs. These peoples did not construct permanent roofed temples but probably created sacred enclosures as a focus for ritually damaged votive deposits to be offered to the gods. Many rites may have been performed at sites of natural, religious significance – by the side of rivers, springs, in woods, and on mountains. In other words, places endowed with sanctity, a central component of Celtic magico-religious practices.

Castlerigg in Cumbria is one of the many stone circles in Britain and northern Europe that are believed to be ancient sites of Celtic worship.

The Druids were Celtic priests, prophets, soothsayers and magicians, and were written about by a number of Graeco-Roman authors, who derived their information from Posidonius. Caesar says that the Druids officiated in the worship of the gods, regulated sacrifices and ruled on religious questions.

An ancient carved head at a natural spring, in Clwyd, Wales, probably once a shrine to a water spirit or god.

It appears that these tribal peoples had a wide variety of deities, which were focused on appropriate tribal gods and the locality. Weird-shaped rocks, gnarled trees, springs and bogs were all places where the gods could be contacted. Female deities may have had some association with fertility; they could also have been endowed with healing attributes. However, their greatest powers were likely to have been associated with their relationship with a magical otherworld.

MYTHS AND LEGENDS

The Celts had an oral tradition and so the only information we have about their beliefs comes from early Christian monastic scribes who collected accounts of pre-Christian beliefs in the eighth and ninth centuries. One such Irish story concerns a vengeful goddess called the Mórrigan. When the hero Cú Chulainn ignores her sexual advances she gets her revenge by trying to distract him while he is engaged in battle with Lóch:

So the Mórrigan came there in the guise of a white red-eared heifer accompanied by 50 heifers ... Cú Chulainn made a cast at the Mórrigan and shattered one of her eyes. Then the Mórrigan appeared in the form of a slippery, black eel swimming downstream and went into the pool and coiled herself around Cú Chulainn's legs ... Then the Mórrigan came in the guise of a shaggy russet-coloured she-wolf. While Cú Chulainn was warding her off, Lóch wounded him. Thereupon Cú Chulainn was filled with rage and wounded him ... and pierced his heart in his breast.

A great weariness fell on Cú Chulainn. The Mórrigan appeared to him in the shape of a squint-eyed old woman milking a cow with three teats. He asked her for a drink and she gave him milk from the first teat. "Good health to the giver!" Cú Chulainn said. "The blessing of God and man on you." And her head was healed and made whole. She gave him milk from the second teat and her eye was made whole. She gave him milk from the third teat and her legs were made whole. "You said you would never heal me," the Mórrigan said. "If I'd known it was you I wouldn't have," Cú Chulainn said.

This story illustrates an essential magical world view – that there is no permanent boundary between the human and the animal worlds. The tale demonstrates the Mórrigan's powers to change her shape or "shape-shift" into a red-eared heifer, a black eel and a she-wolf; and by her metamorphosis into an old woman she tricks Cú Chulainn into healing her from the wounds that he has inflicted upon her.

THE CELTIC CHARACTER

Much romance has been built up around the Celts and they have, in modern times, become the focus of a particular nostalgic view of the past. They have been portrayed as a distinct cultural group displaying characteristics such as chivalry, courage and dauntless bravery. The Celts have also been viewed as posessing a sensitivity to music and poetry, and are thought of as being prone to philosophizing. However, recently some archaeologists are now questioning how far it is possible to see the Celtic people as originating from a single common source possessing a uniform culture. Other scholars are pointing to

A highly imaginative artist's impression from the 1700s of a Druidic ritual.

the fact that "the Celts" have been romanticized as an "imagined community" based on a certain shared identity that has more to do with the concerns of modern life than of peoples who existed more than 2,000 years ago.

SHAMANIC ELEMENTS

A story concerning Taliesin the Bard, which comes from the Welsh *Mabinogion*, is widely held to offer a profound insight into the deeper mysteries of the Celts, and is popular among modern-day witches. This myth,

A romantic portrayal of a Celtic bard.

which also comes from an oral tradition that was recorded by Christian scribes, demonstrates the same magical technique of shape-shifting utilized by the Mórrigan.

During the reign of Arthur, there lived Tegid Voel of Penllyn and he had a wife called Ceridwen who was a witch and a sorceress. They had a son named Avagddu who was ugly, and so Ceridwen decided to compensate him for his looks by giving him wisdom. Casting the necessary accompanying spells and uttering incantations, she brewed a concoction in a magical cauldron. The potent mixture had to be kept boiling for a year and a day and was watched over by Gwion Bach, Ceridwen's second son, and Morda, a blind man, who was charged with keeping the fire going. One day, towards the end of the alloted brewing time, a drop of the mixture flew out of the cauldron and landed on the finger of Gwion Bach, who tasted the liquid and became gifted with supernatural sight. Realizing that this was not intended for him, Gwion Bach took flight but was hotly pursued by his mother. Gwion Bach saw Ceridwen chasing him and turned himself into a hare. Ceridwen changed into a greyhound, whereupon Gwion Bach became a fish. Ceridwen turned into an otter and the chase continued. He became a bird and she a hawk. Eventually Gwion Bach turned himself into a grain of wheat but Ceridwen became a black hen and ate him. Nine months later Ceridwen gave birth to a beautiful baby son whom she wrapped up in a leather bag and cast to sea in a coracle. The baby was found by Gwyddno, named Taliesin, and raised as his own. Taliesin became a wizard and a bard and had the skill of prophecy.

In this story Ceridwen and Gwion Bach change shape in a chase that is characterized by its interchange of shamanic-type metamorphoses, or shape-shifting. Ceridwen, as a sorceress mother, by accident confers wisdom and inspiration upon her second son, Gwion Bach, who then has to undergo initiation – through gestation in the womb – and rebirth, before he can realize his magical inheritance as the legendary Taliesin.

Northern European Magic

It is difficult to be specific about the magico-religious beliefs of the Germanic and Norse peoples. Historians and archaeologists are now coming to the conclusion that rather than there being a clear contrast between the religions of the Celts and the Germanic peoples, there was, in fact, a wider spectrum of beliefs in existence.

Germanic Tribes

During the years of empire, the Romans called the tribes living east of the Rhine the "Germani". The culture that grew up in the region of Copenhagen was described by the Roman, Tacitus, writing in the last decade of the first century AD. Tacitus describes German society as being "heroic". The leading characters were the kings and chiefs and their companions, élite warriors who were bound to their lords through honour, courage and generosity.

Tacitus divided the peoples of this area into western Germani, who he said had a cult of symbolic atonement, and eastern Germani, who had a religion that seems to have had much more of a shamanic nature, as it involved trance and possession. All the Germani believed in women's prophetic powers, and the prophetesses of their society were sometimes thought of as divine. Divination was apparently carried out through the use of strips of wood, cut from a nut-bearing tree and carved with special signs that were called sigils. The sigils were spread out at random on a piece of white cloth. Later, a similar procedure was adopted using strips of wood with special symbols called runes carved on them.

English Tribes

According to Tacitus, the English were a separate tribe conforming to the general Germanic pattern, apart from the fact that they worshipped an earth mother, Nerthus. The English believed that she intervened in human affairs.

The god Odin, who had a central role in Nordic mythology, and was also called Wotan or Wodin, astride his horse and accompanied by his hunting dog.

Viking Mythology

During the period AD780–1070 the Danes, Norwegians and Swedes, because of a system of primogeniture that forced

A Viking memorial picture stone showing the god Thor, son of Odin.

younger sons into looking for fortune abroad, mounted Viking raids and invaded the coasts of Britain and France. They settled in Iceland in about AD870 and the Icelandic sagas reveal this Norse influence. The word "saga" is related to the English "say" and in Icelandic it refers to something said in a narrative. The Icelandic sagas concern human dilemmas and conflicts that arise out of everyday life – robberies, thoughtless words, loves and jealousies, arguments about property – things that set people against each other before there is reconciliation. Based on aristocratic and chivalric conceptions of honour, they often told of strength and courage in battle. Heroes could perform magical curses and cures through their poetry, and their inspiration was gained from the one-eyed god Odin, who had given his other eye away in order to gain wisdom by drinking from the underworld well of the wise god Mimir.

Norse cosmology tells that life was created though the union of ice from Niflheim in the north and fire from Muspellheim in the south when they met in the chasm of Ginnungagap. The first creatures made were a frost giant called Ymir and a cow called Audumla. The cow licked a man, Buri, out the ice. His three grandsons, the gods Odin, Vili and Ve, killed the giant Ymir and created nine worlds from his body.

In mythology, the nine worlds are organized on three different levels. On the top is Asgard, the realm of the Aesir or warrior gods. Here the gods and goddesses have their halls, and one can also find Valhalla, the hall of warriors who had died valiant deaths and now feast each evening while they await the final battle. Vanaheim, where the fertility gods live, and Alfheim, the land of the light elves are also on this level.

Midgard forms the middle level and is inhabited by humans. Jotunheim, the citadel of the giants, Nidavellir, where dwarfs live, and Svartalfheim, the land of the dark elves, are also located here. Asgard and Midgard are connected by Bifrost, a rainbow bridge.

Alberich curses Odin and Loge in an illustration for Wagner's opera on Nordic myths, The Ring.

The third level comprises Niflheim, the world of the dead, which is always dark and bitterly cold and has a citadel called Hel. It is nine days' ride northwards and downwards from Midgard.

The ninth world may have been Muspellheim, the land of fire and the first world to exist, according to the thirteenth-century writer Snorri Sturluson, but it is not given a position in the cosmology.

Yggdrasill, a mighty ash tree, stands at the axis of the three levels and has branches that spread out over the whole world and reach up to heaven. Its roots spread under the three levels: one is linked to Asgard and is guarded by three Norns or goddesses of destiny; another connects to Jotunheim, and the Spring of Mimir, whose waters are a source of wisdom; and a third goes into Niflheim and the Spring of Hvergelmir.

ANGLO-SAXON BELIEFS

Literature from the Anglo-Saxon era tells of the notion of "Wyrd", an all-powerful sense of destiny that shapes the world, which may be visualized as a web in which all of life is interconnected. Wyrd means "destiny" and also "power" and "prophetic knowledge" in Anglo Saxon. It is a term used to express the magical interconnectedness of all life.

Hermod, son of Odin, at the barred gates of Hel, pleading for the return of his brother.

MAGIC AND THE JUDAEO-CHRISTIAN TRADITION

Judaism and Christianity are monotheistic: they both focus on a belief in one creator God and both condemn magic and sorcery. Magic was seen to be a way of manipulating supernatural power for human ends, and was often described as *maleficium* ("evildoing").

Darius I of Persia and Ahura Mazda, flying above the chariot, hunting.

ZOROASTRIANISM:

This monotheistic faith was developed around 1200BC by the Persian religious reformer Zoroaster, who saw the world as a battleground between the principle of good, embodied in the creator god Ahura Mazda, and the force of evil represented by Angra Mainyu.

GNOSTICISM:

This Palestininan cult of the first century AD held that salvation was possible through the secret knowledge of the true nature of things, or gnosis, and the corrupt nature of the physical world. A transcendent and hidden God is opposed to an ignorant demiurge. All matter is part of satanic darkness and it is necessary to rise above evil matter to transcendent light.

NEOPLATONISM

Plotinus (c.205–c.270), a Roman born in Egypt, viewed divinity as a transcendental spirit and the source of all things. His philosophy taught that all existence emanated from the one and the aim was to become one with divinity.

The spirit of Samuel appearing to Saul at the house of the Witch of Endor.

The early religious philosophies of Zoroastrianism, Gnosticism and Neo-platonism all had an influence on the development of Christianity as a world religion. Magic has co-existed in an uneasy and tenuous relationship with both Judaism and Christianity, despite being at odds with scriptural orthodoxies. Magic was generally condemned in the Old Testament: God was averse to divination, augury, necromancy (the art of predicting by means of communication with the dead), mediums and wizards, and all forms of enchantment and shape-shifting.

The Old Testament includes an account of the witch of Endor who gives Saul advice, gained through her familiar spirit, as to why God has deserted him and why the Philistines are successful in battle against him. Despite Saul having punished wizards and "those that had familiar spirits", he seeks out the witch, and she conducts a seance to conjure the spirit of Samuel:

Then said the woman, "Whom shall I bring up unto thee?"
And he said, "Bring me up Samuel."
And when the woman saw Samuel, she cried with a loud voice: and the woman spake to Saul, saying, "Why hast thou deceived me? for thou art Saul."
And the king said unto her,
"Be not afraid: for what sawest thou?"
And the woman said unto Saul,
"I saw gods ascending out of the earth."
And he said unto her, "What form is he of?"
And she said, "An old man cometh up; and he is covered with a mantle."
And Saul perceived that it was Samuel, and he stooped with his face to the ground, and bowed himself.

Zoroaster, the founder of a cult that was formative in developing Christian ideas about good and evil.

handed on to initiates and concerns the "mysteries" that were not explained in Genesis. The Cabbala consists of numerous writings by various anonymous authors. The most important are the *Sepher Yetzirah* (Book of Formation), probably written in Babylonia around 2,000 years ago, and the *Zohar* (Book of Splendour) written in Spain in the thirteenth century.

In the Cabbala the universe is seen as encompassing different levels of reality at the same time. In the symbolism of the "Tree of Life" the ten "sephiroth", or spheres, are emanations from En Sof, or the will of God and impersonal ground of Being, through which the infinite relates with the finite. By meditating on the sephiroth a person is said to be able to link up with the greater plan of the universe and so become closer to God.

Samuel told Saul he had not obeyed the voice of the Lord and Israel would therefore be delivered into the hands of the Philistines.

Monotheistic religions and philosophies tend to see a gap between humanity and divinity, and in its most extreme form it is usually seen to be a religious duty for humans to reach out to God, and to rise from the earthly material world to God's realm of transcendent spirit.

THE CABBALA

In Genesis, primordial humans disobeyed God and were driven from Paradise for eating the fruit of the Tree of Knowledge. This disobedience led to the human fall from a state of divine grace. In order to overcome the radical separation from God, the Cabbala (also spelt Kabbalah and Qabalah), a form of Jewish mysticism, was developed to reunite human beings with divinity. Mystics have tried to describe levels of awareness beyond the ordinary and everyday world of the senses. Sometimes they have used myth to articulate what seems like indescribable religious experience.

The Cabbala is said by some to have been taught to Adam and Eve by God, while others say that it was given orally by God to Moses. It is a secret doctrine

Adam and Eve in Paradise. Eve is shown handing the fruit of the Tree of Knowledge to Adam.

The study of the Cabbala encourages a direct and unmediated relationship with God and may be seen to be heretical because it may challenge religious interpretations based on a study of texts.

Hermetism is the term used to describe a collection of beliefs, doctrines and practices that derive from a set of Greek texts written in Alexandria between the first and third centuries, setting out the teachings attributed to Hermes Trismegistus, a Greek name for an Egyptian priest identified with the god Thoth. Called the *Corpus Hermeticum*, many of these treatises describe the soul's ascension through the celestial spheres. In essence, much

A sixteenth-century engraving showing a Jewish Cabbalist holding the Tree of Life.

magicians of the Renaissance were Marsilio Ficino (1433–99), Giovanni Pico Della Mirandola (1463–94) and Giordano Bruno (1548–1600). Ficino, who was a priest and a physician, developed a system of "natural magic" concerned with drawing down the natural powers of the cosmos. His theory of magic was based on the guiding of spirit from the stars using the natural sympathies running through nature. Pico was influenced by Ficino's natural magic but, in an attempt to increase its power, he incorporated the Cabbala to tap the higher powers of angels and archangels. Bruno sought to return magic to what he saw as its purer pagan source in Egypt. He also used the Cabbala but in contrast to Pico, who wanted to work only with angelic forces, Bruno attempted to unlock demonic forces.

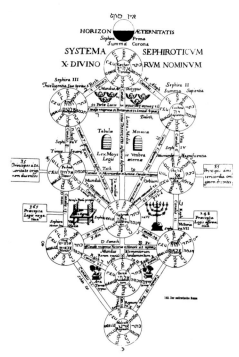

The Cabbalistic Tree of Life, representing the relationship between the microcosm (all the cosmic forces within the individual) and the wider macrocosm as an all embracing totality.

of Hermetism seeks to unite the the microcosm of the human being with divinity and the macrocosm.

During the Renaissance the writings of the Cabbala were interpreted by Christians and magic was used as a means to bring higher angelic forces down to the ordinary world. This changed the status of the magician from evildoer to agent of God and good. Three important

The Renaissance magi Pico Della Mirandola (centre) and Marsilio Ficino (right).

The corruption of nature after the Fall and humanity's supreme position within the created world became central to Christian teachings, but not all Christians agreed with this view. St Francis of Assisi (c.1181–1226) taught that all life formed part of the fellowship of God; all creatures were equal and interrelated and there was no dualism between God and his creation but a seamless web of life. While St Francis cannot be called a magician in the strict sense of the word, he reintroduced a spiritual view of the world which is magical, where God and creation are not separated:

Most High, omnipotent, good Lord,
All praise, glory, honour, and
blessing are yours.
To you alone, Most High, do they belong,
And no man is worthy to
pronounce your name.
Be praised, my Lord, with all
your creatures,
Especially Sir Brother Sun,
Who brings the day, and you give
light to us through him.
How handsome he is, how radiant,
with great splendour!
Of you, Most High, he bears the likeness.
Be praised, my Lord, for Sister
Moon and the Stars.
In heaven you have formed them, bright,
and precious, and beautiful.
Be praised, my Lord, for Brother Wind,
And for Air, for Cloud, and Clear,
and all weather,
By which you give your creatures
nourishment.
Be praised, my Lord, for Sister Water,
She is very useful, and humble,
and precious, and pure.
Be praised, my Lord, for Brother Fire,
By whom you light up the night.
How handsome he is, how happy,
how powerful and strong!
Be praised, my Lord, for our Sister,
Mother Earth.
Who nourishes and governs us,
And produces various fruits with
many-coloured flowers and herbs.
Praise and bless the Lord,
And give thanks and serve him with
great humility.

St Francis of Assisi, a Christian monk with a unique spiritual view of the world,
who preached of a seamless web of life.

Divine nature

Some writers have blamed the Judaeo-Christian Bible for encouraging an anti-ecological position. By denying a magical world view, nature ceases to be regarded as divine. In addition, it is sometimes argued, the Bible is strongly anthropocentric, or human-centred – human beings are divinely ordained to rule over and dominate all other species, in contrast to an animistic view, which sees nature as permeated by spirits that inhabit natural phenomena such as trees, rivers, animals, mountains and planets.

Adam and Eve are banished from
Paradise after eating the forbidden fruit.

ISLAM AND MAGIC

Magic in Islam forms part of the occult sciences, which include divination, astrology and prophecy. It is seen as a fragment of the celestial knowledge that was given to humans by fallen angels who revealed secrets. Thus humans have come to know what they should not know, and divinatory magic uses these secrets. Spells and incantations are also used to compel the spirits and demons called *jinn*, or *djin*. Two types of conjuring are distinguished. The first is bad and involves directing the mind toward an object rather than God, thus being unfaithful and acting in a manner that is wicked and harmful to others. The second concerns the conjuring of spirits with piety and lawfulness and in surrender to God, the spirits acting like angels: this is viewed in more positive terms.

A healer tapes up the toes and fingers of a person possessed by a jinn spirit to "lock it in".

RELIGIOUS VALUES

Islam was instituted as a recall to monotheism, from which Jews and Christians had drifted away; it was not a new religion but a call to Muslims to return to a strict path. It recognizes Jewish and Christian prophets but believes that their messages have been tampered with and are thus based on the work of humans rather than God.

There is one God, Allah, who is separate from humans: he has no likeness and no divine Son; he is transcendent but present everywhere.

A herbalists' souq in Marrakesh. Herbal remedies have been in use for centuries.

A Moghul prince speaking to a Dervish.

Allah is seen to preside over two worlds: the visible *al shahada*, which is accessible to humans; and the unseen *al ghaib*, which is accessible only to humans through special revelation. In the visible world, the earth, moon, stars and animals are not autonomous but are evidence of the unseen creative force – the signs by which Allah reveals himself. The reality of the unseen world is unknowable and mysterious and can be revealed by miracles, which show the unseen but true form of what is beneath. Miracles are a sign of God's power.

THE SUFIS

In Islam there has been a strong emphasis on the difference between human beings and God, but Sufism, so-called because the earliest followers of the movement wore woollen garments (*suf* means wool), developed as a form of personal mystical training that aimed at overcoming this distinction. The Sufis brought an inner spirituality into Islam. By the purification of consciousness, the self and God could merge. The mystical poet Jalal ad-Din ar-Rumi was born in what is now Afganistan in 1207 and was the founder of the sect known as the Dancing Dervishes. Its members were adherents of a form of Sufism that was developed around AD800–900 as a way of attaining union with God:

> I died a mineral and
> became a plant.
> I died a plant and rose an animal.
> I died an animal and I was a man.
> Why should I fear? When was
> I less by dying?
> Yet once more I shall die as
> man, to soar
> with the blessed angels; but
> even from angelhood
> I must pass on. All except
> God perishes.
> When I have sacrificed my angel soul,
> I shall become that which no
> mind ever conceived.
> O, let me not exist! for Non-
> Existence proclaims,
> "To Him we shall return".

The founder of the Dancing Dervishes, Jalal ad-Din ar-Rumi.

The Sufi mystical tradition claimed descent by a chain of grace that linked the holy men to the family of the Prophet. The Sufi saint, who acts as a spiritual teacher and master, is said to have the ability to foresee the future, control spirits and know what is in human hearts. The saint's knowledge is a concrete manifestation of divine grace demonstrated by his power over nature, and he uses his mystical powers to perform miracles.

From about the twelfth to the nineteenth centuries, Sufi brotherhoods, under the direction of a shaikh, were widespread. The aim of the ascetic practices of the Sufis is not to earn themselves credits in the next world by the mortification of the flesh, but rather to liberate the spirit for improved communication with the divine. The idea of union with God is seen by some as blasphemous, and the idea that the individual could in some sense become God is resisted by more orthodox Muslims.

Members of the Whirling Dervish sect, performing the dance that they believe helps them to find union with God.

CHINESE MAGIC

Magic was very important in the Chinese royal ancestral religion of the Shang and early Chou (between the sixteenth and eighth centuries BC). The wu was a shaman or sorcerer who sacrificed to and invoked the spirits, and effected cures by means of medicinal plants and spells. The wu tradition is connected with individuals known as fangshi – "persons of techniques". These were outsiders, marginal or peripheral from the point of view of official Confucianist doctrine. They specialized in astrology, medicine and geomancy, as well as methods for achieving a long life. They were usually solitary seekers who tried to find the laws behind natural phenomena.

Increasingly, a differentiation evolved between magic, as archaic religion dealing with spirits, and a developed theory of symbolic correspondences.

Lao Tzu, the legendary founder of Taoism, is presented with the baby Confucius.

Some rulers, such as Liu Chíe (140–87BC), favoured shamans and established shamanic cults, and the court became a gathering place for those who claimed to possess magical powers and the secrets of immortality. Li Shaoweng, a psychopomp (a conductor of souls to the place of the dead), gained Liu Chíe's favour by conjuring the ghost of the ruler's recently deceased concubine, but was executed after he was exposed as a fabricator of portents. Near the end of Liu Chíe's reign the court was paralysed by an outbreak of shamanic witchcraft known as *ku*, a type of demonic affliction which attacked its victim as the result of witchcraft. Sometimes shamans were hired to work black magic, and accusations of charlatanism and fear of witchcraft were widespread during the Han period.

During the periods of the Warring States (403–221BC), Chíin (221–207BC), and Han (206BC–AD220) there was a decline in the prestige of shamanism and the practice became associated with witchcraft.

TAOISM

Chinese religion is said to be a mixture of Taoism, Confucianism and the later arrival of Buddhism from India. Taoism and Confucianism share the same system of divination called the *I Ching* (Book of Change). This consists of 64 six-line figures, which represent every possible combination of hexagrams, and eight three-line figures, or trigrams. In order to consult the I Ching, a hexagram is constructed by determining each line (which may be either yin or yang) with the tossing of coins. Explanations attached to each hexagram advise on how to cope with a particular situation.

The *Pa Kua*, the symbolic arrangement of the eight trigrams, is said to have been developed around 3100BC from the inscriptions on oracular shells and bones from an earlier age. Today, the Pa Kua appears on flags, plaques and porcelain and is used as a charm to bring

A belief in spirits is widespread in China and here a pilgrim burns spirit money at the temple of the spirits' retreat.

good luck. It is hung up in Chinese homes to ward off unfriendly spirits and other evils. Often a mirror is placed in the centre to reflect evil influences.

The most harmonious hexagram combinations balance the two elements of yin and yang. Yin and yang are opposites: yin is dark, female, cold, solid and wet, while yang is light, male, fiery, ethereal and dry, but they are inseparable and each is dependent on the other. Each carries the other within it: they are not opposed in a fixed dualism, but combine polarity and ambiguity to produce the dynamic energy of life.

Everything is interconnected, as the interaction of the seasons shows. Autumn and winter are yin, but at the moment when yin triumphs in the heart of the cold dark winter, it also begins its inevitable decline and yang forces begin to arise, leading to the yang times of spring and summer. When summer reaches its high point, the seasons begin to change and yin is once more in the ascendant.

The altar of the Yap Kongsi temple in Penang showing the eight-sided Pa Kua, *the symbolic hexagrams and trigrams of the* I Ching.

Heaven has four seasons, to allow cultivation, growth, harvesting and storing, and five elements: wood, fire, earth, metal and water. It produces cold, heat, drought, humidity and wind. Humans have five vital organs that transform the five influences of the elements to engender happiness, anger, vexation, sadness and fear. The five elements represent forces that react against each other. Wood brings forth fire, fire produces ashes, earth brings forth metal, metal produces steam when

heated and water produces trees. On the other hand, earth is broken by wood, water is contained by earth, fire is extinguished by water, metal is melted by fire and wood is shaped by metal. The five elements are linked to nature and to humans by a whole series of connections. For example, wood corresponds to spring, germination and wind, and to the liver, gall bladder and mouth, as well as to anger.

NATURAL TRANSFORMATION

The Taoist system inspires a sense of confidence in the normal course of nature, and a mistrust of human intervention. This is expressed in the Taoist notion of wuwei – meaning a positive non-intervention with the Tao. The Tao is not a deity but simply the innateness of life. From the Tao comes the One, which is the primal essence of being, the core of innateness. The One splits and forms the two – yin and yang. Lao Tzu, the legendary founder of Taoism, explains the meaning of Taoism to Confucius:

> Human life between Heaven and
> Earth is like a white colt
> glimpsed through a crack in the wall,
> quickly past.
> It pours forth, it overwhelms,
> yet there is nothing that does not emerge.
> It drifts, it swirls,
> yet there is nothing that does not return.
> Life is transformation, death is
> also transformation.
> All living creatures are saddened,
> all humanity mourns.
> However, it is simply the releasing
> of the Heavenly bowstring,
> or the emptying of the Heavenly satchel,
> a yielding and a changing which
> release the soul, as the body follows,
> back at long last to the great Returning.
> That without shape comes
> from shape, that with shape
> returns to the shapeless ...

This philosophy reflects one of the great magical themes of transformation: of life and death and a constant interplay between form and formlessness as part

A Taoist weather manual depicting fire (yang) and cloud (yin) from the nineteenth-century Qing dynasty.

of a universal pattern of energies. The similarities between this strand of Chinese wisdom and the Egyptian myth of Osiris and Isis, the Greek underworld versus overworld rhythm of Demeter and Persephone, and the Celtic death and rebirth theme of Gwion Bach/ Taliesin are apparent.

An Immortal plays a flute in the Tao paradise.

JAPANESE AND KOREAN MAGIC

The magico-religious thought of these countries cannot be viewed in isolation from China. Japanese spiritual beliefs are a combination of indigenous Shinto, Confucianism and Buddhism, with Taoism as a secondary Chinese import.

JAPANESE SHINTO

In the early centuries AD, Japan was organized into clans, each with its own mythology and *kami* – gods or spirits of nature. Gradually a central core of myths centred on Amaterasu, the great goddess of the sun, and ancestress of the royal family. The kami of mountains, streams and the sea blended with tutelary kami who were associated with particular clans. Only gradually did Shinto emerge as a self-conscious religion. Shinto means the "way of the spirits" and is the name for a collection of myths and rites that are rooted in conceptions of kami. Kami are associated with natural phenomena, deified heroes, or anything that may inspire awe; worship is designed to please the gods. Purity is central – the *mago koro* or "true heart" is sincere and pure, and the divine light that illuminates the kami is also found within the human heart.

A Shinto priest from Northern Honshu, Japan.

There are two categories of religious leaders who deal with spirits: the *miko*, who are female shamans and mediums through whom the spirits descend and who are associated with witchcraft; and the *kannushi*, spirit controllers or priests who oversee the worship of the spirits and officiate in the state cults. Buddhism was introduced into Japan in the sixth century and it blended with Shintoism as part of the fabric of Japanese life with kami being viewed as manifestations of Buddhas and Bodhisattvas.

KOREAN SHAMANISM

Chinese religion, as well as Chinese magic and occultism, was part of the general flow of Chinese culture into Korea. The Korean religious culture includes Confucianism, Buddhism, Protestant Christianity and cults formed around female shamans who were a source of native Korean magic that was known as *Mu-sok* ("shamanic customs"). All religions co-exist and a Korean Buddhist may consult a shaman. People tend to participate in the rites of several of these religions for different purposes.

Korean shamanism is centred around the individual shaman or *mansin* and her household gods. Men are not generally shamans but they do conduct formal rites of ancestor worship. The few men who are shamans perform in women's clothing, including long silken pantaloons. It is the role of the shaman to seek out the gods, communicate with them, lure them into houses and bargain with them. The mansin is one who invokes gods and ancestors, speaks with their voice, uses their power to interpret dreams and visions, and deals with potentially dangerous spirits or ghosts.

The mansin purifies the dwelling and invites the gods and the ancestors inside to possess her. They vent their grievances and give divinations, exorcise the sick and banish lingering ghosts. The gods receive tribute, while the ancestors are given sustenance. The anthropologist Laurel Kendall describes the role of a shaman called Yongsu's Mother:

Garbed in the red robes of an antique general or wielding the Spirit Warrior's halbard as she drives malevolent forces from her path, Yongsu's Mother claims an imposing presence. Even in everday dress and sprawling comfortably on the heated floor of her own home, she speaks with authority. By virtue of the powerful gods who possess her, she can summon up divination visions and probe the source of a client's misfortunes, exorcise the sick and chronically unlucky, remove ill humors

A South Korean shamanic ritual held on a boat.

Wooden good luck charms hung in a Shinto temple in Kyoto, Japan.

from those who have difficulty finding mates, and coax a reluctant birth spirit into an infertile womb. The professional shaman makes the gods and ancestors a vivid presence in the home; she spots them in her visions and gives them voice in trance. In kut, her most elaborate ritual, she garbs herself in their costumes and in their person scolds, banters, advises and commiserates with the mortal members of household and community.

Korean shamans use horoscopes to link individual afflictions to the household. They believe that when the gods are angry the household's defences are lowered, and the individual who will suffer at this time is the person whose horoscope indicates vulnerability. The goal of many shamanic rituals is to discover which household god has been offended and to make amends in order to restore harmonious relations between humans and spirits.

A present day female Korean shaman performing a rite involving the gods of a household.

In this photograph, taken in 1919, a Korean shaman (lower right) tries to drive evil spirits out of an old man (lying on floor).

Magic and ritual in India

What has been called the Vedic phase of Indian history began with the influx of Aryans, a tribe of pastoral nomads from central Asia, who settled on the plains of the Ganges around 2000BC. They had an agrarian culture that was dependent on the forces of nature and this was reflected in the canonical body of texts called the Vedas (*veda* is Sanskrit for "what is known"). The Vedas praised and appeased the forces of nature as well as higher beings depicted as gods. In Indian tradition, the human being is a part of incarnation where everything has the power of sense perception, and where the highest good is identified with the total harmony of the cosmic order.

The Vedas are a rich source of magical ideas; no fundamental distinction is made between substances or beings and their qualities. Reality is built up from various networks of affinities or connections, which can be evoked and controlled by human beings. The Vedas

Indra, the Aryan god of war, seated on an elephant.

show the unity of creation as a mysterious interconnectedness and co-dependence of everything. Each bio-organism, element or species has a purpose in a larger scheme and is sacred.

Gods and Ritual

Like the Greeks and Romans, the Aryans were polytheistic – they believed in many gods, as well as spirits and demons. They had four main gods: Indra, a weather and warrior god; Varuna, who maintained order; Agni, a fire god; and Soma, a plant god who is also concerned with the visible and invisible world, and the different aspects of experience.

Rituals, which were performed by the Brahmin class, were conducted not to control nature but to restore equilibrium. Competition, struggle and tension were seen as healthy, a point of incentive for the growth of the natural world to overcome malignant spirits.

The aim of ritual was to keep the life processes of the universe moving and to maintain good relations with the powers of the unseen. Rituals were held on special occasions, such as festivals, and for specific ends, such as the curing of disease or the exorcism of malevolent spirits. The ritual might include divination, witch-finding and the manipulation of spirits or deities. There was a sacred power implicit in the action of sacrifice, and the sacrifice itself was supposed to have a beneficial effect on the person on whose behalf it was made; it was thought to have within it a power that the priest manipulated, and which was also in the priest himself.

Vedic Spells

The Atharva-Veda, one of the oldest collections of Hindu scriptures, contains a rich collection of spells and magical

Varuna, keeper of moral order, as portrayed on a stone carving on the Konark Sun Temple, Orissa.

Agni, a fire god associated with sacrifice. Fire was of central importance in Vedic ritual: it was through the consuming flames that sacrifices were sent to the heavens.

A modern day Hindu ascetic chanting a mantra – or spell.

A coin holding an impression of the goddess Kali.

The god Varuna.

rites. These were later divided into those that were concerned with positive welfare or the pacification of evil influences, and those directed against hostile powers or individuals. The Hindu goddess Maya, who is an aspect of Kali, refers to a creative capacity for magic or transformation that may be turned to good as well as evil purposes, and may be used to beguile or subjugate a victim.

A key to hidden reality is the realm of sound, which can be manipulated by the power of the sacred, ceremonially uttered word or mantra. Usually such spells contain invocations of deities who are ordered to carry out the magician's commands. Some mantras can be obtained only under the guidance of a guru and may involve preparation, astrological readings, long recitations and the regulation of breath.

A Pakhandi ritual showing participants using the plant soma.

Pakhandi

The magico-religious use of the plant soma shows that great importance was given to the use of drugs and intoxicants to induce experiences that were beyond those of the everyday and that were seen to have a sacred quality. Juice was prepared from the soma plant and drunk during ritual, and a hymn extols its beauty.

*Men beautify him in the vats, him
worthily to be beautiful,
Him who brings forth abundant food.
Him, even him, the fingers ten and the
seven songs make beautiful,
Well weaponed, best of
gladdeners.*

HINDUISM, BUDDHISM AND MAGIC

What is now called Hinduism developed out of Vedism. Towards the end of the Vedic period there was an increased interest in ascetic practices concerned with self-discipline and yoga techniques aimed at individual spiritual development.

THE BRAHMAN

In Hinduism, there is one and only one being in existence: the absolute Brahman, who is without form and is both immanent (within) and transcendent (beyond), and creates the world out of himself. The individual soul, or *atman*, is a part of this reality. Hinduism developed a number of orthodox systems of philosophy concerned with salvation and attaining oneness with God. In the post-Vedic Hindu tradition, supernatural powers are seen to derive from Brahman and the whole world is understood as divine action welling forth from this mysterious supreme power.

ASCETICISM AND DESIRE

The *Upanishads* were composed between 800 and 400BC and were a synthesis of Vedic and contemplative ideas and yoga practices aimed at training the mind and

A Hindu woman practising Padmasana yoga meditation.

A devadasis or sacred temple prostitute.

The god Brahma (right) looks on as Siddhartha Gautama, the Buddha, cuts off his hair as a sign of his asceticism. He later came to abandon asceticism and developed his own path to enlightenment.

body. The Upanishads led to the development of Buddhism and Jainism, as well as a more devotional form of Hindu religion expressed in the *Bhagavadgita*, a sacred text composed around 200BC and incorporated in the epic *Mahabharata*.

Hinduism embraces asceticism (*tapas*) and desire (*kama*) and these are not necessarily opposed but are frequently seen as interchangeable forms of energy. Asceticism is viewed as beneficial but in certain circumstances may generate a dangerous amount of magical "heat", which might cause fires, droughts or earthquakes. In Indian folklore, water is associated with sexuality and opposed to heat and asceticism. On occasion, sacred temple prostitutes called *devadasis* would be called on to seduce an ascetic and thereby dispel the heat.

SALVATION

Buddhism is a religious tradition associated with the teachings of Siddhartha Gautama, the Buddha, who was born around 563BC. The Buddha's world-view and teaching is concerned with a practical path to salvation. This is based on the assumption that the world is suffering and that liberation comes from the elimination of desire or craving by following the Noble Eightfold Path, a set of moral and ethical teachings leading to Nirvana, an enhanced state of awareness and enlightenment.

SPIRIT CULTS

In Hinduism and Buddhism the manipulation of superhuman powers motivated by worldly ends is seen to detract people from their proper purpose, which is the release from ordinary existence. In practice, Hinduism and Buddhism have co-existed with many spirit cults and folk religions and are often concerned with the problems and trials of everyday life. One example of how spirit cults exist alongside orthodox Buddhism is given by the anthropologist Stanley Tambiah. In *Buddhism and the Spirit Cults in North-East Thailand* (1970) he writes that the orthodox Buddhism of the monastic order concerns the withdrawal from the world, and a concentration on following an individual path that leads to Nirvana and the release from reincarnation. However, among lay people Nirvana is not a goal, for they cannot hope for salvation, only a better rebirth.

Ordinary people are involved with Buddhist practices but they also engage with spirit cults. At village level, spirit cults are concerned with the family, household and community; they involve the animistic, pre-Buddhist cult of guardian spirits who are concerned with good crops and healing.

There are a large number of specialists in the village who cure disease and communicate with spirits. Most are

A spirit priest prays before a sacrificial post during a funeral ceremony at the village of Pa Bu.

called by names that have the prefix *mau*. There is mau song, who acts as a diviner or diagnostician; a mau du, or mau lek, who is an astrologer or fortune-teller; a mau mau, who is a discoverer of lost property; a mau ya, a physician or herbal doctor; mau ram, a spirit medium; and mau tham, who acts as an exorcist. Spirit mediums officiate in rituals to appease the spirits; they have to be chosen by the spirits and undergo repeated possessions by them. Assistant mediums deal with individual cases of illness. Many of these mediums are female and serve as oracles of the guardian spirit. They inform the victim whether the spirit is responsible for the illness and what offerings it requires.

Prayers performed in the shade of the Bodhi Tree which grows at the site of the tree under which Buddha sat.

TANTRIC RITES AND BELIEFS

Magic in Hinduism and Buddhism is most prominent in the esoteric practices of Tantrism. The mystic combination of Hinduism and Buddhism, Tantrism originated in India around 700BC. Tantric goddesses are particularly highly valued and are seen as divine forces from which the universe emerged. The coming together of god and goddess in sexual union is central to Tantric rites, and men and women took on the qualities of the deities in the pursuit of enlightenment. *Tantra* represents the magical generation of life in the material and spiritual dimension. It is a Sanskrit word meaning "web" or "weaving" and can be interpreted as a practice that expands understanding; Hinduism and Buddhism each have their own versions. There are Tantric elements in the *Vedas*, and the Upanishads include descriptions of Tantric ritual sex.

Tantra developed in India in small cult groups centred around a particular set of deities and practices that were based

The Hindu god Shiva.

on either private meditation aimed at self-development, or public ritual performance. A central practice was the evocation of a Tantric deity through which the practitioner learnt to replace

their ordinary view of the world with a different "pure" vision. Enlightenment was not achieved by denying the world or the self but by merging with a transcendental reality.

Everything in both the ordinary and the transcendental world is seen to be generated by the interaction of the goddess Shakti and the god Shiva, and the universe is seen to be born of their desire. Tantrists, unlike orthodox Hindu Brahmins, do not moderate their desire but redirect its energy. The cosmos and the human body are intimately linked and, by a process of training, the Tantric practitioner can attune his or her body to progressively higher levels of cosmic awareness until she or he becomes one with the deity. The process involves activating the energy of the opposite sex in the individual body. In some traditions this is effected by meditation,

A linga, *or* phallus, *symbol of the god Lord Shiva. The* linga *is the main object of worship in Saivite temples and family shrines. This example shows one of the five faces of Shiva carved on its top.*

Shiva and Shakti in sexual embrace. In Tantrism, the Universe is born of their union.

the recitation of spells and words of power; in other traditions it is pursued through ritual sexual intercourse.

MAITHUNA

A form of ritual sex, Maithuna forms the last part of a ceremony known as the "five Ms". The preliminary stage involves taking wine, fish, meat (all forbidden to Hindus) and parched grain for their aphrodisiac properties. Maithuna is said to be a ritual during which Shakti and Shiva are united in the practitioner and this is believed to cause a transformation of consciousness. The ritual is usually carried out in a circle of initiates guided by a guru and it may incorporate meditation, yogic postures, the recitation of mantras, visualizations of diagrammatic representations of energy fields called yantras, and the invocation of many deities.

The basic theory is common to Buddhist and Hindu yogic traditions and involves *prana*, a flow of psychic energy through the body via the *chakras* (or energy centres) and channels. This forms a psychic model of the body, which relates the person to the wider spiritual world. Hindu Tantra identifies chakras at the base of the spine, the genitals, the navel, the heart, the throat, between the eyes and at the crown of the head. Buddhist Tantra locates chakras at the base of the spine, the navel, the

Padmasambhava (AD721–c.790), a Buddhist monk who spread the Tantric belief system to Tibet when he visited as a missionary in AD777.

throat and the crown of the head. Enlightenment is achieved when the energy located at the base chakra rises to progressively higher states of awareness. In Hindu terms, the female *kundalini*, represented by a serpent manifestation of Shakti, shoots up through the body to the crown of the head where it finds union with Shiva.

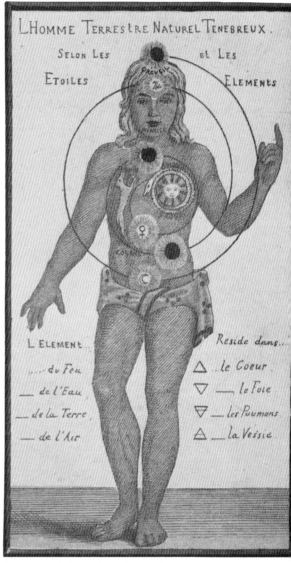

The seven chakras shown in an illustration from the nineteenth century.

Tantrists carrying out a ritual with corpses.

Tantrikas

Tantric practices can be concerned with the breaking of social taboos, which is believed to liberate much power. Some Tantrists have made their homes in graveyards, and some have meditated inside rotting corpses. This practice is intended to demonstrate the impermanence of the world, and to help the Tantrists to conquer their fear or disgust of death; it also openly flouts the caste divisions of Hindu society (the work of handling corpses is carried out by members of the lowest caste).

AFRICAN RELIGION AND MAGIC

African religions have complex cosmologies and display a strong sense of connection with a spiritual force that permeates the universe, as we have already seen with the !Kung of the Kalahari Desert. Early missionary zeal led to the mistaken view that African religion was primitive and undeveloped. In fact, the first missionaries erroneously described the magical practices they saw as a form of deception.

THE SPIRITUAL AND PHYSICAL WORLD

There is no body of beliefs and practices common throughout Africa and it is therefore very difficult to generalize, but in most African societies the spiritual world is seen to be a part of the everyday world. Many societies hold a pantheistic world-view that expresses life as an on-going process that includes living and dead ancestors. Pantheism is a view whereby everything in the natural world has a unity and is seen to be divine.

African cultures are very diverse, but they are all similar in the way they connect human beings (both living and as ancestors) and the natural world with a strong magical power.

This power is viewed as a kind of vital force, which flows through the universe and permeates all aspects of life. Some societies see it as originating from a creator spirit, and in Tanzania and Kenya, for example, the notion of a supreme named god is well established. The Janjero of Ethiopia believe in a supreme being that they call Hao. The Swahili word for God is Mungu or Mulungu, whereas the Kikuyus and the Masai of Kenya call him Ngai. The Nuer in the Sudan pray to Kwoth and the Nupe in Nigeria say that their god Soko is in the sky.

There is often a hierarchy of spirits: from the nature spirits of rivers, rocks, trees and animals, through ancestor spirits, to divinities who derive their power from the creator spirit. The Lugbara have a cult centred on the

The pastoralist Masai of Kenya depend on cows for their subsistence. Here a cow is ritually killed.

A Zulu diviner.

spirits of the dead, in which the living are seen to belong to the "outside" world and the dead belong "in the earth". If they are neglected, the dead punish their descendants by inflicting misfortune and sickness.

A female witch doctor of the Usumbura, 1929.

THE EARTH GODDESS

In African thought, complex systems of magico-religious beliefs, myths and cosmologies are interlinked with moral rules of behaviour. This is illustrated here by the myth of the great earth goddess Dzivaguru, who was once worshipped by the Korekore people of Zimbabwe. Dzivaguru lived in a palace by a lake, wore goatskins and possessed a long horn filled with magical substances that gave her everything she wanted. Nosenga, the son of the sky-god Chikara, became jealous of Dzivaguru's wealth and decided to drive her away. He descended into her valley but Dzivaguru surrounded herself with fog so Nosenga could not see her. Nosenga tied a magic red ribbon around his head so that he could see Dzivaguru's palace and he entered it to search for her. However, Dzivaguru had taken to the hills with all the light of the earth. Nosenga was surrounded by darkness. He cut fibres from a plant and made a snare, which he set up by the lake to catch sunbirds. As dawn came Nosenga could see Dzivaguru standing on the hill. She said that she would take the lake with her and told Nosenga that as he had brought the sun out it would soon become so hot that the forest would dry out. Dzivaguru warned that if any of Nosenga's sons commited incest she would withhold the rain from the land, and that if they wanted to pray to her they would have to slaughter a sheep first.

SPIRITUAL POWER

Most African societies believe that spiritual power can be manipulated by humans for good or bad. Positive mystical power is productive, can cure illnesses, and is protective, while negative power eats the health and souls of its victims and causes misfortune. Witches and sorcerers employ this power for antisocial ends.

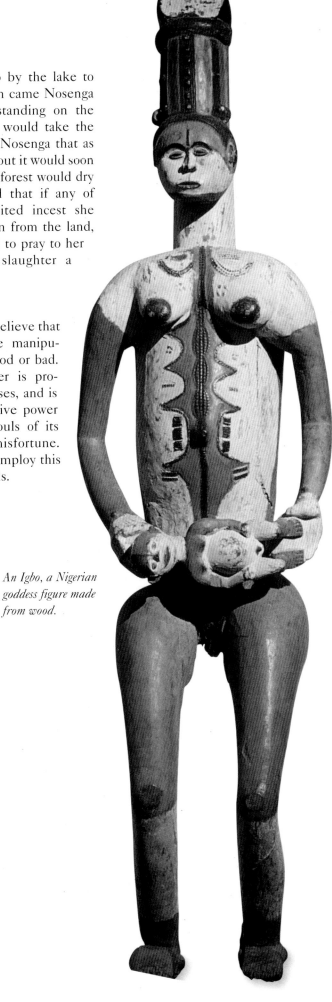

An Igbo, a Nigerian goddess figure made from wood.

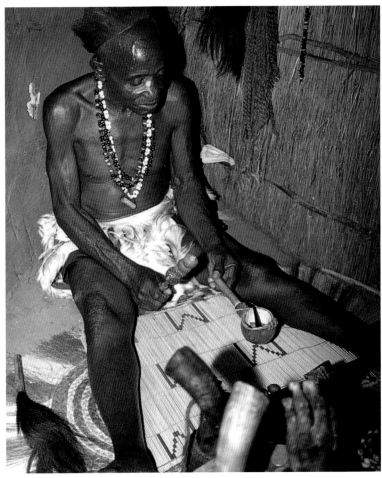

A witch doctor from Zimbabwe.

MAGIC AND MEDICINE

It is generally acknowledged that words can be powerful. They can "cause" good fortune, success or blessing, or they can curse and bring sorrow. It is usually specialists such as witch doctors, medicine men, diviners or rain-makers who use their knowledge of this magical power. The words are seen to work through the actual herbs of the medicine and are thought to cure or prevent misfortune. Medicines may be used to prevent rain from falling, to delay sunset, to aid hunting – by making a hunter invisible or preventing a wounded animal from escaping – for success in love affairs, or to find stolen property.

Medicines may also be used for treating illnesses. The diviner or medicine man may protect people by using spiritual power in amulets or charms. Magic involves rites using medicines made from trees and plants, and the magician addresses the medicines and tells them what he wants them to do: they are commissioned to carry out the task. Success is not seen to be due to magic but unusual success is.

A wooden Senufo kunugbaha mask used in anti-witchcraft rituals on the Ivory Coast.

Nganga is the term used in most Bantu languages to refer to a medicine man, magician, herbalist or shaman. In Zimbabwe, a young man becomes a nganga if his father or some other male relative will train him, and a young woman will become a nganga if some female relative will teach her the art of recognizing diseases and their cures. The nganga goes into the forest to collect herbs, roots, bark, flowers and leaves needed for the practice.

Knowledge about plants is wide spread, but what is secret is their magical properties and uses, and this information is inherited from nganga to nganga. Some nganga families have a tradition of healing going back many generations and the living members receive guidance from their ancestors, who speak to them in dreams. For example, the spirit of a grandfather may tell his grandson where to find the herbs that will cure an illness, and which spirit has caused it. The spirits tell the nganga how to prepare the herbs, and also reveal the person responsible for the disease. This information is important because healing may involve not just one person but sometimes the whole village or clan. The authority of the ancestors is necessary in order to make the medicines effective.

A Kikuyu witch doctor from Kenya.

A witch doctor with fetishes, Zimbabwe.

A traditional healer's medicines, as used in Zimbabwe.

A healer casting out devils during a ceremony in Zimbabwe.

THE MORALITY OF MAGIC

Magical power is seen to come either from the creator spirit, or through the spirits of the ancestors, or as part of the invisible force of nature in the universe. When spiritual power is used in antisocial or bad ways it is termed "sorcery" or "black magic". This type of magic may be used, for example, to send animals, such as lions, flies or snakes, to attack a person or carry disease; it might be used to send spittle laced with secret incantations; or to possess a person's spirit. Many misfortunes are the result of this type of magic. Sorcery is bad not because it can destroy health and property, but because it is immoral and flouts the law. Good magic may also be destructive but it strikes only at those who have commited a crime, it cannot be used for evil purposes. Oracles may be used to determine witchcraft, illness or misfortune.

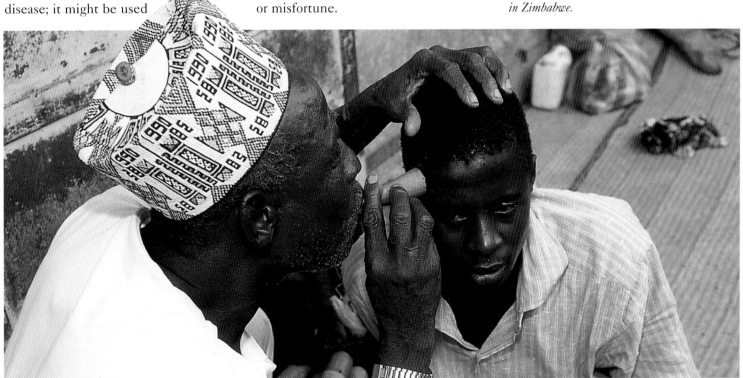

A healer treating a man for migraine in Mali.

VOODOO RITUALS AND BELIEFS

Voodoo (sometimes also spelt vodu or vodou) is the word for the gods in the Fon language of Dahomey (now Benin). The Fon people differentiate between three regions for the gods: the sky, the earth and the clouds in between. The first god, the Creator, lives in the sky and created twin gods: Lisa, the sun god of day, strength and endurance, and his sister, Mawu, a moon goddess of night, peace, joy, fertility, mother-hood and rain. The two eldest children of Lisa and Mawu were Sagbata and his twin sister who were sent to earth to populate it with their children.

The younger brother, Sogbo, was sent to the clouds to become the ruler of thunder and lightning, but in spite of his power, he was jealous of his elder brother who was the ruler of the earth, and withdrew rain. Nothing could grow and the people were starving. The prayers of the people moved Mawu to send Lega, a god of fate and the youngest son of Lisa and Mawu, to earth. He took the Otutu, a songbird, with him and told it to sing as soon as fire broke out. Soon the angry Sogbo caused a fire on earth with his lightning, but Otutu began to sing and this informed Mawu who sent rain and saved the earth.

COLLECTIVE SPIRITUAL CREATION

Voodoo, vodu or vodou is also the name for the religion of former slaves from West Africa imported into Haiti in the West Indies. The diverse magico-spiritual beliefs of peoples from the African states of Dahomey, Loango, Ashanti, Yoruba and Mandingo, whose cultures were deliberately broken up and scattered through Haiti, have been brought together to form a sense of religious identity and continuity out of fragmentation. Voodoo is a collective spiritual creation born out of the inhumanity of the slave system, and it brings together ancestor worship, spirit possession, dance, song and drumming.

A Fon bocio figure, which is believed to embody a potent magical power.

HAITIAN VOODOO

Today, voodoo is a peasant religion practised by 90 per cent of Haitians but regarded with contempt by the small Westernized ruling class. It is a fusion of African spirit beliefs and Catholic Christianity. The Christian God (called Bondye in Haitian Creole) presides over the ritual and sends down his angels in a variety of performances, which range from the lighting of candles to animal sacrifice. Much of the ritual and liturgy is of Chrisitan origin and the *loa*, who are also called "saints" or "angels", are seen to be a part of Christian cosmology. Santeria is a Caribbean practice similar to voodoo, and is also centred on the worship of African gods within a Christian religious framework.

The human being is seen to consist of a material body animated by spirit, and may achieve the status of divinity or loa, which possesses the body. When a loa possesses a new devotee it has to be baptized and take holy communion. The loa moves into the head of an individual and displaces his or her *gros bon ange* or "good angel" soul, one of the two souls

An ancestor-worshipping ceremony in Ghana, West Africa.

Haystack-like mounds that will become spiritual village guardians when worn by Voodoo worshippers at a festival. The guardians, called zangbetos, are said to contain the spirits of the village.

that a person carries, causing trembling and convulsions. The spirit incarnates into its earthly host and rides it like a horse (like the Greek Pythia at Delphi who were mounted by Apollo, who rode on the nape of their necks). This spirit union may be marked by a celestial marriage whereby the possessed person may seek the permanent protection of the loa. When the god and his or her mortal partner have undergone a wedding, they then share a common destiny. The spirit's duty is to protect its spouse, but it must be given presents in return.

The spirits help to deal with the ordinary problems of life and maintain African roots and identity. They help to heal relationships, putting problematic human relationships into an external form where they can be worked out.

Voodoo initiates in "kapame", a secret ritual enclosure, near Lomé, Togo.

Fetishes for sale at Lomé Voodoo market, Togo.

THE MAGIC OF ABORIGINAL DREAMING

The religious life of the Native Australian peoples is focused on what Europeans term the "Dreaming" or the "Dreamtime", and what Aborgines call *jukurrpa*. The Dreaming relates to a state of reality beyond the everyday in which ancestral creators – such as the Wauwalak Sisters and the Wandjina – travelled across the unshaped world in human and non-human form, classifying it as they went and bringing laws of social and religious behaviour.

THE WAUWALAK SISTERS

Myths about the Dreaming show how humans are related to the land. The myth of the Wauwalak Sisters shows how the spiritual heritage of the Dreaming is passed on through rituals and ceremonies.

A bark painting depicting a Wandjina, one of a group of ancestral beings from the sea and sky that bring rain and control the fertility of the animals and the land.

A Churinga, a sacred disc believed to be a transformation of the ancestors of the Dreamtime and their weapons. They represent each person's spirit, while the design is a totemic pattern of the associated sacred site. They could only be viewed by initiated men and had to be handled with the correct ritual songs.

An Aboriginal shaman of today. The patterns of the body painting across his chest represent the Oruncha, the mythical creature from whom his shaman's powers are derived.

Two sisters left their homeland after the elder of the two became pregnant through an incestuous relationship. They travelled to the sacred waterhole of Muruwul and on the way named all the animals, birds and plants. As they walked along they killed lizards, possums, bushrats and kangaroos, and dug yams. They placed the animals and plants in their dilly bags.

When they stopped to rest at Gruawona, the elder sister gave birth to a baby girl. They made a fire and attempted to cook the food from the dilly bag. They put the animals on the fire but as soon as the creatures warmed they came back to life, escaped to the sacred waterhole and in the process became sacred themselves. In the waterhole lived the great rock python Julungul, the rainbow serpent. Julungul slowly emerged from the waterhole smelling the birth blood of the eldest sister. The sisters danced to keep the snake at bay, and this dance caused the younger sister to start menstruating. Attracted by the blood, the snake swallowed both of the sisters and returned to the waterhole. Later the snake vomited up the sisters, saw that they were still alive, beat them with her song-stick, and swallowed them again.

Julungul then returned to all the other snakes in the sacred waterhole and the spirits of the Wauwalak Sisters spoke to them through Julungul. In this way the snake delivered to her people the spiritual heritage of the Dreaming: the sacred law, ritual, dance and song. When this was done she retired to a cave and never emerged again.

A WEB OF DREAMINGS

Australia is covered by an intricate web of Dreamings. Some relate to a particular place, while others reside within individuals. On one level, the Dreaming is shrouded in the mists of time; people claim to be descended from a particular region without actually tracing the links through specific ancestors, and exact names and dates add little to their perceptions of the past. What is stressed, however, is the relationship to others, their Dreaming affiliations and ritual associations, and this is a way of focusing on relationships with the land and with the people. Individuals derive their identity from the land. Relationships are stated and affirmed in terms of rights and responsibilities in the country of their ancestors. During the Dreamtime an all-encompassing law bound people, flora, fauna and the natural world together. One native Australian elder has described the Dreaming in the following manner:

Dreaming,
The first ones lived, those of long ago.
They were the Wandjinas –
Like this one here, Namalee.
The first ones, those days,
Shifted from place to place,
In the Dreaming before the floods came.
Bird Wandjinas, crab Wandjinas
Carried the big rocks.
They threw them into deep water,
Then piled them on the land.

All kinds –
She the rock python,
He the kangaroo,
They changed it.
They struggled with the rocks,
They dug the rivers.
They were the Wandjinas. They talk
With us at some places
they have marked.

Where the sun climbs, over the hills
And the river they came,
And they are with us in the land.
We remember how they fought
Each other at those places they marked.
It is Dreaming there.
Some Wandjinas went under the land,
They came to stay in the caves
And there we can see them.
Grown men listen to their Wandjinas.
Long ago, at another time,
These Wandjinas changed the bad ones
Into rocks
And the spring we always drink from.
These places hold our spirits,
These Ungud places of the Wandjinas.
There a man learns
Who his child really is:
Its spirit comes when he is dreaming
And tells him its name.
Then the man has been given his child:
It has its own name
Beside the land-name of its father ...

A petroglyph incised in the rock at an aboriginal sacred site. These designs are believed to have been made by clan ancestral beings during the Dreamtime.

A bark painting depicting three spirit figures, legendary supernatural beings of the Dreamtime.

An aboriginal bark painting of two crocodiles appearing as a shaman might see them.

SCIENCE AND MAGIC

Human beings have always tried to make sense of the world around them. In modern times we often look to science to give us explanations for the way things are. Way back, in the distant past, our ancestors probably would have turned to the spirits and what we would now call magic as a source of information. Today, in Western societies, this way of seeking knowledge has been devalued. Magic has often been contrasted with both science and religion. However, magic is similar to science in the way that it offers an explanation of the world, although it uses the medium of spiritual connection, which cannot be observed or measured in a laboratory; the cause-and-effect relationship between an act and its consequence is spiritual, rather than scientifically validated and observable. More recently, there has been a shift from comparing magic and science to looking at different ways of thinking. All human beings are capable of exercising two ways of thinking: these are logical, analytical thought, the thought required to work out a complex mathematical formula, for example, and analogical or magical thinking, the state of mind required to enter a trance, such as a shamanic journey. Both can be examined and understood through a scientific world-view.

Alchemists in the middle ages believed they used scientific methods to control natural magic.

Sir James George Frazer, Scottish social anthropologist, classicist, folklorist and author.

JAMES FRAZER (1854-1941)

An early anthropologist and the author of *The Golden Bough* (1890), James Frazer saw the relationship between magic, science and religion in evolutionary terms. Frazer thought that magic was the first stage in the evolution of the human mind, and that both magic and religion, which grew from the mistakes of magical thinking, would eventually be superseded by science. As people came to realize that magical techniques were ineffective, they created omnipotent gods that controlled nature and needed to be supplicated. Finally, as humans began to recognize the existence of empirical natural laws, religion would join magic as superstition.

A depiction of a witch doctor discovering an unfavourable sign, c.1870.

Frazer thought that magic was formed from the association of ideas, and developed the notion of sympathetic magic – the belief that everything is connected in a state of sympathy or antipathy. Magical rites were based upon the idea of "homeopathic magic", founded on a "law of similarity" that "like produces like"; and "contagious magic", based on a "law of contact", which holds that things that have been in physical contact continue to act upon each other at a distance.

LUCIEN LÉVY-BRUHL (1857–1939)

The French philosopher Lucien Lévy-Bruhl thought that while modern Western societies were scientifically orientated, what he termed "primitive" societies were mystically oriented, and he used the supernatural as an explanatory framework. Lévy-Bruhl saw pre-scientific or magical thinking as "pre-logical" (a term he later abandoned). He said that "primitive" societies were "pre-scientific" because their collective representations inhibited the development of a scientific world-view. Lévy-Bruhl thought that there was a special primitive way of thinking that explained collective life, and which every individual unconsciously accepted as a result of the influence of society. He was interested in how collective beliefs explained what seemed to be irrational religious views such as witchcraft.

EDWARD EVANS-PRITCHARD (1902–73)

The anthropologist Edward Evans-Pritchard, in his study of the African society of the Azande in the 1920s, was interested in Lévy-Bruhl's ideas but questioned his view that "primitive" people had a special way of thinking that was "pre-logical". He asked why the Azande still believed in magic despite its frequent failure and came to the conclusion that they attributed failure to a particular magician's performance and not to the magical world-view itself. This led him to speculate that the Azande had a closed system of thought, which inhibited scientific verification. He saw the Azande magical system as rational in itself, but ultimately inferior to science.

The Polish-born British anthropologist, Bronislaw Malinowski, working among the people of the Trobriand Islands, 1914–18.

BRONISLAW MALINOWSKI (1884–1942)

An anthropologist who conducted fieldwork among the inhabitants of the Trobriand Islands (now part of Papua New Guinea), Malinowski emphasized that magic was both material and spiritual and was similar to both science and religion. He claimed that magic was used in high-risk situations, such as when fishing in the open sea, but not in the safe waters of the shallow lagoon. He argued that the Trobrianders used both magical and scientific knowledge in the way that they planted yams: they grew yams with a great deal of technical expertise but also employed magical spells to protect them.

In a painting from 1913, a witch doctor in Swaziland goes round the village "smelling" for the sorcerer who is using magic against his client.

ASTROLOGICAL KNOWLEDGE

Astrology derives from the magical practice of linking the individual human being with the wider universe, as microcosm to macrocosm. Astrology is said to have its origins in Egyptian and Chaldean astral lore, and in the revelations of the Egyptian god Thoth, a scribe of the gods and divinity of wisdom who was identified by the Greeks with Hermes. It has also been attributed to the mythical Egyptian pharaoh Nechepsos and the priest Petosiris. Eudoxus of Cnidus (c.408–353BC), said to be the father of Greek astronomy, was also versed in the principles of astrology. The astronomer Hipparchus (second century BC) studied the correspondences of planetary signs with the people and the geographical features of the earth.

THE DEVELOPMENT OF ASTROLOGY

According to the historian Frances Yates, astrology developed from a collection of Greek writings called the *Corpus Hermeticum*. During the Renaissance, these writings were believed to be by an Egyptian priest known as Hermes

Hipparchus in his observatory in Alexandria.

Trismegistus, but have since been identified as largely Greek and dated between the first and third centuries BC or AD. This large body of magical writings concerned astrology and the occult sciences; it involved the drawing down of the powers of the stars, and the understanding of the secret virtues of plants and stones. A form of sympathetic magic, it was a way of connecting the material everyday world with the influence of the stars and planets.

An understanding of the astrological pattern in the cosmos enabled the positive influences of the stars pouring down on to the earth to be captured in talismans and used by a magician with the right knowledge. The magician who wished to capture the power of the planet Venus must know what plants belonged to Venus, what stones, metals and animals to use when addressing Venus; images inscribed on talismans had to be made of the right materials, and used at precisely the right astrological moment. Talismans were believed to capture the spirit of the star and to hold or store it for use.

THE SIGNS OF THE ZODIAC

The cosmos was divided into 12 signs of the zodiac, each with its own complicated correspondences and associated animals, plants and other attributes. The magician was the person who knew how to operate this complex system of links

The Ibis-headed Egyptian god Thoth is associated with the beginnings of astrology. Thoth is depicted here with the pharaoh Seti I.

between the celestial and the earthly realms. The powers so derived could be used to obtain material benefits, or to gain insight into the worship of the divine forces in nature. Knowledge gained from the celestial realms could be used to predict a person's future based on a cosmological analysis of their past, or it could indicate the future of whole societies or nations.

WORLD ASTROLOGY

Greek ideas about astrology spread around the world, reaching India between AD100 and 300. Chinese astrology may have derived from Indian astrology. Astrologers predicted cultural and political events, and connected every important moment in history with the movements of the planets, comets or eclipses. The discipline had a prominent place in Renaissance science, but it gradually lost this position after the Christian church disassociated itself from astrology during the Reformation of the sixteenth century. Today, many people read their "stars" in popular newspapers and magazines, but such horoscopes constitute a form of entertainment rather than a serious study of a person's connections with the planetary

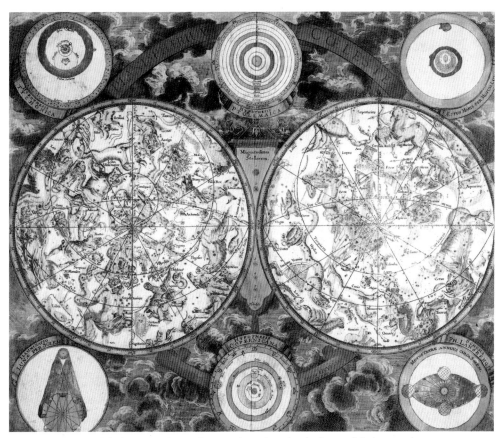

A representation of the heavens: the northern and southern hemispheres with the star signs. A copper engraving of c.1700.

sphere. The link uniting the individual with the wider connections of the cosmos has largely been lost.

Signs of the Chinese zodiac surrounding the symbol of yin and yang.

A Christian allegorical depiction of the planetary system.

THE SCIENCE OF ALCHEMY

Alchemy is an esoteric technique and has spiritual goals similar to many magical traditions. Appearing as a term of reference in the West from the twelfth century, it referred to a quest for either an "elixir of immortality", a universal cure, or for a means of transmuting base metals into gold. It has been seen as a speculative precursor of chemistry, but it is very different to chemistry: chemistry deals with the scientifically verifiable while alchemy, as a magical practice, is concerned with a hidden reality underlying ordinary perception.

Through an alteration of consciousness, the ordinary way of seeing the world (which is likened to the metal lead) is changed to a more subtle perception, which is thought to penetrate the secrets of nature, life, death, eternity and infinity (associated with the sacred metal gold).

The bible of the alchemists, *The Emerald Table*, is attributed to Hermes Trismegistus. It states that "that which is above is like what is below", and that all things come from the infinite, eternal

A portrait of Paracelsus who sought to found a medical science based on a relationship between human beings and the cosmos.

One, symbolized by Ouroboros, a snake or dragon eating its own tail, which represents the cycle of the universe and the infinite eternal.

PARACELSUS

A dominant figure of sixteenth-century medicine and philosophy, Paracelsus (1493–1541) was an alchemist. He argued against the position of seeing reason as the basis of medicine and sought to found a new medical science based on the spiritual relationship between humans and the cosmos. He believed that he could convert base metals into gold by "curing" them of their impurities. Paracelsus compared alchemy to medicine and the baseness of metals to disease. Alchemy was a way of perfecting what nature had left in an imperfect state. Paracelsus saw humanity as the crown of creation and believed in personal free will and power to the extent that it could influence the stars. He wrote that:

Medicine must be understood and classified internally ... The physician should know how to bring about a conjunction between the astral Mars and the grown Mars [i.e. the herbal remedy]. In this sense the remedy should be prepared in the star and should become a star, for the stars above make us ill and die, they make us healthy ... The physician must therefore ... understand medicine in the light of the heavens, namely that there are stars both above and below. As a remedy cannot act without the heavens, it must be directed by them. Thus you must make a remedy volatile, that is to say, remove what is earthly in it, for only then will the heavens direct it. What should act in the brain will be directed to it by the Moon; what on the spleen by Saturn; what belongs to the heart will be guided to it by the Sun, and to the kidneys by Venus, by Jupiter to the liver; by Mars to the gall-bladder ...

ALCHEMY AND SPIRITUALITY

In every culture where it is practised, alchemy is related to esoteric traditions. In China it is associated with Taoism. The alchemical view of the self in this tradition is associated with practices

The legendary Hermes Trismegistus, the alleged author of The Emerald Table.

An early sixteenth-century woodcut of two alchemists at work.

of a whole, and the aim of the elixir was to preserve the spirit.

In Hinduism, alchemy is concerned with techniques of bodily perfection, invigoration and rejuvenation, whereas in Buddhism there is a greater emphasis on internal yogic processes, and prolonging life is seen only as a means towards realizing total liberation. Islamic alchemy is concerned with the transmutation of the material and the spiritual with the highest form of perfection. The prophet Muhammad is said to have endorsed alchemy, and its origins are traced back to Adam, the major prophets and masters from the ancient world, including Aristotle, Galen, Socrates and Plato.

An alchemist surrounded by his equipment.

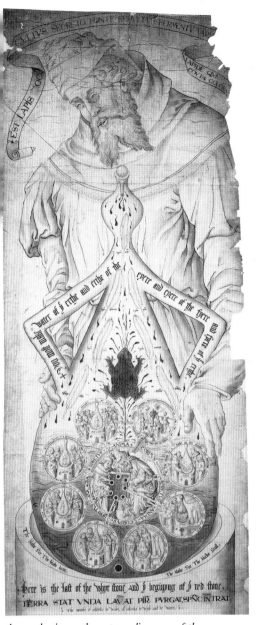

An early sixteenth-century diagram of the alchemical processes for the production of the philosopher's stone (the elixir).

that aim at perfection of the spirit and refining the body to encompass the Way, a mystic path in which the individual is integrated with society and the cosmos.

The Chinese were interested in prolonging life and an "elixir of immortality" appears to have been developed in the fourth century BC. Chinese alchemists were single-minded in their quest and, unlike Indian, Greek or Western alchemists, did not make a distinction between this world and the next, nor did they seek liberation from the cosmos. By contrast, matter and spirit were part

The four elements, zodiac signs and alchemical symbols in conjunction.

WITCHES AND SUPERNATURAL BEINGS

Nearly all societies have some conception of witchcraft in which individuals are thought to possess a form of extraordinary power. A belief in witchcraft is part of a magical worldview that sees powers and forces inherent in the universe, which may be directed by certain people. These people have been called witches but are also known by other names such as sorceror, shaman or witchdoctor. Having all manner of special abilities, these people are often frightening figures that are thought to have the ability to change their shape, fly and sometimes trick and deceive, and they have been the subject of folklore in numerous countries. They have also been used as scapegoats for the unexplained or the unexpected elements of everyday life.

WHAT IS WITCHCRAFT?

If you look up "witchcraft" in a dictionary, you will read that it is the art of bringing magical power to bear, or at least of trying to do so. This magical power can be used to both harmful and beneficial effect, but it is the former quality that is most often thought of in the context of witches. The idea that it is possible for human beings to cause harm to their fellows through the exercise of a special power not possessed by others is widespread throughout the world. Nearly all societies have some concept of witchcraft, in that certain individuals are thought to have supernatural or occult powers, which may be used to do harm or, in some cases, to heal.

A Ndebele shaman, wearing an "isiba" headdress, which features porcupine quills, divines the setting sun to foresee the future.

Various forms of witchcraft beliefs appear from India to the Pacific, but they are most widespread in Africa. In Europe between the fifteenth and eighteenth centuries, witchcraft was seen to be an organized heretical sect, which was opposed to Christianity. Witches during this time were considered to be possessed of an evil power as a consequence of being the Devil's agents. Large numbers of Europeans of all social classes believed in the existence of witches, and witchcraft was defined as a crime: people were prosecuted and executed. The European witch hunts spread to the American colonies in the seventeenth century.

The word "witch" comes from the Old English *wician*, meaning "to cast a spell". The meaning of witch and witchcraft changes from society to society and there is no neat and precise definition with which everyone agrees. A witch is often female, frequently old, although she may also be especially beautiful and lure unsuspecting men by her charms; she may shift between different guises to trick and deceive. In Africa, she may be thought to be fattened on human flesh. She almost always has the ability to change shape or cause others to be turned into other beings. By changing her form or substance she can appear in human form, as an animal or as a feeling of anxiety or horror; she also has the capacity to become invisible and to fly, often on a broom.

A witch is often believed to be capable of being in two places at once: she can act at night while her physical body lies sleeping at home. In Nigeria, the Yoruba believe that witches are generally women who fly about at night and meet in secret places. They are associated with birds, especially the nightjar, and they suck the blood of their victims until they die. For the Ibo, also of Nigeria, witches fly as balls of fire or as night-birds to their meetings. Witches are not entirely human.

They are associated with the dark, with night and with the reversal of normal human lives. A witch could be an envious neighbour who wished ill will or could be envy itself, as a powerful force for evil might take on any particular shape or guise. Witchcraft frequently

A witch doctor in Bulawayo, Zimbabwe.

represents greed, depravity, corruption or unrequited love, and it is also associated with sexuality. Witches turn against their neighbours and delight in "unnatural" practices such as incest or bestiality; they may eat their own children or dig up corpses. In short, they are immoral.

Witches have supernatural power or strength, and frequently have a knowledge of herbs and plants. A witch is a human being who incorporates a non-human power. How a witch's power is acquired varies: to Christian intellectuals at the period of the witch hunts it was derived from a pact with the Devil; in other places the power is acquired through an association with carnivorous predators, or it is gained through a skill that can be learnt; sometimes it is thought to be inherited, as in the African society of the Azande. The evil power of witches may work on their victims immediately or it may take some time to take effect. Witches can be recognized by particular signs such as a red eye or some kind of devil's mark, or they may have a snake in their belly or a special witchcraft substance.

One of the marks of witches around the world is that they are able to fly; their flight takes place at night-time.

A fifteenth-century English engraving of witches making a spell to brew up a hailstorm.

A sharp distinction between witchcraft and sorcery is impossible to maintain. Sorcery is also associated with maleficent magic, evil spells and injury. Some scholars and writers on witchcraft do not make a distinction between witchcraft and sorcery, while others differentiate between conscious harming, which they call sorcery, and unconscious harming, which they term witchcraft. Others have used the word "wizard", which comes from Middle English "wis", meaning "wise woman or man". The choice of terms is arbitrary.

A popular portrayal of witches in the seventeenth century. Here they are associated with the darkness, death, cannibalism and nakedness.

THE CLASSICAL WORLD

From writers such as Homer, Apuleius and Ovid, we learn that magic was a central and necessary part of Graeco-Roman society. It was commonly practised by a variety of people, including doctors and priests of specific deities. The state employed diviners to predict the future, and political and military decisions often depended on what the diviners foretold. Although magic was acepted as a part of everyday life, any spells that were intended to cause harm were actually illegal, and it was considered a serious, punishable offence to engage in maleficent occult acts.

The gods of the Greeks and the Romans were held to be largely subject to the same physical and spiritual laws as humans. Ideas about good and evil were related to physical feelings and experiences, which were common to gods and humans. There was no strict division between divinity and humanity, unlike the mono-theistic religions of Judaism, Christianity and Islam.

ANCIENT NATURE GODS

Early Greek religion was based on the power of nature. Peoples' lives were subject to external powers – of which some could protect and some cause harm – which made up a universe of order and harmony. Greek religion was polytheistic – many gods and goddesses were worshipped – and the powers of nature were personalized. The gods dwelt in the fields, woods, rivers and springs, and later in the sea. Rivers were few and sacred: each had its deity in the form of a bull or a horse. Spirits peopled the countryside in semi-animal and semi-human form. The centaurs had the bodies of horses and the heads and torsos of men, and were probably tutelary spirits of the mountain torrents.

A nature spirit, or nymph, in the form of a beautiful young woman.

Nymphs were spirits in the form of young women: they were enchanting but they might also become threatening.

The centaur Chiron, half man and half horse, and one of the archetypal nature gods of the classical world. Chiron was renowned for his musical gifts, which were so seductive he could even bewitch the Sirens themselves.

ROMAN WITCHCRAFT

Acceptable magic acts took place in daylight; the night was considered to be the time when evil magic was practised. Roman literature is full of references to a creature called a *strix* (a word of Greek origin meaning "to screech"), which flew about at night uttering its ear-piercing screams, and feeding on the flesh and blood of human beings. The strix was usually thought of as an owl and had feathers and laid eggs, but it was more than a bird as, according to popular belief, it was able to suckle its young, and one of its evil acts was to offer its teats for human babies to suck its poisoned milk. When a *strix* found an unprotected baby it dragged it from its cradle and tore out and ate its entrails.

Witchcraft was portrayed in works such as *The Golden Ass*, in which the writer, Lucius Apuleius, writing in the first person, was transformed into an ass when he tried to imitate a witch. He describes how he observes her change herself into a bird so that she is able to fly into her lover's bedroom at twilight:

An illustration from an edition of The Golden Ass *in which Lucius Apuleius has succeeded in changing himself into an Ass.*

I ... watched Pamphil' first undress completely and then open a small cabinet containing several little boxes, one of which she opened. It contained an ointment which she worked about with her fingers and then smeared all over her body from the soles of her feet to the crown of her head. After this she muttered a long charm to her lamp, and shook herself; and, as I watched, her limbs became gradually fledged with feathers, her arms changed into sturdy wings, her nose grew crooked and horny, her nails turned into talons, and soon there was no longer any doubt about it: Pamphil' had become an owl. She gave a querulous hoot and made a few little hopping flights until she was sure enough of her wings to glide off, away over the rooftops.

Lucius cannot believe his eyes: he thinks he was dreaming, or perhaps going mad, but he nevertheless wants to try the ointment himself. However, instead of becoming transformed into a witch he metamorphoses into a donkey, a lesson to those who might experiment with forces they can't control.

In an illustration from an Italian edition of The Golden Ass *from the early 1800s, Lucius watches the transformation of the witch into an owl.*

THE CLASSICAL WITCHES

The three most famous witches in the classical world are Hecate, Circe and Medea. They are witch-goddesses that are also associated with darkness and the night. These magical beings were not the completely evil hags that witches later became under the influence of the Christian Inquisition, but represented a necessary component of the life/death interaction that went back to much earlier times. Witches were believed to be able to call down the moon from the sky with chanting, to make waxen figures move, to invoke the spirits of the dead and to make love philtres.

Among the Romans it was thought that men were more prone to thieving, while women were more inclined to witchcraft and poisoning. However, in their original form witches represented part of a wider totality, before dark became totally separated from light.

Hecate (right) and Persephone, two classical goddesses associated with darkness and the underworld, as depicted in the fifth century BC.

HECATE

The witch-goddess Hecate was associated with the night and the moon. Hecate was called the "Queen of Night" by the poet Sappho in the sixth century BC. She was the goddess of the dark phase of the moon (while Artemis, the huntress virgin goddess, represented the new moon, and Selene, or Demeter, the full moon). Hecate was looked upon as queen of the spirits of the dead; she lived in tombs, although she might also sit by the hearth. She was believed to be

The witch-goddess Medea with one of her murdered children beside her.

Hecate, witch-goddess of darkness and the queen of the spirits of the dead.

Odysseus lands on the island of Aeaea, the home of Circe. A group of Odysseus' men enter Circe's palace. They are invited in and Circe gives them a drug that changes them into pigs, though their minds remain human. She drives them into pigsties. Odysseus sets off to rescue the men, and on the way meets the god Hermes, who gives him a drug that will make him immune to Circe's magic. When Circe finds that she cannot enchant him, Odysseus persuades her to release his men, and she uses an ointment to restore them.

They stay in Circe's palace for a year until Odysseus is reminded by his men that they must go home. Circe tells Odysseus that he must first make a journey to Hades, the world of the dead, and consult Teiresias, a blind prophet from Thebes, who will reveal his future

A sixteenth-century depiction of Circe as a sorceress, sitting in a magic circle, wand in hand, a flaming chalice at her side.

present at a person's birth and death – when the spirit entered and left the human body.

Hecate appeared at crossroads on clear nights with a following of spirits and dogs, who were sacred to her and barked at the moon. Her power was threefold and extended to heaven, earth and the underworld. Witches were said to gather at crossroads and invoke Hecate, and offerings of the remains of purifying sacrifices were placed each month at crossroads to appease her. The women who were believed to invoke Hecate in this manner were held to be experts in the manufacture of poisons.

CIRCE

Witches feature in the works of the Greek poet Homer, to whom the *Iliad* and the *Odyssey* are attributed. These two epic poems, composed in the eighth century BC, were based on the legends surrounding the Trojan War. The former describes part of the war and the latter tells how Odysseus struggled to find his way home. The *Odyssey* is a tale of the hero Odysseus' mastery of nature. It is an inner quest for illumination in which the journey to reach "home" works as a metaphor for finding the treasures of the soul.

The sorceress Circe with the companions of Odysseus that have been transformed into animals.

to him. The north wind will carry his ship to the ends of the world, across the river of the ocean where he can enter Hades. Odysseus must dig a trench and pour in honey, milk, sweet wine and water as offerings to the dead. He must also sacrifice two sheep, being careful not to let any ghost near the blood until he has consulted the prophet. Odysseus follows Circe's instructions and meets various spirits, including the fallen heroes of the Trojan War and his dead parents, as well as Teiresias.

On his return to the witch's palace, Odysseus is warned by Circe of the dangers that he and his men will meet on their journey. The first of these is

Odysseus tied to the mast of his ship so that he can hear the song of the Sirens but is unable to answer their call.

the Sirens, nymphs who attract and enchant. The voices of the Sirens are divine, but the land where they sing is strewn with human bones. Circe tells Odysseus to instruct his men to put beeswax into their ears so they will not hear the Sirens' song, and if Odysseus wishes to hear their singing, she says that he must get his men to tie him to the ship's mast. Circe also warns him of the wandering rocks where he must pass between the monstrous Scylla, who has twelve feet and six heads at the end of long necks and will snatch any sailors whose ship comes within her reach, and Charybdis, a whirl-pool that sucks in passing ships.

Medea helps Jason to flee with the stolen fleece as they are pursued.

Circe symbolizes the woman who seduces men by enchanting or bewitching as well as by her skill. She is the gateway to the dark and she instructs Odysseus to journey to Hades, to enter the underworld. This has been interpreted as an inner quest to find the "treasures of the soul". Circe gives Odysseus advice about how to deal with magical pitfalls in the shape of the Sirens, Scylla and Charybdis. She is a witch in the sense that she is mistress of the dark, but she will assist those whom she favours to find illumination or enlightenment through an encounter with the underworld.

MEDEA

Medea, like Circe, has a knowledge of spells, potent brews and concoctions for causing sleep or changes in consciousness. She is the dark power that is uncontained and that, in the stories told about her, eventually creates chaos and destruction.

In Ovid's *Metamorphoses*, Medea invokes the night at the point of commiting an evil action: "O night, most faithful guardian of my secrets, and golden stars, who, with the moon, succeed the brightness of day ...". At other times she also calls on Hecate, the "night-wandering queen of the world below".

Medea's most famous role in legend is in the expedition of Jason and the Argonauts, when she falls in love with Jason and helps him to gain, and then keep, the Golden Fleece:

The monster in his sheath of horny scales rolled forward his interminable coils, like the eddies of black smoke that spring from smouldering logs and chase each other from below in endless convolutions. But as he writhed he saw the maiden take her stand, and heard her in her sweet voice invoking Sleep, the conqueror of the Gods, to charm him. She also called on the night-wandering queen of the world below to countenance her efforts. Jason from behind looked on in terror. But the giant snake, enchanted by her song, was soon relaxing the whole length of his serrated spine and smoothing out his multitudinous undulation, like a dark and

Medea after the dreadful murder of her own children, the darkest evil imaginable.

silent swell rolling across a sluggish sea. Yet his grim head still hovered over them and the cruel jaws threatened to snap them up. But Medea, chanting a spell, dipped a fresh sprig of juniper in her brew and sprinkled his eyes with her most potent drug; as the all-pervading magic scent spread round his head, sleep fell on him. Stirring no more, he let his jaw sink to the ground, and his innumerable coils lay stretched out far behind, spanning the deep wood. Medea called to Jason and he snatched the Golden Fleece from the oak.

When Jason beds the daughter of Creon, King of Corinth, Medea is full of vengence. She invokes Hecate and is filled with magical power, which she uses to torture the woman. Medea sends her children with a rich enchanted wedding robe that is steeped in poison and will cling to the princess's flesh and kill her. Then, in the madness of jealousy, Medea kills her own sons before she is borne away through the air in a chariot drawn by dragons.

Circe pouring poison into a vase and awaiting the arrival of Odysseus, whose ships can be seen in the background.

THE EUROPEAN TRADITION

In Europe, as elsewhere, people believed in witches. Witches were a normal part of everyday life for most people. If something went wrong, such as a cow dying or the butter failing to churn, it was due to witchcraft. People looked to their immediate neighbours to see who might be responsible. During the fifteenth to the seventeenth centuries the Christian church claimed that witches were members of a devil-worshipping cult who flew to night Sabbaths to feast on the bodies of children and indulge in orgies. Witches were said to be responsible for all types of misfortune, and they were tried and condemned to death for their supposed evil ways. Ideas about witches are still deeply embedded in folklore, literature and fairy stories.

Kit's Coty, one of the sites in England that bear witness to the folkloric prevalence of witches.

FOLK BELIEFS

Witchcraft beliefs form part of a magical world-view in which powers and forces inherent in the universe may be directed for good or ill. This is a world where everything is seen in terms of spirits and where certain persons specialize in their control. This was the case until the eighteenth century in Europe, when the Enlightenment – an intellectual movement that cast aside what it saw as the dark mysteries of religion in the pursuit of scientific research based on reason – changed the way that people thought. The process was aided by the development of rationalism, a particular way of thinking that sees all knowledge of the world as based on reason and logic. Magical beliefs came to be seen as superstition based on ignorance.

Ideas about witches, witchcraft, wizards, magic and sorcery are deeply embedded in European culture in the classical world and also in fairy tales and folk beliefs, and the countryside.

In Kent, England, for example, a megalithic chamber tomb was for centuries said to have been raised by four witches, and was known as Kit's Coty. Likewise, at the Rollright Stones in Oxfordshire, England, legend tells of a local king and his knights who were going to war. It was prophesied that if he reached a place called Long Compton he would be king of all England. However, as he was making his way up a big hill he met an old witch who turned him and all his men to stones. It is still said

A portrayal of the three witches of Shakespeare's Macbeth *as they work their magic.*

that ill-luck will fall on anyone who tries to move them. This folk tale holds echoes of the witches' role in the play *Macbeth*.

Shakespeare wrote *Macbeth* at the beginning of the seventeenth century, and in it he describes the role that three witches play in Macbeth's ambition to be king. The portrayal of the "weird sisters" is how most Europeans at that time would have viewed witches. The three women were isolated from society, living outside the community, and they were strange, both physically and behaviourally, taking on almost unhuman aspects. The witches exercised a certain amount of power and prophecy, but were only potent on their own ground – it is Macbeth that comes to them rather than the other way round: their territory is the wasted heath. Their activities are also typical of contemporary thought. They work in the dead of night, around a fire, they make plans for future meetings, and they cook a spell in a huge cauldron that is the receptacle for all kinds of unlikely ingredients. They also invoke Hecate, a Roman witch from classical times whose reputation as the witches' queen had lasted until this time:

3rd Witch: *Scale of dragon, tooth of wolf;*
Witches' mummy; maw, and gulf,
Of the ravin'd salt-sea shark;
Root of hemlock, digg'd i' th' dark;
Liver of blaspheming Jew;
Gall of goat, and slips of yew,
Sliver'd in the moon's eclipse;
Nose of Turk, and Tartar's lips;
Finger of birth-strangled babe,
Ditch-deliver'd by a drab,
Make the gruel thick and slab:
Add thereto a tiger's chaudron,
For th' ingredients of our cauldron.

2nd Witch: *Cool it with a baboon's blood.*
Then the charm is firm and good.

ENTER HECATE

Hecate: *O, well done!*
I commend your pains,
And every one shall share i' th' gains.
And now about the cauldron sing,
Like elves and fairies in a ring,
Enchanting all that you put in.

Hansel and Gretel outside the witch's house made of bread, cake and sugar.

As queen of witches, Hecate was the epitome of evil in the classical world, invoked in rites of black magic. Here she is the antithesis of good and plays a central part in Macbeth's downfall.

FAIRY STORIES

Tales of witches abound in fairy stories. They are almost always portrayed as evil old women who must be defeated by the innocent heroes or heroines. The German folk tale of Hansel and Gretel typically expresses these kinds of popular ideas about the witch. In this story Hansel and Gretel are the children

of a poor woodcutter. When famine strikes, their stepmother persuades their father to take the two children into the wood and abandon them. The children wander in the wood for three days until they come to a clearing where there is a house made of bread, cake and sugar. The children begin to eat the house and an old woman comes out and invites them in for a meal and shelter. The following morning, however, she locks Hansel in a cage and forces Gretel to work for her. She feeds Hansel to fatten him up to eat but she starves Gretel. Each day she makes Hansel hold out his finger to see how fat he has got, but he holds out a bone instead. The witch decides to eat him anyway and she orders Gretel to stoke the oven, however, Gretel tricks the witch into climbing into the oven herself. The two children return home to find that their stepmother has died and they are welcomed home by their father.

This fairy tale shows how in folklore the witch is associated with the female and with evil; she can be seen at one and the same time as the stepmother in the home who is trying to get rid of the children and as the outsider, a sinister inhabitant of a dark and frightening wood. One is a threat from within, the other represents a world of anxiety, chaos, darkness and terror.

Macbeth encountering the three witches who foretell his rise and fall as King of Scotland.

ORIGINS OF EUROPEAN WITCHCRAFT

Where did the idea of a witch come from? Scholars have seen witchcraft in terms of superstition, peasant credulity or female hysteria. They have focused on the persecution of witches without looking for the origin of such beliefs. The historian Carlo Ginzburg has criticized this approach and has looked to folklore to find the origins. He studied the *benandanti*, men and women in sixteenth- and seventeenth-century Italy who claimed that in their dreams they were wizards who fought against witches in order to protect their community. Other examples supported Ginzburg's belief – the *kresniks* of Slovenia and the *táltos* of Hungary. Together with the benandanti, he described these peoples as the surviving elements of shamanism – those who use their spiritual powers for protective purposes.

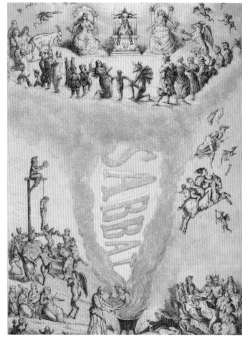

A popular stereotype of witches, showing scenes of sacrifice, orgy and night-flying to sabbaths to worship the Devil and his countless demons

Carlo Ginzburg discovered documents of the Inquisition relating to these persons known as benandanti of the region of Friuli in north-east Italy, ranging from 1575 to the second half of the seventeenth century. Originally writing in 1966, Ginzburg described how the benandanti fought against the harmful activities of witches. They identified witches, cured the bewitched and used counter-magic against witches' spells. Four times a year they went into a trance while their souls left their bodies and, armed with fennel stalks, fought for the fertility of the fields against male and female witches armed with canes of sorghum. The spirits of the benandanti left their inanimate bodies and took the shapes of mice or butterflies. Sometimes they rode hares, cats or other animals to battle against witches or to join a procession of the dead.

A person had to be born a benandanti, and the sign of their vocation was a caul, or portion of the amniotic sac, covering their head at birth. The parents generally had the caul baptized with the child, and either preserved it until the child grew up, or made the child carry it around the neck or shoulder. When they were around twenty years old they were initiated during a visionary soul journey, during which another benandanti or an angel of God appeared to them, beating a drum, and called their soul to an assembly of the benandanti.

The inquisitors were baffled by the strange beliefs of the benandanti,

Witches and their familiars, according to a seventeenth-century view.

An erotic seventeenth-century portrayal of a witches' Sabbath, which became stereotyped by the inquisitors as a meeting for female witches who renounced their Christian faith and indulged in sexual orgies.

THE KRESNIKS

In later works, Ginzburg attempted to find other folk beliefs like those of the benandanti, and found that the beliefs of the kresniks in Slovenia and Istria were closely related. Yugoslavian and Hungarian folklorists have collected much data on the beliefs associated with the kresniks. They were people who acquired the power to confront witches because they, like the benandanti, had been born with a caul. During the night the kresniks fought witches in the shape of dogs, horses or giants. In another version, the kresnik fell into a sleep, and a big black fly flew out of his throat to fight the witches. Yet another version states that kresniks fought witches with sticks in the air near a crossroads, or they crossed the sea in eggshells to fight in Venice above St Mark's Square.

Every clan had two kresniks, one who did good, and one who did harm. They could take the shape of any animal, although they mostly fought in the form of goats, bullocks or horses. A natural opponent of the kresnik was the *vucodlak* or werewolf. The vucodlaks were also capable of soul journeys during which they transformed into wolves. It has been suggested that the fights of the kresniks and the vucodlaks were not, in fact, encounters between positive and negative forces, but the clash of "sorcerers" who represented different communities or regions.

especially the fact that they claimed that they were fighting for God and Christ. The inquisitors tried to shape the beliefs of the benandanti into what they knew about demonology. They likened their assemblies to the witches' Sabbath. The Sabbath became stereotyped as a night meeting of witches, who were usually female, and flew to the nocturnal gathering astride broomsticks, or on the backs of animals. This spirit flight was seen to be aided by the application of unguents made from children's fat. The first time a witch went to the Sabbath she had to renounce the Christian faith, desecrate the sacrament and pay homage to the Devil. They had banquets with dancing and sexual orgies.

A much less erotic image of a witch was the old crone. Here the Lancashire witch Mother Chattox rides to Pendle Hill, England, a notorious meeting place for witches, according to folklore.

The shamanic basis of ideas about witchcraft lies in the concept of the soul leaving the body and transforming into animals.
In this Scandanavian illustration from 1555, men are transformed into wolves in a ferocious flying hunt.

THE TÁLTOS

The Hungarian táltos were, like the kresniks, rivals of witches, and they fought for the fertility of their own village or region with adversaries from neighbouring regions, diverting drought, hail or animal plague from their own locality to that of their adversary. These fights are mentioned in accounts of witch trials. In 1741, a female táltos said that the ability to transform into animals was not necessarily related to the fights. She described how sometimes she looked into a plate filled with water and turned into a fish, disappearing for three days. On other occasions she could become a dove or a fox if she wished.

SHAMANIC LINKS

Ginzburg makes the connection between the benandanti and shamans, and a case can be made for seeing the benandanti, kresnik and táltos as various surviving elements of shamanism in central and southern Europe. Shamans use their power to communicate with the spirit world for the benefit of their social group. They are protectors of their community from magical aggression and natural calamities. They can also heal sick people, communicate with the spirits of the dead, find lost objects and predict the future. They do this by entering into a trance during which their soul leaves their body and changes into spirit forms such as various animals, to battle with spirits or forces or to gain information.

The soul of a witch was said to leave the apparently lifeless body of the witch through the mouth and take the form of a butterfly, a fly or other small animal, returning some time later. Ginzburg argues that it is shamanic folk beliefs that were reinterpreted by the Inquisition as witchcraft, because the Christian church took a hostile approach to any form of magical activity. There emerged an image of a heretical witch sect, which was identified with evil and maleficence. The witches' Sabbath had two cultural aspects. The first, which was the view of the inquisitors and lay judges, was that there was a hostile social group conspiring against the Church and the forces of good. The second was that elements of shamanic origin were rooted in a folk culture of magic flight and animal metamorphosis. The result was a conflict between folk beliefs

Witches were said to have a close association with animals. Here three witches are shown with their familiars in a seventeenth-century woodcut.

and the learned culture of the inquisitors. The belief that a witch could fly through the air and transform into various animals has its roots in an earlier magical world-view. Perhaps these ideas go back to societies where shamans engaged, through trance, with spiritual other worlds to protect the community from harm, to resolve problems like the whereabouts of animals to hunt, or to heal. These shamanic activities were reinterpreted by the Inquisition as the work of witches and labelled as harmful rather than beneficial to society.

MAGIC AND FLIGHT

How did these shamanic beliefs change into ideas about witches? The cannibalistic night witch was a part of traditional European folk beliefs. The notion of cannibalistic witches or *strigae* flying at night was familiar to many Germanic peoples of the early Middle Ages. At this time there was also a cult of the night-flying goddesses Diana, Herodias and Holda. These goddesses were beneficent female protective spirits who were sometimes associated with the souls of the dead and had no association with witchcraft or evil.

Diana was worshipped as goddess of the moon, lover of the night and associate of Hecate. She rode out at night followed by a train of souls disguised as women. These were souls of the prematurely dead, those who had died by violence, or of those that had never been buried.

Diana is equated with Herodias, the wife of Herod the tetrarch and the instigator of the murder of John the Baptist. According to a twelfth-century Latin poet Reinardus, Herod's daughter, who is referred to as Herodias rather than Salome, falls in love with John the Baptist. Unfortunately, her love is not returned and when his head is brought to her on a platter she kisses it, but it shrinks away. Herodias is blown into outer space where she must hover for ever. From midnight until cockcrow she is permitted to rest from her eternal travelling through the air by sitting on oak trees and hazel bushes.

Holda, or Hulda, is a fertility goddess who circles the earth and is particularly active in the depths of winter. She travels in the 12 days between Christmas and Epiphany bringing fertility to the land for the coming year. The historian Norman Cohn suggests that originally Holda was a pagan goddess who was associated with the winter solstice and the rebirth of the year. She is a patroness of husbandry, assisting with the crops, and the plough is sacred to her; she is also interested in spinning, weaving and childbirth. She can become terrifying if angered, but will reward hard work. When she rides out on nocturnal journeys she takes with her a train of the souls of the dead, including those who have died without being baptized.

Holda's cult followers imagined that their souls were joining this night flight, not for destructive purposes but rather for positive and sustaining ends. However, according to the *Canon Episcopi*, written in the tenth century, the women who sent their souls to ride in such a train were wicked; they had been seduced and deluded by Satan, and by the illusions and phantoms of demons, into believing that they really were riding with Diana:

… [they] openly avow that in the hours of the night they ride on certain animals, together with Diana, the goddess of the pagans, with a numberless multitude of women; and in the silence of the dead of night cross many great lands; and obey [Diana's] orders as though she were their mistress, and on particular nights are summoned to her service.

The canon reminds priests to warn their congregations that this is an illusion inspired by Satan. Thus folk beliefs of the night-flying goddesses Diana, Herodias and Holda were equated with those of cannibalistic strigae, and the wicked stereotype of the witch flying to the sabbath was created.

The cult of the night-flying goddess Diana was one manifestation of a social preoccupation with the possibility of human flight, and its association with the divine or the magical.

THE WORLD OF FAIRIES

Ideas about witches are sometimes associated with those concerning fairies. European folklore tells of worlds inhabited by little people called by various names such as elves, fairies, pixies or goblins. The land of faery is a magical place and special human beings were intermediaries between this enchanted realm and the ordinary, everyday world. In other cultures these people may have had a shamanic role to play in their communities. These fairy tales have often become mingled with tales of witches and sorcery, and at times the two have become indistinguishable.

As we have discussed, the origins of European witchcraft beliefs may lie in the shamanic elements of folklore. According to Carlo Ginzburg, the benandanti of northern Italy told their inquisitors that they were good wizards who fought against witches. In Romania, the historian of religion, Mircea Eliade, found information on another group of healers who cured diseases caused by fairies. The folklore of certain areas of Europe shows fairy cults in which special individuals

Fairies take possession of the human world at night, and their flickering, unearthly lights would act as a warning to humans to keep away.

served as intermediaries between the world of the fairies and the human world. They had elaborate rituals for curing people and animals stricken by illness because they had offended the fairies.

THE FAIRY KINGDOM

The words "faerie" and "fey" are of French derivation, and started to replace the Old English *elf* during the fourteenth century, so the words "faerie" and "elf" are interchangeable. The world of faery is said to be a world of enchantment, captivating beauty, humour, mischief, laughter and love; it is also a world of darkness, ugliness, callous superficiality, terror and tragedy. Faery is an otherworld, a place of magical power that can reveal itself to certain people. Many fairies were said to live inside hollow hills or barrows of the dead and

Fairy kingdoms were said to be places of beauty, mischief and love, ruled over by the fairy king and queen. Note the interesting depiction of the god Pan in the top right hand corner of this painting of Titania and Oberon.

The fairy kingdom was inhabited by weird and wonderful creatures, as this procession of curious sprites and goblins illustrates.

these were thought to be entrances to the otherworld. There are many types of fairy, including pixie, elf, goblin, lubberkin and hobgoblin; banshee, sidhe and leprechaun in Ireland; fynodere on the Isle of Man, gruagach, urisk, brollachan and fuath in Scotland. They range in height from the size of a human to minute proportions, and their appearance varies from extreme beauty to grotesque ugliness.

ROYAL FAIRIES

The fairies have kings and queens. Gwyn ap Nudd is a fairy king and lord of the underworld. In Celtic folklore Gwyn ap Nudd is a wild huntsman who rides a demon horse and hunts in waste places at night with a pack of white-bodied and red-eared dogs of hell. The Wild Hunt is the generic name given to numerous folk myths associated with such "soul-ravening" chases. There are many

The goddess Diana in her hunting role, with her bow and arrows, horn and dog.

leaders of the Wild Hunt in folklore, including Woden (Odin or Wotan) and Herne the Hunter. The leader of this ghastly rout is sometimes female and associated with the goddess Diana.

A later derivative of Diana is Titania, queen of the fairies in Shakespeare's *A Midsummer Night's Dream*. Also known as Mab, she probably derived from the Celtic Medb, or Maeve, queen of Connaght, who fought against Cú Chulainn. In sixteenth- and seventeenth-century literature Medb was the fairy queen who gave birth to dreams in humans. Oberon, a king of the fairies, also features in *A Midsummer Night's Dream* in which he is the estranged, and later reconciled, husband of Titania . His first appearance is in a medieval French romance called *Huan de Bordeaux* where he is called Alberon, a dwarf-king, the son of Julius Caesar and the witch queen Morgan le Fay, who helps the hero in an impossible task. His origins probably derive from Alberich, the king of Teutonic dwarfs.

Morgan le Fay, sometimes called a witch, sometimes a dark fairy, whose lust for power brought about the end of King Arthur's reign.

FAIRY CAPTIVES

Humans may be lured to the otherworld, as in the Scottish ballad of Thomas the Rhymer. One day as he lay down on a bank, the Queen of Elfland rode past on a horse whose mane was plaited with silver bells:

> *True Thomas lay o'er yond grassy bank,*
> *And he beheld a ladie gay,*
> *A ladie that was brisk and bold,*
> *Come riding o'er the fernie brae*
> *Her skirt was of the grass-green silk,*
> *Her mantel of the velvet fine,*
> *At ilka tett of her horse's mane*
> *Hung fifty silver bells and nine.*

Human beings – usually men – were said to be lured into the otherworld by irresistibly beautiful female fairies, and were often never seen again.

> *True Thomas he took off his hat,*
> *And bowed him low down till his knee:*
> *'All hail, thou mighty Queen of Heaven!*
> *For your peer on earth I never did see.'*
>
> *'O no, O no, true Thomas,' she says,*
> *'That name does not belong to me;*
> *I am but the queen of fair Elfland,*
> *And I'm come here for to visit thee.*
> *But ye maun go wi' me now, Thomas,*
> *True Thomas, ye maun go wi' me,*
> *For ye maun serve me seven years,*
> *Thro' weel or wae as may chance to be.'*
> *She turned about her milk-white steed,*
> *And took True Thomas up behind,*
> *And aye whene'er her bridle rang,*
> *The steed flew swifter in the wind.*

Thomas dwelt underground for seven years before returning to the ordinary world where he wrote poetry and made prophecies.

The fairies of Ireland are called sidhe (pronounced "shee") and are thought to be the descendants of the Tuatha dé Danaan, the original Irish. Their music is said to be a joy to listen to and their Queen Maeve is so beautiful that it is dangerous to look at her. The sidhe live happily if left undisturbed, but if they are molested or have any of their taboos broken, they can be very dangerous.

Their touch can sicken or madden a human being and their elf-arrows can cause instant paralysis or death. Contact with the sidhe should be avoided on 1 May and Hallowe'en when they are moving homes, at twilight, before sunrise and at noon. It is wise never to walk inside sidhe circles or over sidhe hills. Cutting down a thorn bush or leaving something on their path also invites disaster. If angered they will sometimes kidnap people and make them their slaves inside their hills. Even a short stay with the sidhe can change a person completely and they may not return. If they do, they are likely to be either mad, or come back as seers, healers or prophets.

In one story a girl heard music and was enticed into fairyland by the song – it made her think of things far away and of rivers flowing slowly to the sea. Her encounter with the sidhe was to have serious consequences for her.

As she was gathering nuts in the forest, a girl heard music of a kind different from any she had ever known. It warmed her heart and made her forget the half-gathered nuts lying beneath the tree. The soft whisper of the wind was loud in comparison with this music, and she thought of things far away and of the neighbours came to the wake, they found a hag with long teeth in her place. She was so old and so wrinkled that she could have been 100. That night the music was heard again. The mother saw flashing coloured lights outside every window and heard for the last time the music of the pipers who had taken her daughter away.

In this story, the music drew the girl into the magical land of fairy, her place in the ordinary world being taken by an old hag. Did she die as the hag or did she go to live with the sidhe in a different place and time? We do not know, we can only imagine. Such is the enduring magic of these tales.

FAIRIES AND HUMANS

Fairies were said to be fond of dancing in circles, and if a person took a walk outside at night they might actually see the fairies enjoying themselves, feasting and dancing. Fairies could be mischievous or even cruel, capable of stealing human children for their own breeding purposes and leaving substitutes or changelings in their place. If anything angered them, they could use their magical powers to inflict disease, but they could be kept friendly by offerings of food or drink. Iron objects were said to repel them. They were sometimes said to live in a fireplace and help with housework, if the fireplace was kept clean for them. They could lend farmers cattle that yielded unending milk. Fairy women were said to marry mortal men and bring much happiness, and they could also bestow good luck, beauty and talent on children.

The fairies were associated with nature; they were said to inhabit wilderness, heaths and forests. They were akin to the "wild men and women" who combined human, animal and spirit, and were believed to roam the forests in medieval times. Elements of the wild woman, who was often portrayed as a childeater and bloodsucker, lingered in the folk tales of the lonely witch who dwelt in the forest. Gradually, the characteristics of wild women were transferred to witches.

Fairies were said to be able to entice humans into their magical realms, and children were warned never to step into a fairy ring by superstitious parents.

rivers flowing slowly to the sea, until twilight darkened around her and she could hear no more.

She told her mother of the music and left even earlier the next day for the woods. She stood there beneath the nut tree, listening until the last echoes of the song had faded and the stars glittered in the night. She went again the next day to listen and the music overwhelmed

her and followed her home, filling her room with its magic. Then suddenly it stopped. When the girl emerged from her room, her mother asked her about the strange sounds. 'There was no music, mother. You must have imagined it.' With a doubtful shake of her head, her mother turned back to her work and said no more about it. The next day she found her daughter dead in bed. When

Faires and witches were often interchangeable. This is a painting of a fairy tale witch from the early 1900s.

FAIRIES AND WITCHES

It is often difficult to make distinctions beween fairies and witches, and ideas about both have merged at certain periods and changed over time. Eliade discovered that the Romanian healers, who cured diseases caused by the fairies, met in night gatherings ruled over by Doamna Zónelor, the "Queen of the Fairies", a Romanian version of Diana or Aradia, both of whom have connections with Western European beliefs in witchcraft and the Wild Hunt. Satanic elements of these beliefs about night-flying goddesses may have been forcibly imposed during the trials, when they were associated with maleficent witchcraft.

The historian Gustav Henningsen studied Sicilian fairy cults. In the archives of the Spanish Inquisition he found accounts of trials of Sicilian witches between 1579 and 1651 documenting beliefs about the *donna di fuora*, who was a mixture of fairy and witch. The Inquisition material reveals that the Sicilians had two meanings for the term *donna di fuora*. The first was as a supernatural fairy-like creature of either sex who accompanied witches on their night-time excursions, and the second was associated with accused witches who adopted the name.

FAIRY CULTS

According to the Inquisition trial records, fairy cults were organized in companies. Those who attended were described as beautiful women dressed in black or white with cats' paws, horses' hooves, or "round feet". Some also had pigs' tails. Sometimes one of the group was a male fairy, who played the lute or the guitar while the others danced with linked hands.

In 1588 a fisherman's wife from Palermo confessed to the Inquisition that in a dream she and her company rode on billy goats through the air to a country called Benevento, which belonged to the Pope. They worshipped a king and a queen who, they were told, would give them wealth, beauty and young men to make love with. After the worship there was feasting, drinking and lovemaking. She also told about another witches' assembly called "The Seven Fairies". These witches had the habit of transforming themselves into dogs, cats and other animals, before going out to kill boys and commit other misdeeds. The fisherman's wife confessed the error of her ways and said that at the time she did not know that it was devilment. However, in spite of this she went on doing it because of the pleasure it gave her and because the king and queen gave her remedies for curing the sick.

In 1627 a 36-year-old wise woman related how she was taken by her "company of the Romans" to many places, including Rome, Messina and a "vast plain with a big walnut tree in the centre". The "Romans" were the "wise Sybil's people" (Sibil was King Solomon's sister) who came from a cave in the tower of Babylon. The woman talked about her experience and this was recorded by the inquisitors:

She had instructed the others together with the bliss-crowned Virgin Mary, and had received the impression that she herself must be the Mother of God. But when she saw that it was not to be her, but the bliss-crowned Virgin, she threw all her books on the fire. But Mary kept hers under her arm.

The company toured around the houses of the town each Tuesday, Thursday and Saturday night. The "Matron" leading the procession carried a torch to light the way, which was visible only to members.

Members of these secret assemblies were poor: they were farm labourers and their wives, workmen and their wives, fishermen's wives, a tailor, a shoemaker and his wife, a deacon, two Franciscan begging nuns, a charismatic healer, a washerwoman, two prostitutes, two gypsy women, some widows and various other people. There were more women involved than men.

The majority of the accused were practising wise women who were skilled in sorcery and magical healing rituals and who were known to cure misfortune brought about by the fairies. *Tocadura de brujas*, or "witch-touching", was the term for these illnesses, which could take every possible form, from indisposition to epilepsy, and which were caused by offending the fairies. For example, a young man who suffered an attack of cramp while playing the guitar was told by a wise woman in Noto that he had pushed some fairies with his arm who had gathered around him to listen to the music. The wise woman would explain the cause of the illness or misfortune to the patient and explain that she would attend a nocturnal meeting and persuade the fairies to make the sick person well. In the meantime the fairies could be mollified with offerings of a ritual meal. The wise woman would decorate the sick person's room, covering the bed with a red cloth and perfuming the whole room. On a table she would put water, wine, sweetmeats, loaves and a honey-cake. The fairies would usually visit at night when everyone was asleep, but the wise woman, or *donas*, would come when the family was present. She would walk up

Fairies carried out their work invisibly, and one talent of the wise women was to be able to "see" or sense their presence.

Fairies were not just ephemeral, lacy-winged beings, they were often grotesque and hostile too, such as these hobgoblins up to no good.

and down near the sick person playing her tambourine, and picking up food from the plates as if to feed the fairies. She told the family that she was being instructed in how to make the sick person better. The tocadura de brujas could also strike horses and donkeys, and rituals would be carried out in the stable. Sometimes rituals would be performed to bless the fields.

SHAMANIC LINKS

We can see from this that ideas about fairies have become intermingled with those about witches. Both fairies and witches were thought to have an association with a magical otherworld – the fairies as otherworldly beings and witches as gaining power from a supernatural realm. In reality, these ideas were probably a particularly European interpretation of an older shamanic pattern, whereby a specialist in dealing with spirits would go into trance to visit these otherworlds for information, advice or knowledge.

AFRICAN WITCHCRAFT

In most African societies witches are described as morose, unsociable people; they eat alone so as not to share their food, but are dangerous if food is not shared with them. They are arrogant and pass people without greeting, but are also easily offended if the same is done to them. Witches are often said to have the evil eye. Explanations of witchcraft rest on the boundless possibilities of human misdeeds and antisocial acts due to rivalry, jealousy, prejudice or any personal grievance of which you can think. Magical charms, spells and objects, such as fetishes, are often employed as protection. Witchcraft is seen as evil and it is often motivated by ill feelings generated by a quarrel, which may be remembered when someone becomes ill or suffers some misfortune. Witchcraft is always unjustified – a person may have good cause for anger, but anger should not be expressed as witchcraft.

Fetishes, magical objects used as protection against witchcraft, in Akodessewa market in Lomé, Africa.

Many African peoples believe that certain relatives might, if provoked, curse, and this inevitably has dire consequences. Relatives must accordingly be treated with respect. In Ghana, some peoples think that the power of witchcraft is inherited, and witchcraft is thought to flow along the recognized line of inheritance of property, succession to office etc; it can pass through the mother's or the father's line. Other societies believe that witchcraft power is transmitted by the parent other than that from whom property is inherited. The Tallensi of Northern Ghana believe that witchcraft powers are transmitted to persons of both sexes by their mothers.

PROTECTIVE SHRINES

In the Akan-speaking parts of Ghana, people go to shrines for protection against witchcraft. Shrine deities possess those persons who act as their priests and mediums. Talisman or fetish shrines are common in western Africa where medicines of protection are dispensed in rituals. A person thought to be bewitched is taken with the suspected witch to the shrine, where the witch is forced into making a confession. A new medium for the spirits is created when a person becomes possessed and runs wild in the bush, and is then taken to a priest of a shrine where the name of the possessing spirit is revealed. The objects in which the spirit power is embodied are thought to fall from the sky and they are captured by a diviner in a brass pan before the new medium enters the priesthood. A temple is built to the responsible spirit and people who are victims of witchcraft come for protection. The shrine is the focus of a village, and people bring offerings with requests for protection and help.

Medicines may be used as protection against witchcraft.

Night witches and animals

The night witches of the African tradition were witches who worked only in the hours of darkness. Their night time activities meant that they were associated particularly with the nocturnal owl. The hooting of owls was said to warn the night witches of someone approaching, and owls were therefore feared by the people, who saw them as bad omens. Night witches were also associated with hyenas, which they were said to ride on to distant places. When riding the hyena the witch would keep one leg on the ground and put the other on the animal's back, this had the effect of progress at great speed. Some people said that the witches were even capable of making their own hyenas by creating the body from porridge and bringing it to life with special medicines.

Potent magical symbols of the Azande people, of Sudan.

MAGIC AS A SOCIAL RULER

Witches, fairies and other spirit beings abound in European folklore; they are a central part of a magical view where a spirit world co-exists with ordinary, everyday reality. In African beliefs about witches and magic, similar ideas can be found. Magic and beliefs about witchcraft regulate many African societies. They allow grudges to be brought out in

the open and provide a formula for action in misfortune. Accusations appear where tensions between neighbouring rivals could not otherwise be resolved.

NIGHT WITCHES

The Tswana of Botswana, studied by the anthropologist Isaac Schapera in the 1930s, believed in "night witches" and "day sorcerers". The night witches were mainly elderly women who bewitched people. By day they went about their everyday activities but at night they gathered in small groups, visiting one homestead after another carrying out wicked practices. They were naked and smeared their bodies with white ashes or the blood of dead people. Before a woman was admitted to the group she had to prove that she had caused the death of a close relative, preferably her own first-born child. Once initiated, she was given an ointment to smear on her

A stool shrine of the Omanhene of Anomabu, Ghana, which is associated with the spirit of the tree. Such shrines are seen as sources of spiritual power, and are often used as protection against the presence of witchcraft.

A shrine of an Ashanti spirit medium. Here, a witch and those thought to have been bewitched are brought together and a confession is extracted from the witch. Shrines are also spiritual centres of the village and offer help and protection to people.

body, which would make her wake up immediately when her fellow witches came to call. In some tribes, it was said that a special medicine was injected into a witch's thumb to make it itch when she was required to attend a night gathering.

Night witches were said to dig up newly buried corpses with the aid of a special magic that made the grave open by itself and caused the corpse to float to the surface. The witches would then take parts of it to use in their medicines. It was said that they had special medicines that would put the inhabitants of a homestead into a deep sleep so that the witches could enter and find a victim. They inserted small stones and fragments of flesh into the victim's body that would make him or her fall ill and ultimately die unless counter-magic was applied in time.

DAY SORCERERS

Not everyone believed in the night witches but day sorcerers, on the other hand, were taken very seriously. Sorcerers did not belong to bands but they did use magic to harm and bewitch specific people. They might sprinkle the blood of their enemy's sacred totem animal over their courtyard. If the victim stepped on the blood it was said to affect their feet, leading to death or the loss of a limb. The sorcerer might hide rags containing special roots in the eaves of a victim's hut, or bury them at the entrance of their homestead. The sorcerer might take some dust from his victim's footprint to work magic upon it with medicines, or he might blow special powder in the direction of the victim, calling their name; he might send an animal such as a lion, snake, ox or leopard to cause bodily injury; or put special medicines in food to poison them. By using the appropriate medicines, the sorcerer was said to direct lightning so that it struck its victim, or their hut or cattle. Some sorcerers were believed to be able to fly through the air and then descend on their victims in the guise of lightning.

NIGHTWATCHMEN

Many African peoples have chiefs or village headmen whose duty is to watch over the community by day and by night. The night watch is sometimes described as a war against witches. Among the Nyakyusa witches, power is thought to derive from the python in their entrails, and so the chiefs or headmen must also have pythons in theirs. A part of the accession ritual for chiefs and headmen involves them drinking medicines made from the flesh of a python, this is thought to give the power to see and to fight witches.

A shaman of Botswana with a small animal skin, about to perform a divination, perhaps to detect the presence of witchcraft.

A divining instrument for the detection of witches, used in Zaire. The instrument is held in a diviner's lap and springs forward when a witch's name is mentioned.

THE AZANDE – A CASE STUDY

African studies of witchcraft have been influenced by the work of the anthropologist Edward Evans-Pritchard (1902–73), who carried out research among the Azande of central Africa in the late 1920s. Evans-Pritchard's book *Witchcraft, Oracles and Magic Among the Azande* is a study of Sudanese tribal kingdoms ruled by the Avongara and indirectly ruled by the British colonial administration. Evans-Pritchard showed how witchcraft played a major part in all parts of Azande life, from agriculture, fishing, hunting and domestic life to law, morality, technology and language. He wrote that witchcraft, which he likened to bad luck, was ever-present in Azande life: there was no niche or corner of Azande culture where it was not apparent. If blight seized the groundnut crop it was witchcraft; if there was no game in the bush it was witchcraft; if there were only a few small fish to catch it was witchcraft; if a wife was unresponsive to her husband it was witchcraft; if a prince was cold and distant with his subject it was witchcraft; if a magical rite failed to achieve its purpose it was witchcraft. Any failure or misfortune that could befall anybody at any time in relation to any activity might be because of witchcraft. Witchcraft was intertwined with everyday happenings and was a part of the ordinary world.

There was nothing remarkable about a witch – you might be one yourself, as might your neighbour.

Evans-Pritchard took witchcraft beliefs seriously and described how they structured Azande thinking; they provided a philosophy by which relations between humans and unfortunate events were explained. For example, a granary collapsed because termites had eaten the supports; it crushed the people sitting underneath. Rather than blame the rotten wood this was said to have happened because of witchcraft. The Azande knew that termites had undermined the supports of the granary and did not call this disaster witchcraft in its own right; they also knew that people were sheltering from the heat of the sun and that they were not there due to witchcraft. But they then asked why the two events happened at once: and the answer to this was witchcraft. Witchcraft explained the coincidence that the granary collapsed at the time when people were sitting under it sheltering from the sun. To the Western way of thinking these would be two independent factors.

An Azande ritual of cleansing a baby after birth by passing it through the smoke of a fire to banish evil spirits.

An Azande shaman and diviner holding a rodent's skull in his mouth as part of a ritual.

The Azande used common sense as well as magical explanations. For example, where there was a clear law or moral code witchcraft was not involved, and witchcraft could not make someone lie or commit adultery.

Witchcraft explained what we would call coincidence. Evans-Pritchard described how a boy knocked his foot against a small stump of wood in the centre of a path and suffered pain and inconvenience as a result. The boy declared that witchcraft had made him knock his foot in this way. Evans-Pritchard argued with the boy, saying that it was his own carelessness that had made him knock his foot and that witchcraft had not placed the stump in the path – it had grown there naturally. The boy agreed that witchcraft had nothing to do with the stump of wood being in the path, but argued that because he had been bewitched he had not been able to see it. He added that the cut had festered and not healed quickly and this was proof of witchcraft.

An Azande chief pictured here with members of his family.

Another example was provided when he noticed that a hut had been burnt to the ground. Evans-Pritchard spoke to the owner, who was overcome with grief because it had contained beer he was preparing for a mortuary feast. He explained that he had gone to examine the beer the previous night, lighting a handful of straw to cast light, and this had ignited the thatch. He was convinced that the disaster had been caused by witchcraft.

Likewise, a woodcarver explained the splitting of wooden utensils he was carving as due to the witchcraft created by his jealous neighbours. Similarly, a potter would attribute the cracking of his pots during firing to witchcraft. As an experienced potter, he knew that his pots would not crack as a result of error because he selected the proper clay, kneaded it thoroughly to extract grit and pebbles, and built it up slowly and carefully. On the night before digging the clay he abstained from sexual intercourse, so he should have had nothing to fear, and yet the pots cracked.

WITCHCRAFT AND THE SOUL

Evans-Pritchard claimed that the Azande made the distinction between witchcraft as a hereditary quality within a person, which might be unconscious and remain inoperative, and sorcery, the conscious and deliberate performance of a magical rite to cause injury. *Mbisimo mangu*, or the soul of witchcraft, might leave the body at any time, but especially at night when the victim was asleep. The Azande thought of a witch sending his soul on errands at night when his victim was asleep. It sailed through the air, sending out a bright light. During the daytime this light could only be seen by witches and witch doctors who were primed with medicines, but anyone might be unfortunate enough to see it at night. It was said to be like the gleam of firefly beetles but larger and brighter. If a person happened to see the light they picked up a piece of charcoal and threw it under their bed so that they would not suffer misfortune from the sight.

Only once did Evans-Pritchard say that he had seen witchcraft on its path. Around midnight, before retiring to bed, he went for a stroll in the garden at the back of his hut. He noticed a bright light passing at the back of his servants' huts towards the homestead of a man called Tupoi. He followed the light, running through his hut in order to see where the light was going, but he lost sight of it. On the following morning he learnt that an old relative of Tupoi had died. This event fully explained the light he had seen in terms of witchcraft: the light was coming from the body of the witch. The witch remained on his bed while the soul of his witchcraft was dispatched to remove the psychical part of his victim's organs – the *mbisimo pasio*, the soul of his flesh – which he and his fellow witches would devour. Evans-Pritchard never discovered the real origin of the light but speculated that it was possibly a handful of burning grass lit by someone on their way to defecate.

The soul of witchcraft, the mbisimo mangu, which was said to devour its victim's organs slowly, needed conscious direction to determine its route or else it

The Shilluk of Sudan constructing the thatched roof for a mud hut.

would return. The witch could not send out his witchcraft and leave it to find its victim for itself, he had to define its objective and determine its route. A sick man could elude its ravages by withdrawing to the shelter of a grass hut in the bush, unknown to all but his close relatives. The witchcraft would search at his homestead in vain and return to its owner. Sometimes a person would leave a homestead before dawn to escape witchcraft when witches were asleep and

The Pende of Zaire, dancing at a festival.

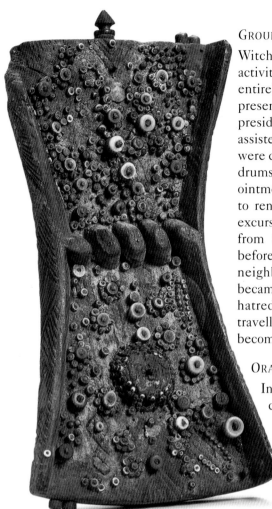

Oracles, like this divination board, are consulted to determine who is responsible for witchcraft.

GROUP WITCHCRAFT

Witches cooperated in destructive activities: a witch might not kill a man entirely on his own initiative but would present proposals to a witch meeting presided over by a witch leader. They assisted each other in their crimes and were called to congress by the beating of drums. They possessed a special kind of ointment that they rubbed into the skin to render them invisible on night-time excursions. Knowledge had to be gained from the experience of elder witches before a man was qualified to kill his neighbours. When a witch died he became an evil ghost and showed a hatred of humanity by bedevilling travellers in the bush, causing them to become confused.

ORACLES

In order to combat more serious cases of witchcraft, or to find out about possible misfortunes in the future, the Azande consulted oracles. If the oracles told of inauspicious circumstances or said that witchcraft hung over them, their plans were abandoned or postponed until the oracles had been consulted again. An oracle would be asked about suitable sites for a homestead or land for particular crops. If the oracle decided against one site it was asked again until it announced that one was auspicious and that there was no danger associated with it. An Azande man would ask the oracle if particular witches were threatening a future marriage and if they were he would try to persuade them to withdraw their ill will. He would leave things for a time before asking the oracle again if there was still danger ahead.

The main oracles used by the Azande were the poison oracle, the rubbing board oracle, the termite oracle, and the stick oracle. The poison oracle was by far the most important and the Azande relied on its decisions, which had the force of law when obtained on the orders of a prince. It was important in collective understanding, serious legal disputes and all life crises. A poisonous liquid, similar to strychnine and made from a forest creeper mixed with water, was given to small domestic fowls. The doses sometimes proved fatal but often the fowls recovered. In some cases, the birds were completely unaffected by the poison. From the behaviour of the birds the Azande received answers to the questions they placed before the oracle.

The rubbing board was the most frequently used oracle and it might be consulted when a man was on a visit to a friend's homestead. When the visit was finished he asked the oracle whether he should leave openly during the day or secretly at night, so that any witch wishing to send witchcraft or cause misfortune on the journey would be unaware that he had left. The rubbing board, although considered inferior to the poison oracle, had the advantage of being portable, and some were carried around in a leather or plaited-grass bag. It consisted of a miniature table-like construction in two parts – the flat surface of the table and a lid that fitted over it. The oracle answered questions

would therefore not see his departure. Witchcraft worked only at close range. If a person fell sick visiting relatives then the source of the witchcraft would be sought there.

A witch destroyed his victim slowly. It was only when a witch had completely eaten the soul of a vital organ that death resulted. A witch made frequent visits over a long period and consumed only a little of the soul of the organ on each visit. Alternatively, he might remove a large portion, but he hid it in the thatch of his hut or in a hole in a tree and ate it slowly. Witches also shot objects called *ahu mangu* into the bodies of those they wished to injure. This led to pain in the place where the missile was lodged and a witch doctor would be summoned to extract it. The missiles might be material objects or living organisms such as worms or grubs.

Belief in witchcraft is part of a rich oral tradition, here a Dinka storyteller tells a tale.

put to it by either allowing the lid to slide freely on the surface or by causing it to stick and not move.

When making a rubbing board, a man was subject to taboos. He must not have sexual relations for two days before he started to make it. He cut the wood, shaped it and blackened it with a red-hot spear. The rubbing board was then given its magical potency: it was anointed with medicine derived from boiled roots, whose juices were mixed with oil and boiled again while the following words were said over the pot:

This is my rubbing-board oracle,
which I am going to doctor.
When I consult it on a man's behalf may
it speak the truth, may it foretell the
[threatened] death of a man.
May it reveal things to me,
may it not hide things from me.
May it not lose its potency.
If a man eats tabooed food, such as
elephant [and comes near my oracle],
may it not lose its potency.

He then took the mixture off the fire and rubbed some of it into cuts in the table of the oracle. The remainder of the oil and juices were mixed with the ashes of various plants and rubbed on to the face of the table. The oracle was then buried to give the medicines time to sink in. It was wrapped in a piece of new barkcloth or the skin of a small animal and placed in a hole dug in the centre of a path where people would walk over it to remove all the "coldness" from the rubbing board.

The termite oracle came second only to the poison oracle. Often, preliminary verdicts were obtained from it before consulting the poison oracle. A termite mound was found and two sticks from two different trees were pushed into two holes. When the questioner returned to the mound the next day he or she received an answer according to whether the termites had eaten one stick or both. If both were left untouched, this meant that the termites had refused to answer. The Azande said that the termites did not listen to all the talk that was going

A group of Himba widows in Namibia in a healing trance, being exorcised of a lion spirit by a healer.

on in the homesteads and heard only the questions put to them.

The stick oracle consisted of three small pieces of wood or three sticks. Two pieces of stick were placed side by side on the ground and a third was placed on top of them. They were generally arranged just before nightfall in a clearing at the edge of a garden or at the back of a hut. When asking about a new homestead they were arranged in a small clearing at the proposed site. The oracle gave its answer by either remaining in position – generally an auspicious sign – or by falling, which was frequently seen as inauspicious.

Oracles are consulted to determine the site of a new homestead.

WITCH DOCTORS

Witchcraft is an activity that cannot be detected by everyday means, and so the actions of witches have to be discovered by divination. Some divination is revealed to men or women who are thought to have special powers and who speak as the mediums of the spirits.

These people are often called "witch doctors", although the term can be misleading. In many African societies the same word is used for a person who professes to cure sickness by physical means and one who claims to detect and counter the activities of witches. Many such people say that they are called to the service of the spirits; others simply receive the appropriate training from an already qualified practitioner.

A witch doctor among the Ashanti in western Africa is typical of many in the role that he performs in detecting witches. Possessed by a monster who is believed to be in league with the witches and the enemy of the good spirits, the witch doctor could discover who was responsible for committing an act of witchcraft.

The Azande witch doctor was a diviner and a magician who exposed witches and cleared areas of witchcraft. The Azande believed that witches brought sickness and death at any time and they sought to control their evil powers. A witch doctor was one who knew what medicines to use to be able to see witchcraft with his own eyes and how to drive it away.

Witch doctors held public seances at which they danced and divined, usually at the request of someone who was suffering or feared misfortune. Members of the audience would pose questions to a particular witchdoctor who responded by dancing alone. When he had become exhausted he signalled to the drummers to stop drumming at which point he began his revelations. After he had finished one question he would take another question and the whole process would start again.

Azande witch doctors wore hats that were decorated with feathers and carried

A traditional healer is often called a witch doctor, this is a Pedi healer from Transvaal, South Africa.

Ideas about witchcraft shape much African thought. They form part of a moral order which initiates learn about during rituals. Here boys take part in the circumcision dance, part of a puberty ritual in Tanzania.

large bags containing skins, horns, magic whistles, belts, leglets and armlets made from various wild fruits and seeds. They often worked together and the seances were led by the eldest, most experienced magician, who may have initiated the others into the practice. Edward Evans-Pritchard notes that it was not usual for women to become witch doctors, but a few, usually older and widowed, were qualifed to act as leeches, and some gained a considerable reputation as healers.

Evans-Pritchard called witchcraft accusations an all-purpose social device for restraining uncharitable behaviour and bringing grudges out into the open. He explained how witchcraft acted as a stabilizing influence on the social and moral systems of the society, insulating its beliefs from social conflict. Only commoners could be accused, and a son could not accuse his father without accusing himself, so authority remained unchallenged. Evans-Pritchard was keen to show the meaning of witchcraft as a way of seeing the world, as well as describing the way it worked to order and regulate society.

Sociological explanations of witchcraft are concerned with how witches represent immoral forces and how these ideas work to order society. Some scholars have seen witchcraft beliefs only in terms of ordering social relations. Others are critical of this approach and say that comparisons between European and African witchcraft are limited and that witchcraft must be studied within its own environment; witchcraft should be analysed as part of a larger cultural scheme particular to each case.

Right: Witchcraft beliefs structure everyday life in African societies.

A fetish priest, believed to have special powers to cure sickness, makes a libation at a shrine in the Volta region of Ghana.

NATIVE AMERICAN WITCHCRAFT

As in other parts of the world, witches among the Native Americans are viewed as antisocial people who can inflict harm and cause injury to people. A witch is someone who uses magical powers for their own ends rather than working in harmony with the good powers of the universe and helping their community. North American shamans had to know about working with the helpful and benign spirits of the universe; they also had to know about those spirits that could bring harm and illness. A good shaman would harness beneficial spirits and control those who had ill will. In some cases though, a shaman could turn his or her knowledge of such matters to antisocial ends. This was viewed as witchcraft and as such was considered to be illegal.

A portrait of the famous Black Elk, a shaman of the Oglala Sioux.

To the Native American Indians, the links that the tribe had with the spirit world was a central part of their culture. Not only did it link them with their past and the wisdom of their ancestors, it also provided them with a means of communication with the animal spirits and the spirits of nature on whom their survival depended. It was the tribal shaman who, through trances and vision quests, was responsible for maintaining these links between the community and the spirit world.

Various rituals and artefacts were used as tools by the shaman to aid trances. In the following extract Black Elk, a

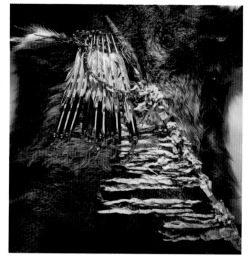

A traditional medicine pipe used by a shaman.

shaman of the Oglala Sioux, who dictated his life story to John G. Neihardt in the 1930s, used the ritual smoking of a pipe used in the propitiation of the spirits to send an offering to the Spirit of the World and to call on all the good spirits of the universe:

… I will first make an offering and send a voice to the Spirit of the World, that I may help me to be true. See, I fill this sacred pipe with the bark of the red willow; but before we smoke it, you must see how it is made and what it means. These four ribbons hanging here on the stem are the four quarters of the universe. The black one is for the west where the thunder beings live to send us rain; the white one for the north, whence comes the great white cleansing wind; the red one for the east, whence springs the light and where the morning star lives to give men wisdom; the yellow for the south, whence come the summer and the power to grow.

But these four spirits are only one Spirit after all, and this eagle feather here is for that One, which is like a father, and also it is for the thoughts of men that should rise high as eagles do. Is not the sky a father and the earth a mother, and are not all living things with feet or wings or roots their children? And this hide upon the mouth-

The shamans of the tribes of North America would use a drum to help induce a trance.

piece here, which should be bison hide, is for the earth, from whence we came and at whose breast we suck as babies all our lives, along with all the animals and birds and trees and grasses. And because it means all this, and more than any man can understand, the pipe is holy.

Smoking the pipe put Black Elk in touch with all the spirits; these are all a manifestation of the Great Spirit. The Oglala Sioux, like many other North American peoples, share a belief in a great controlling power that is made up of a hierarchy of a series of lesser powers that pervade the universe. This power is frequently called Wakan-Tanka, the "sacred ones". Native American peoples believe in a multitude of spirits who inhabit all natural phenomena – plants, animals, rocks, wind, rain, the stars and so on. Although many aspects of the spirit world have benign features, the world is seen to be full of spirits that can also do great harm. Each individual possesses a guardian spirit that was originally found in a vision quest or a dream, and protects a person through their life. Among the Ojibwa of the north-east, the spirit world is loosely divided into an upper world inhabited by benign spirits represented by the sun, moon and thunderbirds (spirit beings that are half human and half turkey cocks, representing the spirit of rain, thunder and lightening), and an underworld inhabited by underwater

A shaman of the Assiniboin, placating the spirit of a slain eagle.

panthers, and a cannibal giant called Windigo, who searches for people to eat in the winter. These malign spirits are connected to ideas about witchcraft, and witches are thought to know how to use them to cause misfortune.

WITCHES' POWER

It is witches who use these dangerous spirits to cause disease. Evil witches are usually medicine men or healers who called upon the spirit world for help in curing the sick but have come to use

A Sun Dance effigy doll used by the Crow people. These were used in Sun Dance rituals to assist a pledger in obtaining a vision that would lead to the defeat of an opponent. A witch might acquire such a doll to represent a person's spirit.

their power for their own ends, rather than for the benefit of others. They may have become diverted from their previous task of healer, or perhaps they have become mentally unstable by their association with evil guardian spirits. Witches may turn upon people making them suffer from starvation and disease. They may inflict hunger on them by destroying their hunting luck, and they might cause disease by creating an image of their victim on the ground and placing poison over the organ to be damaged. Alternatively, they might tie a carved wooden image of the person they want to destroy to a tree, believing that when the thread breaks the person will die.

A witch will try to obtain an object connected with the person they want to harm, such as hair, spittle or nails. Then he or she goes to a burial place and puts the object into a grave where there is a body, or the ashes of a body, and curses it. The witch may make an effigy of the victim's body, making it as thin as a skeleton or deforming its hands.

It is said that over 100 years ago one Plains Indian witch carried a doll wrapped in buckskin attached to his

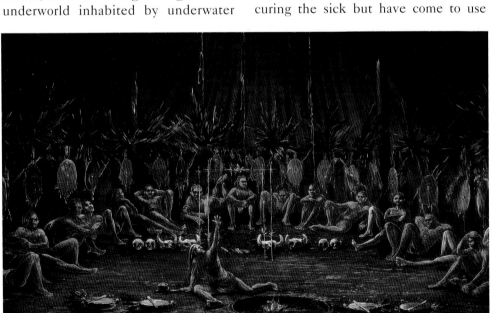

The interior of the Medicine Lodge of the Mandan people, during an O-kee-pa ceremony.

A mid-nineteenth-century depiction of a North American Indian medicine man in a wigwam preparing medicine while holding a gourd rattle and chanting an invocation.

necklace. It represented his guardian spirit, a mountain ogre, and was acquired intentionally to injure people, and he was said to steal people's souls during the Sun Dance ceremonies, which honoured the sun. The witch was finally killed by the stronger magic of a Ute Indian medicine man.

Some witches are said to shoot disease-ridden or pathogenic objects into a person. Among the Coast Salish of the north-west coast, diseases are seen to be due to a malevolent shaman or witch shooting an object imbued with their power into a patient. The object has to be removed, in this case by a medicine man. Witches may inject a piece of flesh from a corpse, a shred of funeral cloth or a splinter of bone, or any sharp or pointed thing such as a cactus point or a shard of glass. It is often the job of the shaman to remove the object that has caused the disease. This is done by sucking it out through a hollow bone or by putting their mouth on the affected part of the ill person's body to suck out the sickness. The disease may also be

pulled out by the shaman using his or her hands, or just by rubbing or touching. Sometimes the shaman may bleed the bad blood out or order the person to bathe the disease away.

Witches might also use soul-stealing procedures to destroy their victims, and then it is the task of the shaman to venture into the spirit worlds to find the soul or parts of the soul and return them to the sick person. Insects are controlled by witches. They can send caterpillars or grasshoppers to destroy crops, and they may send insects into the body of a victim to destroy it. Witches may also attack through the ghosts of members of the family they are persecuting. Witches can also control the weather – they can keep the rain away or cause wind.

According to anthropologist Åke Hultkrantz, the Zuni of the north bank of the Upper Zuni river close to the western border of New Mexico, are likely to have witchcraft societies. Zuni society is horticultural. Since early times they have cultivated corn, squash and beans, and they have elaborate maize

ceremonies. Frequent allegations of witchcraft reveal a strictly ordered social system in which curing societies heal the sick. All members of curing societies have been close to death due to illness, accident, or the effects of breaking taboos. The "beast gods" are the patrons of the curing societies and live in the place where once, at the beginning of time, people emerged from underground. Witches are said to have imitated these curing societies, but instead of curing people they are thought to project disease objects into them. Organized like any other society, the members have to obey the orders of their officers and go out and make people sick. To be initiated, the candidate must bewitch a member of their household to death. In the initiation the candidate allegedly has to go under an arch or bow with a member of the society to metamorphose into spirit animal form. If the initiate wishes to be a witch cat, for example, then he or she must choose a member of the society whose spirit animal is a witch cat. Alternatively, a canditate can put on the skin of the animal that she or he wishes to be transformed into.

In the past, witchcraft was a very dangerous activity, and until the middle of the nineteenth century was punished by death. The witch's own relatives could kill him or her when the shaman

The anthropologist Lewis H Morgan.

had identified the correct person. However, witches of high social rank were not attacked because of their position, and were asked to heal the person they had bewitched in secret. Among the Iroquois, according to the anthropologist Lewis Henry Morgan (1818–81), any person could take the life of a witch when discovered performing witchcraft. If this was not done, a council was called, and the witch was called before it in the presence of the accuser. If the witch confessed fully and promised to amend his or her ways, a discharge was made. However, if the accusation was denied, witnesses were called and the circumstances of the case were heard. If the charge was established, death was sentenced. After the decision of the council, the relatives of the witch gave him up without protest.

Witches and Mythology

Like many other Native American peoples, the Tlingit of the north-west coast of Canada say that all dangerous disease is caused by witchcraft. Witches are said to have learnt their art from Raven. Raven features in North American mythology and is a trickster, rearranger and transformer of the world. Tricksters are beings that deliberately upset order or a certain train of circumstances. Their role in mythology is to cause disruption, and out of the ensuing chaos comes a different understanding. Tricksters have an ambiguous part to play, often they are difficult characters with good and bad qualities, but they are seen to be essential to the overall pattern of life. For example, Raven steals things being hoarded by people and redistributes them. He is associated with origin stories in which he takes the sun, moon, stars and daylight from one person who is unwilling to share them and gives them out to others, and in the process other features of the world, such as rivers, lakes and animals, are created. However, in some stories, Raven is driven entirely by ego, hunger and greed, with no evident good motives. Small birds are lucky to go away hungry but alive

Witches are said to have learnt their art from Raven, the trickster.

after Raven cheats them out of their share of the king Salmon, Bear loses the fat from his thighs in one story and his genitals in another, Cormorant loses his tongue.

Coyote, another trickster, is said to be responsible for the introduction of witchcraft. Coyote assumes a dual personality in most Native American mythologies. Like Raven, he is sometimes seen as having a positive involvement in creation, but he is also a thief and a coward. He bestowed fire but also introduced death. The negative aspects of his image may be attributed to his habit of eating nearly anything and stealing other animals' prey. He is widely regarded as envious, greedy, and easily duped; he is also a bungler and a coward. A powerful spiritual entity, he is associated with illness and witchcraft. Eating a melon that a coyote has previously bitten, or killing a coyote, can trigger an illness. The cure often consists of waving a coyote tail over the ailing person and singing songs. He is believed to cause several diseases, which can only be treated by a shaman.

Native Americans inhabited a world that was alive with spirit powers – theirs was a cosmos that was made up of good and bad entities. Witches were those individuals who worked against the harmonious ordering of the universe by using their powers to disrupt in a wholly negative way.

A shaman of the Zuni Pueblo people blows pollen over a village shrine in a ritual to invoke a spirit.

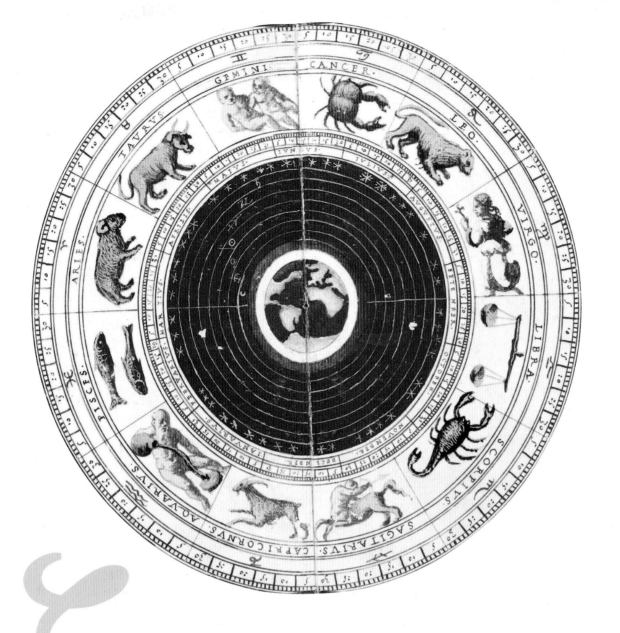

EARLY MODERN WITCHCRAFT

The years 1450–1750 cover a time that is referred to as the early modern period, and in Europe it was a time in which the Christian Church attempted to introduce new ideas about witchcraft. The witch had always been portrayed as an anti-social creature but now she was – according to certain theologians – in-league with the Devil and responsible for many atrocious acts previously attributed to heretics. In fact, those persecuted were probably just ordinary women and men – but maybe some of them were practising folk medicine, and it might have been this that set them apart. The distinction between healers and witches was not always clear: in theory – the authorities felt – a person who knew how to heal also knew how to harm.

[I]

HOW WITCHCRAFT DEVELOPED

In Europe between the fifteenth and eighteenth centuries, a time known as the early modern period, the figure of the witch known in the pagan Greek and Roman worlds took on a different character, as a particularly Christian interpretation was superimposed on older beliefs. For many Christians the world was seen to be divided between good and evil: God represented the good, and an evil realm was ruled over by the Devil, or Satan. Devilish powers were attributed to witches, sorcerers and all those who were thought to follow Satan. Thus Christianity shaped ideas about witchcraft in early modern Europe.

Witches were often associated with lewd behaviour, and were said by their accused to gather in groups with no clothes on.

Witches were thought to be in contact with Satan through their familiars, who would do their bidding and carry out tasks.

From the Saxon period onwards, most of Europe held the same sort of reasonably tolerant beliefs about magic, sorcery and witchcraft, but by the fifteenth century a widespread and popular fear of witchcraft had been fostered by the Church.

Ordinary people were concerned about the practical effects of witchcraft on their daily lives, not where the power of witchcraft came from: this was the preoccupation of the Church authorities. During the early modern period in England, most people lived in rural villages and hamlets and were mainly concerned with the production of food. Society was highly stratified and between a third and half the population lived at subsistence level. Consequently, poverty, sickness and sudden disasters, such as plague or starvation due to crop failure, were familiar events.

Some anthropologists and historians have suggested a comparison between European beliefs in witchcraft and those in Africa. The anthropologist Edward Evans-Pritchard and the historians Keith Thomas and Alan Macfarlane have argued for a dialogue between anthropological and historical approaches. In his study of witchcraft beliefs in Tudor and Stuart Essex in England, Macfarlane discovered that witchcraft allegations were a normal part of village life. Accusations reflected the concerns of yeomen and husbandmen who felt they had been harmed by witchcraft. Witchcraft explained misfortune, so that when a new baby refused to drink its mother's milk, or a child became ill, or farm animals died, the people looked to their social relationships rather than blaming their economic state, to see who might be responsible.

The victims of witchcraft were generally neighbours of the so-called witches. The accused were usually poor women living alone, and accusations tended to follow quarrels that were centred on a refusal to give charity. In a typical case brought on 31 December 1646, Henry Cockcrofte, a member of a yeoman family living in Heptonstall in the West Riding of Yorkshire, gave evidence to two Justices of the Peace about a woman called Elizabeth Crossley. When Crossley had come begging for alms at his door, Cockcrofte's wife had given her something, but she was not pleased with what she had been given.

That night, Cockcrofte's baby son fell ill, partially recovered, but later died. Cockcrofte accused another woman called Mary Midgely of witchcraft. Midgely confessed to being a witch but denied harming his son and blamed Elizabeth Crossley, her daughter and another woman. Cockcrofte's decision to take the affair to the courts prompted his neighbours to make formal accusations against Midgely. In one of these, Richard Wood told how Midgely had begged for wool at his door. His wife had refused her, telling Midgely that she had given her wool three weeks before and would give her no more, but she had given her alms of milk. Midgley

The Devil would summon witches to Sabbaths and would visit their meetings.

Witches were said to have familiars, animals that acted as tools and servants.

had left in an obviously angry mood. After this Richard Wood's cattle had sickened mysteriously.

Such village beliefs about witchcraft would appear to be similar to those of the African Azande studied by Evans-Pritchard. In both cases, witchcraft explained what at that time was the inexplicable, and was a way of understanding social relationships. Thomas argued that witchcraft beliefs helped to uphold traditional obligations of charity and neighbourliness at a time of change, when social and economic forces were weakening communities.

Other scholars have questioned how far it is possible to compare cultures as different in time and place as the Azande and the inhabitants of Tudor and Stuart England. Links can be made between European and African witchcraft if a belief in spirits – a magical or animistic world-view – is accepted as being common to both cultures.

WITCHCRAFT IN POPULAR CULTURE

To ordinary people living during the early modern period, magic and witchcraft were a way of life and witches were a part of European culture. But the Christian church began to construct the image of a diabolical witch, and gradually a stereotype of an anti-Christian follower of Satan emerged. This view of witches infiltrated and merged with older Greek and Roman ones. Magical objects were thought to ward off a witch's attack, and people learnt how to live and deal with those they suspected of witchcraft. Magical practitioners – "cunning folk", wizards and conjurers – were found in every village, and their services were used to identify witches, find lost or stolen goods, tell fortunes and give remedies for a whole host of diseases in both humans and animals.

An eighteenth-century illustration in which a witch is performing a ritual surrounded by herbs, magical grimoires, skulls and bones.

In early modern Europe, witchcraft beliefs were a part of everyday life for ordinary people and they co-existed and intermingled with Christian beliefs. According to the historian Keith Thomas, in a study of popular beliefs in sixteenth- and seventeenth-century England, the hold of orthodox Christianity on the English people was never complete. Although few avoided baptism, matrimony or holy burial, there is evidence to suggest that the poorest classes never became regular churchgoers at any time. Thomas notes that even when they did put in a reluctant appearance, "Members of the congregation jostled for pews, nudged their neighbours, hawked and spat, knitted, made coarse remarks, told jokes, fell asleep and even let off guns".

The poorest people in the sixteenth and seventeenth centuries never became regular churchgoers, and when they did attend were not as orderly as this nineteenth-century congregation.

However, even if they did not attend church or have a religious belief, ordinary people had a view of the world in which the belief in witches was an everyday reality; and they used magical means against the power of witches.

PRECAUTIONS AGAINST WITCHES

Before a witch attacked, precautions could be taken to safeguard a likely victim. Once witchcraft was believed to have been used, cures could be sought. Finally, attempts could be made to locate the witch and either force her to withdraw her power or have her punished.

Precautions to avoid being bewitched included a person regulating his or her life so that a witch was unlikely or unable to attack. This often involved moving out of a "witch-infested" area, or refusing to allow those thought to be witches to live nearby. Sometimes kindness to witches was advocated, and humouring them was thought to ward off an attack.

A witch-doll with an attached written curse, from the late eighteenth century.

SOCIAL SANCTION

Fear of witches acted as a sanction enforcing neighbourly conduct. Alternatively, cutting all contact and avoiding the borrowing or lending of objects through which witches might work magic was another option. It was considered dangerous to receive a gift from a witch as this might cause misfortune. In 1617, the Puritan, Thomas Cooper, in *The Mystery of Witch-Craft*, warned his readers to avoid witches and not give alms:

Be wise in our Liberalitie, and Almesdeedes, not distributing to each sort of poore, because many times Witches go under this habite ... especially, to take heed if any such suspected seeke unto us; to bee straight-handed towards them, not to entertaine them in our houses, not to relieve them with our morsels.

If a witch was seen loitering near a person's house she should be warned off in case she was burying magic under the bedstraw or under the threshold.

Thus, for ordinary people, ideas and beliefs about witchcraft were a part of everyday life. The established church tried to impose a certain view of diabolical witchcraft, which was then incorporated with existing folk beliefs in popular culture.

A modern version of the holed stones that were used as charms against witchcraft.

Magical objects

Charms, objects and gestures were used by most people as protection from witches and evil. Hanging a copy of the first chapter of John's Gospel around the neck was particularly popular, and a woman said to be "haunted with a fairy" was rumoured to wear such an amulet. Certain plants, roots, stones or holy objects were used as amulets against evil. Holed stones, salt, communion wafers, holy water and the sign of the Cross were also used to prevent or cure the effects of witchcraft.

Witches were commonly thought to be able to perform supposedly supernatural feats, such as drawing milk from an axe handle, as shown in this woodcut from 1517.

CUNNING FOLK

Ordinary people relied on the services of "cunning men and women", wizards, wise folk, sorcerers, conjurers or "white witches". These magical practitioners were to be found in every village, and it was common for them to be consulted for help in identifying witches, fortune-telling, finding lost or stolen goods and identifying those who had taken them, and for providing remedies for a wide range of illnesses, both human and animal.

Cunning folk often wore strange costumes, for example dressing in scarlet or, in the case of a well-known cunning man in Essex, wearing "terrifying goggles". They were aided by magical spells and oracles. It was common for people to consult cunning men and women about witchcraft: cunning folk battled against witches – they were "unbewitchers". However, to unbewitch entailed knowing enough about magic to bewitch, and cunning folk were feared as well as respected for their magical powers.

Cunning folk were often quite ordinary members of the community.

The costumes that cunning folk adopted marked them out, such as this outfit shown in a seventeenth-century manuscript.

SOCIAL SERVICE

The distinction between cunning folk and witches is not always altogether clear. Some have called cunning folk "white witches" because they used their magical powers for the good of their community.

If someone was possessed by a spirit they would consult the cunning folk. If the pigs were not doing well, someone might be bewitching them. Practical options were tried first, such as buying another lot of pigs in another name, or nailing a stallion's shoe to the pigsty. Only if the problem persisted would the services of a cunning man or woman be sought. In his study of Essex witchcraft, Alan Macfarlane shows how cunning folk helped people locate their enemies in intimate situations, which prohibited open or immediate accusations. The secret wrongs of neighbours, relatives or supposed friends called for secret detection.

The cunning folk provided an outside, apparently objective and impartial analysis of a person's relationships. They provided a remedy for physical pain and could also explain why the suffering had occurred; they could confirm that the misfortune was due to witchcraft. Macfarlane quotes an account of how, in 1582, a cunning man was believed to have given more satisfaction than an ordinary doctor:

A sailor, landing in Ipswich, found that his daughter was very ill and therefore took a sample of her urine to a local physician. The sailor asked the doctor "if that his daughter were not bewitched", but the latter replied "that hee woulde not deale so farre to tell him", so "not satisfied to his minde", the sick child's father went to a local cunning man, who confirmed that the child was bewitched.

Cunning folk used various techniques in their work, but one practice was common. When a client first arrived to ask for help, they were told that they had come only just in time. The Ipswich sailor referred to above was told that "if hee had not commen with some great hast to seeke helpe, hee had come too late". This created a let-out if the remedies failed.

COUNSELLING AND COMMUNICATION

The cunning folk enquired about the nature of the trouble and sought information about social relationships surrounding the issue, especially who was suspected of inflicting misfortune and whether a particular neighbour was mistrusted. The cunning person's aim was to bring out all information, and if the person was unsure who was the suspect then it was their task to raise suspicions. The Essex writer George Gifford, an Elizabethan clergyman, has given many insights into the workings of popular magic. According to his account, a cunning woman told a client that he was:

Village brawls and feuds were often at the root of accusations of witchcraft, and the cunning man or woman would make it their business to know all such gossip.

... plagued by a witch, adding moreover, that there were three women witches in that towne, and one man witch: willing him to look whom he most suspected: he suspected one old woman, and caused her to be carried before a Justice of the Peace.

Macfarlane says that cunning folk acted as information centres, allocated blame and distributed antidotes to witchcraft. Cunning folk would have gained much information about local witches from gossip, rumour and previous consultations. They divulged this information to their clients, putting them in touch with suspicions circulating in their own village. When the client first arrived at the cunning man or woman's home, they were warned of the difficulties in the task and then told to go away for nine days. In the meantime the cunning man or woman, if they had decided to help, would make enquiries and find out about local gossip. On return, the client would look into a magic mirror and be instructed to see the face of the witch.

The final decision was the client's: cunning folk would not identify the witch themselves, they only provided the situation for the client to discover the witch. Once again, they had created an effective get-out clause.

DIVINATION AND FORSEEING

Oracles were also consulted by cunning folk to determine the location of stolen goods. A common method was to employ a sieve and a pair of shears:

Stick a pair of shears in the rind of a sieve and let two persons set the top of each of their forefingers upon the upper part of the shears holding it with the sieve up from the ground steadily; and ask Peter and Paul whether A, B, or C hath stolen the thing lost; and at the nomination of the guilty person the sieve will turn round.

Subtle questioning and sleight of hand could be used to influence an apparently objective test. Hidden thoughts could be brought into the open and made to appear as if they were dictated by an external power.

Another oracle used was a mirror, basin of water or other reflective surface. One Essex woman went to a conjurer on

A witch, accompanied by a beggar and a fool, curses two terrified sergeants-at-arms in an illustration from the late fifteenth century.

London Bridge to help her to find some lost money. He showed "her in a glass a boye in a sherte gleninge Corne resemblinge the countenance of John Hayes that had her monye". In another account a cunning man took his client out into the hall and:

… browghte with him a looking glasse, (about vii or viii inches square), and did bange the said glasse up over the benche in his said hawle, upon a nayle, and bad the said examinate look in yt, and said as farr as he could gesse, he shulde see the face of him that had the said lynnen.

In several of the cases of theft it was the suspect himself who went to the cunning man to clear his name of suspicion, the cunning man giving him a note vouching for him.

HEALING AND CHRISTIAN ELEMENTS

The remedies for bewitching included using the Christian religion. When Robert Booker informed his patient in 1622 that he had been bewitched by three sources of witchcraft – concealed malevolence ("heart"), bitter words ("tongue") and ocular fascination ("eye") – the cunning man anointed his patient with oil and uttered the following charm: "Three biters have bit him – heart, tongue and eye; three better shall help him presently – God the Father, God the Son, and God the Holy Spirit."

Much healing was conducted with the aid of Catholic prayers. Prescriptions of Paternosters, Aves and the Creed in honour of the Holy Ghost and the Virgin Mary were common. Some cunning folk used debased versions of Christian prayers or bits and pieces of semi-religious

verse, describing supposed episodes in the life of Christ or the saints. These reflected the belief that mythical events could be a source of magical power:

There was a man born in Bethlem of Judaea whose name was called Christ. Baptized in the River Jordan in the water of the flood; and the Child also was meek and good; and as the water stood so I desire thee the blood of [such a person or beast] to stand in their body, in the name of the Father, Son and Holy Ghost.

Religious language possessed a magical power, which could be used for practical purposes. This corresponded with the idea that disease was a foreign presence in the body that needed to be conjured or exorcised out. A fever could be drawn out if the following formula was repeated:

Two angels came from the West,
The one brought fire,
the other brought frost,
Out fire! In frost!
In the name of the Father, Son
and Holy Ghost.

There were also charms for women in labour, mad dogs, sick horses and all aches and pains. The churchwardens of Barnsley, Gloucestershire, reported on a parishioner in 1563:

There is one Alice Prabury in our parish
that useth herself suspiciously in the
likelihood of a witch, taking upon her not
only to help Christian people of diseases
strangely happened, but also horses and all
other beasts. She taketh upon her to help by
the way of charming, and in such ways that
she will have nobody privy of her sayings.

HAUNTINGS AND SPIRITS

The cunning man or woman frequently diagnosed bewitching or "overlooking" as the cause of a patient's illness. The patient might have been haunted by an evil spirit, a ghost or a fairy. If a person suspected that they had been bewitched they would go to a cunning person in the next village. The methods used by cunning folk to diagnose witchcraft were diverse. They might use a technique such as boiling the victim's urine, or burning a piece of thatch from the suspected witch's house to see whether this brought her running to the scene. Alternatively, they would use a mirror, crystal ball, sieve and shears, or a familiar spirit. Sometimes cunning folk said that the fairies told them the answers to their questions.

Keith Thomas gave an account of the cunning woman Elizabeth Page who, in 1555, was asked to cure a sick child who had been bewitched. The cunning woman explained to the child's mother that the cure involved the mother making herself as ill as the child: "... she must cause herself to be in as ill a case as the said child then was [who was then likely to die] ere that she could help her ...". This shows that disease was seen to be a

A seventeenth-century depiction of a witch working inside a magic circle, familiars at hand.

foreign element which could be transferred from one person to another, the second person completely relieving the first one of the illness.

Cunning folk were the specialists in magic that ordinary people turned to in times of distress or illness, and their role in society was an important one.

The wise woman of a French village uses her
powers to discover who has cast a spell on
her client. This is an illustration from a book
published in 1853, showing that folk beliefs
endured for several centuries.

WITCHES, SPIRITS AND FAMILIARS

Witches were said to have special spirit animals or familiars that performed services for them. In return, the familiars demanded milk, or sometimes to suck a witch's blood. Cunning folk were also said to have familiars and these often helped them to diagnose illnesses or find lost objects. The origin of ideas about familiars may lie in a belief in nature spirits – dwarves, elves, fairies etc – and, going farther back in time to our common shamanic heritage, to when shamans communicated with the spirits of the animals that their community was to hunt.

The witch Jennet urges her familiar, the cat Tib, to attack her victim in The Lancashire Witches, *1612.*

The idea that witches were aided by spirit familiars occurred again and again in pamphlets. In the first pamphlet account of an English trial describing witchcraft, one of the accused, Elizabeth Francis, allegedly confessed to having been given a cat familiar by her grandmother when she was 12 years old. The cat, which she called Sathan (Satan), spoke to her, brought her sheep and also a lover. She began to use the familiar for maleficent purposes when her lover refused to marry her and the cat supposedly killed him. Another pamphlet, published in Essex in 1582, portrayed familiars as domestic pets, which had names such as Jack, Robin and Tyffin. One eight-year-old girl described how her stepmother kept her familiars in an earthenware pot lined with wood, and fed them on milk from a black dish.

One sixteenth-century Essex woman accused of witchcraft said that she had three mouse familiars: Littleman, Prettyman and Daynty. Another woman had four mice named Prickeare, James, Robyn and Sparrow. Yet another woman admitted having five familiars: Holt, a kitten; Jamara, a fat, legless spaniel; Sack-and-Sugar, a black rabbit; Newes, a polecat; and Vinegar Tom, a long-legged, greyhound-like creature with an "ox's head and broad eyes, which could turn itself into a headless four-year-old child". Witches were said to take great care of their familiars: they might, for example, baptize toads, dress them, put little bells on their feet and make them dance. They were also said to allow familiars to suck their blood.

Familiars were said to help cunning men and women by assisting in the diagnosis of illnesses and the sources of bewitchment; they were also used for divining and finding lost objects.

Sometimes they were locked into bottles, rings and stones, and these were often sold as charms.

A black cat, a newt and a snake, animals that were often linked to witches and thought to be their familiars.

FAIRY FAMILIARS

Some familiars were said to be fairies. A cunning man said in 1566 that there were three types of fairies: the white, the green and the black. The black were the worst and he found them indistinguishable from malignant devils.

Beliefs about fairies varied, and many traditions give alternative accounts of their origins, including ancestral spirits, ghosts and fertility spirits, as well as pagan gods. Fairies were frequently thought of as malevolent, and were often associated with malignant disease of a spiritual origin, which could only be cured by charming or exorcism. The Anglo-Saxons described a person smitten with such a malady as "elf-shot". It was during the Shakespearean period in England that a view of fairies as a dwarf race of mischievous but fundamentally friendly beings became popular.

SHAMANIC ORIGINS OF FAMILIARS

The origins of witches' familiars lies with dwarves, fairies, trolls and spirits of nature. Robin, one of the first named witch familiars, was probably a version of an Irish folk spirit who appeared as a cat, a shaggy dog or a black man. Going further back in time, the roots of beliefs in spirit beings such as fairies and familiars may lie in the shamanic heritage. Human beings have always had a close association with animals, and in early times everything in the world was seen to possess spirit. Early humans used their knowledge of animals in order to trap and hunt them for food and skins, and it is likely that shamans in these early societies had a particular function as communicators and negotiators with the spirits of the animals. A shaman might have been able to locate or lure game because he or she had been that animal in spirit, or may have been taken and dismembered by that spirit animal at initiation. This relationship between shamans and the animal spirit world may have been behind the folk beliefs about witches' familiars. Later, during the early modern period in Europe, these beliefs were interpreted by the Christian church as relationships with demonic spirits.

A "magic scene" from the seventeenth century showing the familiars that were associated with witchcraft: a goat, bats, snakes and an owl are all part of this illustration of sorcery and the dark arts.

Fairies and elves on their nightly ritual dance in a sixteenth-century "history" of Scandinavia.

OLD WIVES' TALES

Today, so-called old wives' tales are often seen as trivial nonsense, but they have their origins in popular medical lore and reflect the domestic medicine practised by the cunning folk. Some old wives' remedies sound bizarre but they often have a sound medicinal base. By combining remedies with spells or charms, important psychological aspects of curing were included. In our time this is called the "placebo effect" – if a patient believes in the power of the cure, and imagines they are getting better, they often do.

A French village wise woman uses her secret herbal cures to treat a patient.

In early modern Europe the spirit world was at one with the material, everyday world; the two were interconnected. Healers such as cunning folk, wizards and witches used fingernails, hair, amniotic membranes (cauls) and such like, to heal, protect from harm or cause harm, bring luck or cause some sort of magical transformation. Discarded or stolen pieces of a person's body or clothing were seen to be invested with their owner's spiritual essence and might be used in a magical way to identify that person in the spirit world for beneficial or malign purposes. Magical power was gained from a number of different sources to make up a potpourri. Many spells relied on the unauthorized use of Christian prayers, which were thought to give magical potency.

This magical way of healing was often dismissed as old wives' tales. "Old wives", according to modern popular definition, are old women who tell trivial stories and give advice that cannot be relied upon. A more sympathetic view is that old wives' tales have their origins in the popular medical lore and domestic medicine of the cunning folk – the unofficial healers who dispensed their remedies alongside magical lore. It was knowledgeable, outspoken women who were most likely to be accused of witchcraft, and in the witch trials such a woman was often described as a "busy woman of her tongue" or "devilshe of her tonge"; they "scolded" and "railed".

CUNNING CURES

Old wives had many remedies for ordinary complaints. For a headache, for example, cures included fixing "around the head a halter with which one had been hanged"; the application of moss found growing on a human skull, dried and powdered and taken as snuff; bathing the forehead and temples with hot water to which mint or sage had

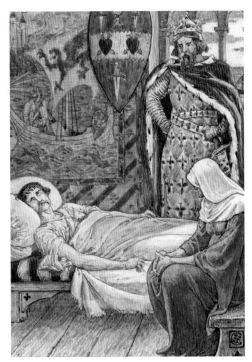

Witches were often called in to heal an apparently hopeless case, as in this illustration from King Arthur's Knights, *depicting a healing from the earlier medieval period.*

been added; soaking the feet in a hot mustard bath; nutmeg in a little water; inhaled pipe tobacco smoke; woodlice "taken as a pill"; and vinegar and brown paper applied to the head. A "thimble-full of whisky rubbed sharply in the hands and held to the nose, cures headache at once, or mix one drachm of sweet nitre, one drachm of sal volatile and two drachms of carbonate soda, in a teacupful of cold water; two tablespoons to be taken three times a day".

The remedies were combined with spells designed to instruct the spiritual agents of disease verbally and symbolically. For example, to cure fever a concoction of four ounces nitre, one drachm camphor, 30 grains saffron, four grains cochineal, all powdered and well mixed together, were to be administered in a small teaspoon each night with the following charm:

I forbid the quacking fevers,
the sea fevers, the land fevers
and all the fevers that ever
God ordained;
out of the head, out of the
heart, out of the back, out of the

sides, out of the knees, out
of the thies.
Free the points of the fingers
to the nebs of the toes. Out sail
the fevers, go some to the ill,
some to the hope, some to the
stone, some to the stock.
In St. Peter's name, St. Paul's name,
and all the saints of heaven.
In the name
of the Father, Son and Holy Ghost.

For epilepsy, the prescription was one ounce each of mistletoe, valerian root, pellitory and black horehound boiled in three pints of water, to which one ounce of tincture of scullop was added. This mixture was to be taken in a wineglass four times a day.

An alternative cure was the powder made from crushing a man's bones, preferably a skull that had been found in the earth. This was accompanied by the chanting of the following charm about the three wise men who attended the baby Jesus:

Gasper with his myrrh beganne
The presents to unfold
Then Melchior brought frankincense
And Balthasar brought gold,
Now he that of these holie kings
The names about shall beare
The fallyng ill by Grace of Christ
Shall never need to feare.

Three witches at the beside of a sick woman. An engraving from the Compendium Maleficarum, *published in 1626.*

HEALING AND SYMPATHETIC MAGIC

During the early modern period the process of healing was based upon what is now called "sympathetic magic", a different way of seeing the world to that of our modern scientific one. Sympathetic magic works on the principle that everything in the universe is in connection with everything else, and that each part has an influence on the whole. Therefore, things could be associated by their colours as well as their physical properties, for example certain metals, such as silver and mercury, were thought to have a special affinity with the moon through their hue, shine, changeability and other characteristics. Healing also had an important social and psychological dimension, one that is frequently ignored today in Western societies.

In 1589 an old woman called Maria Marquart was arrested in Augsburg, Germany. She identified herself as a white witch and gave a full account of her magical powers to her interrogators. Maria Marquart claimed that she used the "natural arts" and these consisted

A sixteenth-century Polish woodcut showing the administration of medicinal herbs.

of spells that used devotional prayers and rituals. Using needles and thread designed for sewing corpses into shrouds for strengthening spells, as well as herbs and crystal balls, her spells imitated and invoked Jesus's sufferings. She proudly described her art as working with the gift granted to her by God. The city council had previously ordered her to stop her healing, and the barber-surgeons' trade had tried to ban her from practising, but to little avail. Finally, however, she was banished from the city for life.

LIKE HEALING LIKE

Healing during the early modern period was based on sympathetic magic, or the notion that like attracts like. Thus, for example, a red flannel was used to draw out a fever, red flowers were used for disorders of the blood and yellow objects were used to cure jaundice. Numbers were seen to have a strong potency, with the numbers three and seven being especially important. The moon and the sun were thought to direct the course of the illness and marked the correct times for gathering herbs as well as for administering treatment. For example, club moss, which was believed to be effective for eye diseases, had to be gathered on the third day of the moon's cycle. The person gathering the moss was instructed to take the knife, show it to the moon and say:

*As Christ healed the issue of blood
Do thou cut what thou cuttest for good.*

When the moon was setting, the gatherer had to kneel to wash the club moss and their hands, and then wrap it in a white cloth. Afterwards, the moss had to be boiled in water from a nearby spring and the decoction used as a treatment for the eyes, or made into an ointment by mixing it with butter made from the milk of a new cow.

A popular cure for juvenile rickets and hernias involved passing a child three times through a young ash tree that had been split down the middle, with the child facing the rising sun as it passed between the two sides of the trunk. The tree would then be bound up and it was believed that as it healed so would the patient.

CONTROLLING THE SPIRITS

Spells gave precise magical directions. For example, a spell for a "tetter" (a kind of skin disease) contained the following instructions:

An early fifteenth-century herbal illustrating the properties and associations of fennel.

A patient visits an apothecary (left), and the insides of a dispensary (right). From a twelfth-century manuscript.

Tetter, tetter, thou hast nine brothers
God bless the flesh and preserve the bone;
Perish thou tetter and be thou gone
In the name of Father, Son
and Holy Ghost.

Tetter, tetter, thou hast eight brothers
God bless the flesh and preserve the bone;
Perish thou tetter and be thou gone
In the name of Father, Son
and Holy Ghost.

And so on, until the last verse:

Tetter, tetter, thou hast no brothers
God bless the flesh and
preserve the bone …

The spell instructs the invading spirits of disease to depart. Invading spirits were often given orders, but sometimes they had to be tricked into leaving their victim, have their attention distracted or be transferrred on to some other person or object. Sometimes disease spirits were sent into animals such as worms, slugs, shrews, mice or cats, the animal being contained until it died. A spell for removing a wart follows this principle: "Steal a piece of meat, rub it over the warts, bury it in the ground, and as the meat decays, so the warts will go."

SYMBOLIC HEALING

Some spells involved a symbolic acting out of sickness as a form of initiation from death into life, a passing on of the sickness into something else. This was often enacted symbolically, with a patient passing through an arch, aperture or hole in a stone. Some healing rituals involved symbolic death, as in this remedy for a cough: "Lay the child face downwards on the turf of a meadow. Cut round the child in the shape of a coffin. Remove the child and turn the turf root upwards. As the turf withers so the cough disappears."

This symbolic acting out of sickness is a common method of healing in other parts of the world, especially in small-scale or tribal societies, and it recognizes important and psychological dimensions of healing.

The zodiacal signs around a herbal dispensary from a 1550 manuscript, showing how connections were made between things in a way that later became known as sympathetic magic.

Collecting plants from a herb garden. Ordinary people would have collected herbs from the countryside.

FAMOUS WITCHES

Dame Alice Kyteler, Mother Shipton and Isobel Gowdie all gained notoriety during their time for being witches, although for different reasons. Dame Alice Kyteler was a wealthy and respected woman who was accused of poisoning. She allegedly headed a band of heretical sorcerers in Kilkenny, Ireland. Mother Shipton apparently had a much humbler background – being orphaned at birth she was brought up by a local woman – and married a Yorkshire carpenter. Having inherited her mother's magical powers, Mother Shipton was famed for her prophecy. It is not certain that she ever existed; the stories surrounding her prophesies may have just been legend, we do not know for sure. The case of Isobel Gowdie is interesting because it is not known why she suddenly confessed to acts of witchcraft. She graphically described attending witches' Sabbaths in which she had sexual relations with the Devil. This demonstrates that ordinary people as well as the witch-hunters had powerful imaginations where witchcraft was concerned.

A fifteenth-century woodcut of the Devil and a witch. It was at this time that Satanic links with witchcraft began.

DAME ALICE KYTELER

Dame Alice was the first person to be tried for witchcraft and heresy in Ireland. In the fourteenth century there were growing ideas about demonic magic and its connection with upper-class sorcery, and the case demonstrates the coming together of witchcraft accusations and demonological heresy. It illustrates a mixture of popular beliefs about witchcraft and magic among the educated elite.

Dame Alice married four times. Her first husband was William Outlawe, a wealthy banker; the second was Adam le Blond; the third was Richard de Valle. Her fourth husband, who was very ill with a wasting disease when Dame Alice was charged, was Sir John le Poer. Sir John's children thought that she might be poisoning him and allegedly found hidden in their home some potions and powders, which could have been used in black magic. Sir John and his children accused Dame Alice of bewitching her first three husbands to death and of depriving her current husband of his "natural senses" by her use of magic. Through sorcery she was said to seek advice from demons during nightly meetings in which she blasphemed the Church. Causing death and disease by ointments made of the entrails of cocks sacrificed to demons and unbaptized boys' brains, amongst other things, she supposedly used sorcery to bewitch to death three husbands, and poisoned her husband of the time.

In 1324 Richard de Ledrede, the Bishop of Ossory, made an inquisition

An illustration from the Compendium Maleficarum, *1626, of sorcerers and witches at a Sabbath dancing to the violin.*

that alleged that Dame Alice was the head of a band of heretical sorcerers in Kilkenny. He indicted them on the following counts:

1 The denial of the faith of Christ.
2 The sacrifices of living animals – allegedly nine red cocks and the eyes of nine peacocks – to various demons, including a low-ranking one named Robin, or Son of Art. The animals had been dismembered and left at crossroads.
3 Using sorcery to seek advice from demons.
4 The holding of nightly meetings during which they blasphemed the church and excommunicated them-selves with lighted candles by naming each part of their bodies and shouting "Fi! Fi! Fi! Amen".
5 Causing disease and death and arousing love and hatred by using evil powders, unguents, ointments and candles. The ingredients of these potions included worms, dead men's nails, entrails of cocks sacrificed to demons, the hair, brains and shreds of shrouds of boys who had been buried unbaptized, various herbs and "other abominations". These had been cooked in a cauldron made out of a thief's skull.
6 That Dame Alice has used sorcery to cause the children of her four husbands to bequeathe all their wealth to her and her favourite son William Outlawe. She has bewitched Sir John le Poer until his hair and nails fell out.
7 That Robin, or Son of Art, or a black man, was Dame Alice's incubus and the source of her wealth.

It was also alleged that Dame Alice swept the streets of Kilkenny with a broom, raking the filth towards the home of her favourite son, muttering, "To the house of William my sonne Hie all the wealth of Kilkennie towne". Bishop de Ledrede tried to arrest Dame Alice, her son William and the other unnamed sorcerers, but because of the family's status the arrest was blocked. Ledrede excommunicated Dame Alice

A witches' kitchen as portrayed in the late 1500s.

A fifteenth-century woodcut of a demon carrying off a child promised to the Devil.

and cited her to appear before him, but she fled to Dublin. The bishop charged William with heresy. Dame Alice brought pressure to bear on influential contacts and had Ledrede arrested and jailed. He was released after 17 days.

He tried several times to get Dame Alice arrested on charges of sorcery but was unsuccessful. Dame Alice fled to England, although in Kilkenny she was condemned as a sorceress, magician and a heretic. Her son William was arrested and spent nine weeks in jail. He decided to confess to all the charges but was let off with a penance of a pilgrimage to the shrine of St Thomas at Canterbury. He was also made to pay for the re-roofing of the Cathedral.

Dame Alice's maid, Petronilla, was then arrested and flogged until she confessed to deeds of sorcery and orgies that involved her mistress. She was excommunicated, condemned and burned alive on 3 November 1324. The others were sentenced to be whipped in the marketplace and through the streets of Kilkenny. Dame Alice was also sentenced in her absence and presum-ably her lands were forfeited. Ledrede was subsequently accused of heresy and had all his lands seized by the Crown. He was later acquitted, but ten years later he was again accused and deprived of his land and possessions.

MOTHER SHIPTON

It is not known whether the English witch Mother Shipton was a real person or a legend, but her predictions are well known. She was said to have been born Ursula Southeil or Sonthiel and, according to different accounts, was born in Yorkshire in either 1448, 1486 or 1488. She married a carpenter called Toby Shipton and lived in the village of Skipton in North Yorkshire. Her mother, who was supposed to have possessed powers of healing, clairvoyance, storm-raising and hexing, had died giving birth to her. Ursula, who was raised by a local townswoman, was said to have inherited her mother's powers, and it was said that strange things happened around her and strange forces were noticed. Furniture apparently moved around on its own; food disappeared from dinner plates; a woman was hung by her toes from a staff floating in the air; men were yoked to the same staff; women found themselves dancing in circles and, if they tried to stop, an imp, in the form of a monkey, pinched them to keep them going.

In a book on her life and predictions, published in 1684, Richard Head described her as having:

Mother Shipton with her cartoon-like nose and chin.

… very great goggling, but sharp and fiery eyes; her nose of incredible and unproportionable length, having in it many crooks and turnings, adorned with many strange pimples of divers colours, as red and blue mixed, which, like vapours of brimstone, gave such a lustre to the affrighted spectators in the dead time of the night, that one of them confessed that her nurse needed no other light to assist her in the performance of her duty.

In a later book of her prophecies, published in 1797 by one S. Baker, she is described thus: "Her stature was larger than common, her body crooked, her face frightful; but her understanding extraordinary …".

Mother Shipton was summoned to court for taking revenge on a group of prying neighbours by bewitching them at a breakfast party. The guests were made to break out in hysterical laughter; they ran out of the house and were pursued by goblins. Mother Shipton threatened the court that if she was prosecuted she would do worse. She is said to have said "Updraxi, call Stygician Helleuei", and soared off on a winged dragon.

Her predictions, published in doggerel verse form, included motor cars, aeroplanes, submarines, iron ships

Mother Shipton depicted with a familiar, 1804.

and gold in California, the Yukon or South Africa:

> *Carriages without horses shall go*
> *And accidents fill the world with woe.*
> *Around the earth thought shall fly*
> *In the twinkling of an eye.*
> *The world upside down shall be*
> *And gold found at the root of a tree.*
> *Through hills man shall ride*
> *And no horse be at his side.*
> *Under water men shall walk*
> *Shall ride, shall sleep, shall talk.*
> *In the air men shall be seen*
> *In white, in black, in green.*
> *Iron in the water shall float,*
> *As easily as a wooden boat.*
> *Gold shall be found and shown*
> *In a land that's now not known.*
> *Fire and water shall wonders do,*
> *England shall at last admit a foe.*
> *The world to an end shall come*
> *In eighteen hundred and eighty one.*

One famous story tells how she predicted that Cardinal Wolsey would never reach York. The Cardinal sent three lords incognito, one of whom was

Mother Shipton casting a horoscope, from a late sixteenth-century pamplet.

Thomas Cromwell, to check on Mother Shipton. However, she knew who they were and told them that the Cardinal would see but never arrive in York. One of the lords allegedly said that when Cardinal Wolsey reached York he would have her burnt as a witch. Mother Shipton tossed her handkerchief in the fire and said that if it burnt so would she. It was said that the handkerchief remained unburnt.

Thomas Cromwell asked her about his own future and she replied that in time he would be as low as she was; Cromwell was later beheaded. Her prediction about Wolsey proved correct too. He arrived at Cawood, eight miles from York, and viewed the city from the top of the castle tower. While he was at the top of the tower he received a message saying that the king wished to see him. He turned back towards London but never arrived, having fallen ill and died at Leicester.

Mother Shipton admonishes Cardinal Wolsey, in a fifteenth-century woodcut.

A fanciful depiction of Mother Shipton's favourite mode of transport.

ISOBEL GOWDIE

Not much is known about Isobel Gowdie as a person, but she is famous for confessing to witchcraft on four occasions in April and May 1662. She is described as an attractive red-headed girl who married a Scottish farmer and lived on a remote farm in Morayshire. Life on the farm was dull, she had no children and her husband was said to be an unimaginative boor. According to her confessions, Isobel began her involvement with the Devil in 1647, when she encountered him in the shape of a man in grey and promised to meet him in the local church. The Devil stood in the pulpit with a black book in his hand and made her renounce Jesus. He baptized her with her own blood, which he sucked from her in the church, renamed her Janet, and gave her a mark on her shoulder. She described him as a big, black, hairy man, who visited her a couple of days later and copulated with

At her trial in 1662, Isobel Gowdie tells how since 1647 she and her companions were visited by "Black John" who chastised disobedient witches.

A scene of sorcery from 1632, in which a gathering of witches with their demon familiars is depicted.

A typical fifteenth-century depiction of a chaotic witches' Sabbath.

her. Isobel Gowdie described witches' Sabbaths with covens of 13 witches. The witches flew to the Sabbaths on corn straws, beanstalks and rushes, which they charmed into flight by shouting "Horse and Hattock, in the Devil's name!". If someone should see them and not cross themselves, the witches would shoot them with elf arrows. She described how she had intercourse with the Devil and other demons, and how she transformed herself into a hare or a cat. She said she had had intercourse with one of her demons while lying in bed beside her husband, that the Devil's enormous, scaly penis had caused her great pain but also pleasure, and that his semen was as cold as ice. He was said to have had sexual relations with all the female witches, sometimes changing himself into an animal such as a deer or a bull. The coven met regularly and when she was away attending the Sabbath she said that she put a broomstick in the bed so that her husband would think that she was still there. Apparently he never knew about her night-time activities.

She told about how she and her coven tormented their neighbours by raising storms; beating wet rags upon stones while reciting incantations; making farmland sterile by ploughing it with a miniature plough drawn by toads; hexing children by sticking pins in dolls; blasting a farmer's crops by digging up the body of an unchristened child and burying it in a manure heap; and shooting elf arrows to kill and injure people. Gowdie seemed to welcome punishment and allegedly said, "I do not deserve to be seated here at ease and unharmed, but rather to be stretched on an iron rack: nor can my crimes be atoned for, were I to be drawn asunder by wild horses."

Isobel Gowdie confessed to witchcraft after 15 years and it remains unclear why she should suddenly do so. It has been suggested that she was a highly sexed masochistic woman with a vivid imagination, and that she turned to her fantasies to alleviate her boredom. In making these fantasies public she increased the excitement by shocking the stolid Scottish community and reinforcing their fears about the evils of witchcraft. It is not known what happened to Isobel Gowdie, or to the other witches that were implicated by her confession.

The case is interesting because it demonstrates the importance of the imagination and sexual desire in the creation of fantasy, and how this is connected with popular ideas about witchcraft. However, to reduce all ideas and beliefs about witchcraft to fantasy would be a simplification that ignores the reality of a magical world-view that sees the universe as consisting of various energies and powers that can be harnessed.

FEMALE STEREOTYPING

Images of women as sorcerers, foretelling the future and attending witches' Sabbaths, were all part and parcel of the popular stereotype of the witch in early modern Europe, and these women's alleged activities represent the dominant ideas about witches of the time.

Dame Alice, Mother Shipton and Isobel Gowdie all conform, in one way or another, to stereotypes of the witch. This standardized idea of a witch had the effect of controlling and shaping the lives of these women, and in later centuries some would say that this was an effect of the patriarchal times in which they lived.

This artist's depiction of a witches' gathering from 1607 is a perfect illustration of how the anti-witchcraft factions fuelled their own fantasies with lurid descriptions, culminating in accusations that demonic influences were leading ordinary women astray.

THE ARISTOCRACY AND MAGIC

Magic was not just the preserve of the common people or the basis of peasant credulity. Magic also formed part of the world-view of kings and queens and those occupying high-status positions in society. Queen Elizabeth I of England took very seriously the astrological advice of her astrologer royal, John Dee, and he was a formidable influence at court throughout and beyond her reign. Her successor, James VI of Scotland, was also affected by witchcraft when a plot against him was declared to have been instigated by witches, but he was eager to introduce a new rationalism to the higher echelons of society and declared himself anxious to establish the unlawfulness of witchcraft. This hostility to magic was partly self protection, as he viewed magicians as a threat to the divine right of kings.

Magical beliefs concerning an interconnected universe formed part of a complex body of knowledge in early modern times. A magical world-view included what today would be called the irrational or the superstitious, but magic was a part of ordinary reality for most people of all social classes. It was not simply a part of folk belief or the "primitive" thinking of common people. Those in the highest positions in society, well-educated scholars and the pioneers of contemporary thought, used this magical world-view as a way of attempting to understand the universe.

Astrology, alchemy and the importance of the spiritual realms were central to the mental world of early modern Europe. The influence of classical culture, elements of Christian thought including demonological tracts, as well as folklore and pamphlets of witch trials, all helped to ensure that magic was a part of everyday life.

The integration achieved by the completed alchemical work – the hermaphrodite, a mixture of feminine and masculine attributes.

NEOPLATONISM

The popularity of Neoplatonism as a quest for the ultimate realities and a universal knowledge was widespread among educated people. Neoplatonism is a spiritual philosophy that envisions a universe full of powers whose secrets can be unlocked by those who seek the answers to life's eternal questions. It formed a body of contradictory elements, most of which were brought together in the *Corpus Hermeticum*, a collection of Greek texts that were written in the early centuries AD. The *Corpus Hermeticum* placed humans in the centre of the universe, acting as the link between the physical and spiritual worlds.

JOHN DEE (1527–1608)

A good example of a scholar, astrologer and early scientist, John Dee published *The Hieroglyphic Monad* in 1564. His scientific interests included navigation, geography, mathematics and astronomy. In 1553 when Mary Tudor came to the

The alchemical macrocosm showing a magical world-view through which all is related.

English throne, Dee was invited by her to draw up her horoscope, and when Mary's sister Elizabeth succeeded Mary in 1558, she chose the astrologically auspicious date of 14 January 1559 for her coronation on the advice of Dee. He acted as astrologer royal and also advised the queen on medical matters. From 1584 he was involved in alchemical experiments and also those designed to raise angels. In 1581 he met Edward Kelly who professed to receive visions from a heavenly stone, which Dee wrote down. In November 1582, Dee claimed to have been visited by an angel in the form of a boy who gave him a stone that was like black crystal. The angels taught Dee the "language of Enoch", which was supposedly spoken by Adam before the Fall. Kelly, in a trance, dictated to Dee *The Book of Enoch*, which revealed the mysteries of creation. Dee was consulted on matters as diverse as assisting in providing a geographical description of the lands to which Elizabeth I had the right to be sovereign in 1580, giving advice to the government on calendar reforms in 1584–5, and helping to cure Elizabeth I when she was ill in 1571.

The historian James Sharpe has observed that there were sporadic accusations of witchcraft among persons of high social class (similar to those made against Dame Alice Kyteler), and that these sometimes

Queen Elizabeth I, a portrait by Isaac Oliver.

involved treason against a monarch. John Dee's life at court was not an easy one in this respect. As early as 1553 his connection with the then Princess Elizabeth was being investigated by the Star Chamber, and he was suspected of trying to kill Queen Mary by poison or magic. In the 1580s his house was attacked by a mob when rumours spread that he was using witchcraft.

In 1604 he petitioned James I asking that he might be cleared of accusations of being a "conjurer, or caller, or invocator of devils".

COURTLY ACCUSATIONS

Beliefs about witchcraft were held by those in the highest social positions, and the case of the 5th Earl of Sussex demonstrates what James Sharpe has described as a magical dimension to aristocratic infighting. A suit that was examined by the Star Chamber involved the marital problems of Robert Radcliffe, the 5th Earl of Sussex. The earl's marriage to Bridget, the daughter of Sir Charles Morison, was problematic. After Bridget was given substantial lands, she allegedly committed adultery and

A portrait of John Dee, the sixteenth-century English scholar and astrologer.

attempted to kill her husband. The couple separated in 1612 and the earl took up with Frances Shute, a woman supposedly of bad reputation. Allegations were made against her that she had tried to injure three of the earl's kinsfolk by magic and that she had used witchcraft to turn the earl against his wife. She was said to have been aided by a magician named Matthew Evans, who, it was alleged, had been involved in her attempts to damage the earl's relatives to favour Shute's children. Evans confessed to helping her by the use of astrology and by casting a horoscope for one of her daughters. He had also been asked to help her gain the affections of the Duke of Buckingham, one of the most powerful men in England.

Another case involving members of the aristocracy and village witchcraft was that against Joan Flower and her daughters Margaret and Phillipa, who were executed at Lincoln on 22 March 1618 for killing Henry Lord Roos and "damnable practises against others the Children of the Right Honourable Francis Earle of Rutland".

Astrological chart with signs of the zodiac from the sixteenth-century Portolan map.

The three women were charwomen at Belvoir Castle in Rutland. Joan Flower was described as "a monstrous malicious woman, full of oaths, curses, and imprecations irreligious … her very countenance was estranged; her eyes were fiery and hollow, her speech fell and envious, her demeanour strange and exotic, and her conversation sequestered, so that the whole course of her life gave great suspicion that she was a notorious witch".

One of her daughters, Margaret, it was maintained, kept "debauched and base company", while the other daughter, Phillipa, was said to have bewitched her lover. After Margaret's dismissal for neglecting her business and indecency Joan cursed all that were the "source of her discontentment". As the court records read:

At last, as malice increased in these damnable women, so his family felt the smart of their revenge and inficious disposition, for his eldest son Henry Lord Roos, sickened very strangely and after a while died. His next, named Francis, Lord Roos accordingly, was severely tormented by them and most barbarously and inhumanly

Above: The crystal ball of Dr John Dee, the best known magician of the Elizabethan era.

Right: An Aztec obsidian mirror, which once belonged to Dr John Dee. It was thought to have been part of the treasure brought back from Mexico by Cortes. It was used as a tool for divination.

tortured by a strange sickness; not long after, the Lady Katherine was set upon by their dangerous and devilish practices and many times in great danger of life thorough extreme maladies and unusual fits; nay (as it should seem and they afterwards confessed) both the Earl and his Countess were brought into their snares as they imagined, and indeed [they] determined to keep them from having any more children. Oh unheard-of-wickedness and mischievous damnation!

THE PRIVY COUNCIL

This body of men acted as England's central governing body and its councillors were aristocrats and high churchmen who were alert to threats of witchcraft, especially any prophesying against the monarch. The Privy Council was often the arbiter in difficult criminal cases and in 1579 ordered the interrogation of a group of witches from Windsor, who, it was claimed, had used image magic, through the use of a bewitched puppet, in an attempt on Elizabeth I's life.

James VI

In 1597 James VI of Scotland published a tract against witches called *Daemonologie*. It consisted of a debate between Philomathus and Epistemon on issues concerning witchcraft, and was concerned to establish the unlawfulness of both natural magic and witchcraft. James executed the work in response to a plot against him by alleged witches, which led to mass trials and executions from 1590-1. During and since his reign, James was held to be a witch hunting fanatic by many, and he did indeed see witches, – thought of as anti-Catholic heretics – as a natural threat to the divine right of monarchs, but evidence shows that he was also interested in the fair examination of women that were accused of the crime.

King James VI of Scotland, later also James I of England.

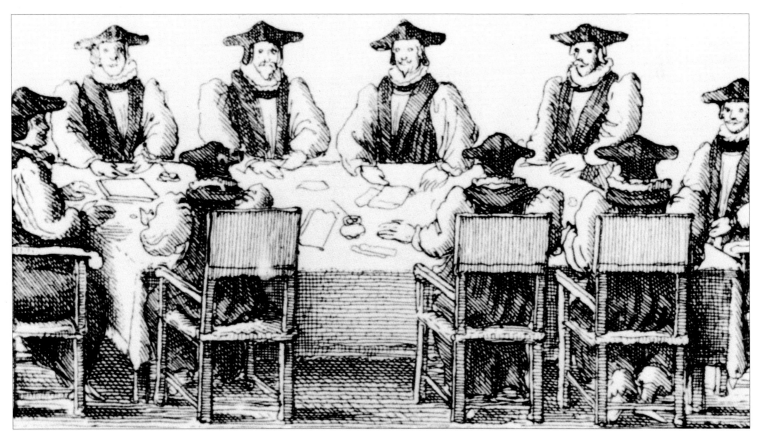

The High Commission Court and the Star Chamber of the sixteenth and seventeenth centuries. It was all-male bodies such as this, both secular and ecclesiastical, that sat in judgement over witchcraft and magic.

REGINALD SCOT AND WITCHCRAFT

Not everyone believed in witchcraft. Reginald Scot, the first English writer to publish a major theoretical work on witchcraft, thought that there were no reasons to believe in witchcraft. Scot, who was probably born in 1538 of Kentish Protestant gentry stock, thought witchcraft was a conjuring art that profaned the name of God. He generally attacked popular beliefs about witchcraft, and said that witches were only able to perform the feats that were attributed to them by trickery and fooling the credulous. He thought that witch hunters were wrong in what they thought about witches, and that the notion that any kind of demonic pact could be established between Satan and witches was absurd.

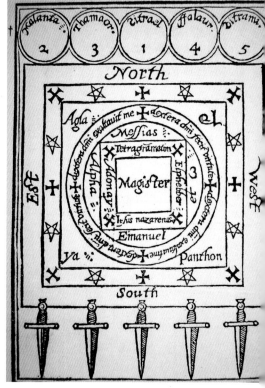

Reginald Scot set out to demonstrate in *The Discoverie of Witchcraft* (1584) that beliefs in witchcraft were superstition and were a sign of an imperfect faith in God. He dismissed descriptions of the Sabbath, shape-shifting and the demonic pact with the Devil. He was concerned with the reality of divine providence and believed that ascribing misfortune to witchcraft was denying the existence of God's master plan. Whatever his views, the book has been influential as a source of magical lore and gives descriptions of rituals, charms and spells, as well as literary references. Shakespeare and King James, among others, used it. The book provides authenticated stories of contemporary village witchcraft. Scot describes witchcraft as:

… a cozening [defrauding] art, wherein the name of God is abused, profaned and blasphemed, and His power attributed to a vile creature. In estimation of the vulgar people it is a supernatural work contrived between a corporal old woman and a spiritual devil.

An illustration from Reginald Scot's The Discoverie of Witchcraft, *"the names written within the five circles doo signifie the five infernall kings".*

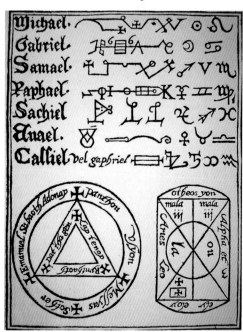

A page of symbols called "the seales of the earth" from Reginald Scot's The Discoverie of Witchcraft.

The Devil is conjured up from a magic circle, an illustration from the Compendium Maleficarum, *1608.*

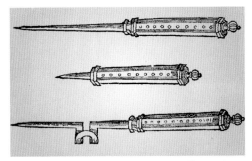

"Trick bodkins" used in torture, an illustration from The Discoverie of Witchcraft.

Witches, according to Scot, are commonly "old, lame, blear-eyed, pale, foul, and full of wrinkles; poor, sullen, superstitious". They are either papists or those in whose minds the Devil "hath gotten a fine seat"; as mad or devilish they "do not differ much from those possessed with spirits". These miserable wretches go from house to house and from door to door for milk, yeast, drink or pottage, and they are feared by their neighbours who feel "they are capable of doing things beyond the ability of human nature".

ALL IN THE MIND

Scot tried to show that the threat of witchcraft superstition could be avoided:

One Ada Davie, the wife of Simon Davie, husbandman, being reputed a right honest body and being of good parentage, grew suddenly ... to be somewhat pensive and more sad than in times past .... But when she grew from pensiveness to some perturbation of mind ... he could not but demand the cause of her conceit [fancy, fantasy] and mourning. But although at that time she covered the same, acknowledging nothing to be amiss with her, soon after, notwithstanding, she fell down before him on her knees, desiring him to forgive her for she had grievously offended ... both God and him. Her poor husband, being abashed at this her behaviour, comforted her as he could, asking her the cause of her trouble and grief, who told him that she had, contrary to God's law and to the offence of all good Christians, to the injury of him and specially to the loss of her own soul, bargained and given her soul to the Devil, to be delivered unto him within short space.

A whole family of witches, including children, are initiated into a Sabbath overseen by two demons. From the Compendium Maleficarum.

Whereunto her husband answered, saying, "Wife, be of good cheer, this thy bargain is void and of none effect, for thou hast sold that which is none of thine to sell; since it belongeth to Christ who hath bought it and dearly paid for it, even with His blood which He shed upon the cross, so the Devil hath no interest in thee". After this, with like submission, tears and penitence, she said to him, "Oh husband, I have committed another fault and done you more injury, for I have bewitched you and your children". "Be content", quoth he, "by the grace of God, Jesus Christ shall unwitch us; for no evil can happen to them that fear God ...".

This was a recurrent theme, although sometimes hidden, that those accused of witchcraft only had to turn back to the Church, and to God, for their misdeeds to be forgiven and expunged.

People's precarious existence meant they were susceptible to superstition and irrational fears.

24 WITCH HUNTS

In early modern Europe, thousands of people were tried for witchcraft; most were poor and elderly women. The Christian Church created the stereotype of a witch as someone who killed babies and engaged in sexual orgies during night-time Sabbats (or Sabbaths) in honour of the Devil, the force of evil that was opposed to the Christian God. The prosecutions, convictions and executions of witches varied in form and number in different parts of Europe but all of them had similarities in the way they were carried out, who they were directed against, and the kinds of people who propagated them. An examination of witch hunts in this period gives a particular insight into a time of significant cultural and religious change.

HOW WITCH HUNTS BEGAN

During the twelfth century, the Christian Church's ideas about witches began to change. Up until that time, women who joined cults of the night-flying goddesses Holda, Diana and Herodias were thought to have been seduced by Satan into believing that they were riding at the dead of night across many lands. This was seen to be an illusion. However, in the twelfth-century the Church became particularly worried about secret organizations plotting its overthrow, and beliefs that had previously been ascribed to vivid imagination inspired by the Devil now came to be seen as having actually occurred in reality. The Church had always been suspicious of dissident sects – such as the Montanists and the Paulicians – but religious dissent had spread and the Church was beset with alternative religious groups claiming their own version of spiritual truth. These groups were branded heretics because their views did not accord with those of the Church. A number were accused of conducting sexual orgies and eating children; their members were persecuted and put to death.

A sixteenth-century illustration of a man who is suspected of sorcery being tortured by the "strappado", a German torture aparatus.

Ideas about witches are found in most cultures all over the world, and a belief in people who had the ability to harm using spiritual forces is probably as old as humanity itself. These ideas can be traced back to societies that relied on a shaman as a specialist who communicated between the everyday world and the spiritual realm. The shaman's special powers could be used for good and helpful purposes – such as finding the whereabouts of food sources – but sometimes, in certain circumstances, these special powers could be manipulated for anti-social or destructive ends; perhaps when they were used to bolster the shaman for his or her personal gain rather than for the good of the group. Thus a shaman who ceased to work for the good of the community was probably the prototype of the witch.

In general terms, a witch is someone who performs antisocial and terrifying deeds, frequently at night. What is different about early modern European witch beliefs is that they became Christianized: witches were not just individuals who were responsible for misfortune and bad things happening, but part of an anti-Christian heretical sect, which worshipped the Devil. They gained their power not through their own wickedness but through a pact with the Devil, the leader of the forces of evil against the Christian God of good.

Ideas about witchcraft and magic were a part of European culture before witchcraft became specifically anti-Christian. Ideas about witches had come from the classical world of Greek and Roman mythology, folk beliefs and fairy stories. In the seventh and eighth centuries there was a widespread belief in the figure of a night-flying cannibalistic female witch called *striga* or *stria* in Italy, *sorcière* in France and *bruja* in Spain. At this early stage, the Christian Church had less emphatic views about witches and witchcraft: St Boniface declared that a belief in witches was not Christian, while Charlemagne ordered the death penalty for those who burnt witches. By the ninth century, Christian authorities had refused to recognize

A sixteenth-century woodcut showing witches being burnt in the market place in Guernsey.

ideas about night-flying witches or beliefs that they could metamorphose into different beings.

The Church's position began to change during the twelfth century with the arrival of popular heresies, according to which Jews, lepers and homosexuals were thought to form secret organizations to plot the overthrow of Christian society. A Western myth of a company of witches that flew to Sabbaths or Sabbats – said to be nocturnal meetings to worship the Devil – was created out of existing folklore.

In early modern Europe, thousands of people – it is not known exactly how many but the estimates of nine million are greatly exaggerated – were tried for witchcraft. The majority were women, usually poor and elderly. About half of those convicted were executed, mostly by burning. Some of the convicts were let off with a warning. The witch hunts represented a very large judicial operation. Some trials took place in ecclesiastical courts while others, especially after 1550, were held in secular courts.

Poor women being hanged as witches. From a seventeenth-century English engraving.

The geographical distribution of witch trials was uneven. In some areas there were few prosecutions while in others thousands may have been tried over a period of 300 years. The witch trials increased in numbers during the fifteenth century, reduced in the sixteenth, increased dramatically in the late sixteenth and early seventeenth, and declined in the late seventeenth and early eighteenth centuries. The historian Norman Cohn suggests that the fully developed stereotype of the witch, as someone who flew at night to Sabbaths, where she engaged in sexual orgies and ritually consumed children, was a by-product of the fierce persecution of Waldensian heretics, who were themselves members of a small reform movement.

Three sorceresses being burnt at the stake in Derneburg in October 1555. Taken from a contemporary leaflet.

THE DEVIL'S ROLE

According to the witch-trial judges there were two main parts to the crime of witchcraft. The first was the practise of harmful magic, or *maleficium* – the practical working of evil or malign magic against other people, which is found worldwide. The second, which marks the difference between beliefs in European witchcraft and that in other cultures, and which became more and more emphasized, was diabolism – the connection with the Devil, the creator and lord of evil in opposition to God, the lord of all good.

The origins of the concept of the Devil may lie in *The Epic of Gilgamesh*, composed in Sumeria during the third millennium BC. This is the first narrative to record the combat between good and evil. Gilgamesh seeks to free the land from the evil inflicted on it by the monster Huwawa, whose roaring is the flood-storm, whose mouth is fire and whose breath is death. Gilgamesh goes with his companion Enkidu to a cedar forest, which is guarded by Huwawa. When Gilgamesh and his companions start felling trees, Huwawa defends his domain by putting Gilgamesh into a deep sleep. Later, when Gilgamesh awakes, he finds Huwawa and kills him. In the poem the underworld is viewed in negative terms, not as part and parcel of the rhythm of life:

Satan gives images to witches to use as charms. A fifteenth-century woodcut.

There is the house whose people sit in darkness; dust is their food and clay their meat. They are clothed like birds with wings for covering, they see no light they sit in darkness.

This vision ruptures the continuity with the past seen in earlier myths, such as that of Isis and Osiris. It marks a separation between the living and the dead, light and dark, and eventually good and evil. God becomes identified with good, while the Devil becomes associated with evil.

THE DEVIL OF JUDAISM

The idea of the Devil is vague in the Old Testament. To the early Jews, God was omnipotent and there was no conspiracy of human beings under the command of the Devil. Yahweh was a tribal god who originally combined light and darkness, good and evil. However, as religious consciousness changed it

Gilgamesh stands between two demigods on this carving from the ninth century BC.

The Sumerian hero, Gilgamesh, holding a captured lion. From an Assyrian stone relief of c.725BC at the Palace of Sargon II, Iraq.

was thought incongruous that God should be responsible for evil. Influenced by the dualistic Persian religion of Zoroastrianism, in which the world is seen in terms of a cosmic warfare between the good god of light and the evil god of darkness, some areas of Jewish religion became more concerned with the Devil. Successive invasions, enslavement and persecution by the Egyptians, Assyrians, Babylonians, Persians, Greeks and Romans led the Jews to view themselves as a people suffering from the gentiles and their associated evil spirits. The Essenes, a Jewish sect, saw the world in apocalyptic terms as a cosmic battle between the

Gradually, Jewish religion became more concerned with the Devil. Here Satan is pictured binding the eyes of the Jews.

Satan and the birth of sin, as portrayed in an eighteenth-century painting illustrating Milton's Paradise Lost.

lord of light and the prince of darkness which would ultimately be won by God who would triumph eternally. However, after the destruction of Jerusalem by the Romans in AD70, which involved the diaspora of the Jews, the Pharisees, as the leading Jewish group, downplayed the Devil's power and influence.

Christianity as a religion was born from a culture of which such dualistic views were a part. In particular, the Gnostic sects combined Iranian and Greek dualism. Unlike the Zoroastrian dualism, which opposed the spirit of

light with a spirit of darkness, the Greeks posited a struggle between good spirit and evil matter. The Devil became creator and lord of evil matter. The early Christians saw life as a struggle against the Devil. Jesus himself was tempted in the wilderness, and the desert in particular became a symbol of evil and the haunt of demons.

SATAN AND WITCHES

By the fifth century, a theology of the Devil was well established. The Devil was increasingly thought to be active everywhere, and was accompanied by demons who were fallen angels. St Augustine wrote that God created intelligent creatures who were given a free choice between good and evil. Adam and Eve were created pure, he declared, but yielded to Satan and so were banished from Paradise.

Up until the thirteenth century, however, although practising magic was seen to be a sin, it was not linked with the Devil. After this time, magic came to be seen as inevitably demonic. Due to the influence of Aristotelian theology, the distinction between the natural and the supernatural was made, and

magic, which was seen to be aided by the work of demons, was placed on the supernatural side. The period from the fourteenth to the sixteenth centuries saw European societies undergoing an enormous amount of social and economic change, and the idea of a widespread conspiracy of witches in league with the Devil took hold.

Satan was reputed to have a voracious sexual appetite and is pictured here having sex with a sleeping woman.

HERETICS

During the third century AD, Christianity ceased to be a militant sub-group and became integrated into Graeco-Roman society. By the fourth century it had become adopted as the official religion of the Roman Empire and was changing its position accordingly to become a part of the establishment. Part of its evolution into a state religion was to extend its authority over its congregation, and as a result it began increasingly to view dissident sects with suspicion and to see them as a threat to its supremacy. All those who deviated from the Church's orthodoxy in any way became labelled as heretics.

Members of a religious sect called the Turlupins being burnt in Paris in the fourteenth century.

MONTANISTS AND PAULICIANS

One such group of dissidents was a Christian group called the Montanists, founded by a man called Montanus. This sect had turned against what it saw as the relaxed, easy-going Christianity of the Greek towns. Accusations were brought against Montanists and it was claimed that they practised cannibalism. At Easter they were said to mix the blood of a child with their offering, sending pieces of it to their supporters. Augustine reported that:

People say that they have most lamentable sacraments. It is said that they take the blood of a one-year-old child, drawing it off through tiny cuts all over his body, and at the same time produce their Eucharist, by mixing this blood with meal and making bread out of it. If the boy dies, they treat him as a martyr; but if he lives, they treat him as a great priest.

Likewise, the Paulicians, an eighth-century sect in Armenia, were condemned as the "sons of Satan" for allegedly coming together under cover of darkness in hidden meetings to commit incest with their own mothers. If a child was born, it was said to be thrown from one to the other until it died, and the person in whose hands it died was promoted to leader of the sect. The blood of such infants was mixed with

Heretics being tortured and taken to execution in the fifteenth century.

Torture being used to obtain a confession in the sixteenth century.

As religious dissent spread from the late twelfth century onwards, legislation was introduced to combat it. At the Synod of Verona in 1184, Pope Lucius III and Empereror Frederick I decreed the excommunication of heretics. In 1215 the death penalty was introduced for impenitent heretics. Inquisitional procedures were established by Pope Innocent III as a way by which the ecclesiastical authorities could take action against any wayward behaviour of clerics. The Inquisition took its name from the inquisitional procedure and adapted it to eradicate heresy, becoming fully organized by the late thirteenth century.

THE WALDENSIANS

In 1173, a rich merchant of Lyon named Peter Waldo gave all his wealth away in a bid to gain salvation. He attracted a group of followers, known as the Waldensians, who were keen to follow a path of poverty. They pledged themselves to observe the law of Christ by renouncing the world, modelling their way of life upon the apostles, being chaste and owning nothing that was not absolutely necessary. The Pope imposed restrictions on their preaching in 1179, and when they failed to stop they were excommunicated in 1181, finally being condemned as heretics in 1184. This

flour to make the Eucharist. The Paulicians were said to worship the Devil by bowing low while foaming at the mouth.

These tales of cannibalism and the workings of the enemies of God were applied to various religious out-groups and became part of a body of Christian demonology. Later, the Devil, or one of his subordinate demons, presided over the nocturnal orgies of heretics, usually in the form of an animal, often a cat. These night meetings were called "Sabbats". The term derives from Judaism, which was regarded as anti-Christianity.

Waldensians fleeing from their burning village.

Illustration of an early Papal crusade against the Waldensians.

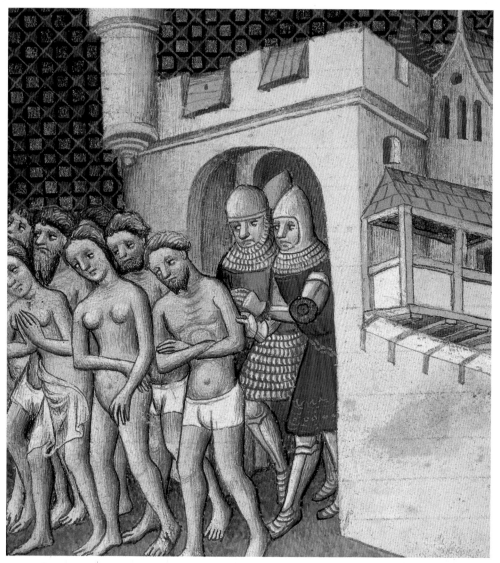

Cathar heretics, stripped and without any possessions being expelled from Cerlesonne by military forces.

failed to stop people being drawn to the sect. Even persecution and the threat of being burnt at the stake did not deter the most persistent, and the movement spread from France into Spain, Italy, Germany and Austria. The members devoted themselves to an intensive study of the Scriptures, and although many were totally illiterate peasants and artisans, they were often able to recite the four Gospels and the Book of Job by heart.

The Waldensians were persecuted for their heresy, and accusations were brought against them. According to one account by a Franciscan monk, they met in an assembly presided over by three strikingly handsome men, wearing shining robes, who were identified as the Father, Son and Holy Spirit. However, when the Franciscan held up the Eucharist, the spirits vanished leaving an evil stink.

THE CATHARS

For the Cathars, all matter was evil and the human body was a container that held a soul struggling to free itself. The Cathars believed that the material world was created by an evil spirit who dominated it. They practised vegetarianism and fasting, and evinced a total revulsion of the material world. Souls, who they saw as angels created by God, had fallen from heaven and

A Christian expedition embarking on a crusade. From a fourteenth-century miniature.

were imprisoned in human bodies. As heavenly beings, souls yearned to escape from the material demonic world and re-enter the world of pure spirit. Thus, for the Cathars, procreation was to be avoided and preventing souls from being brought into the world was seen to be very important. Like the Waldensians, the Cathars were branded as heretics and accused of conducting sexual orgies and worshipping the Devil. Accusations against heretics tended to follow a stereotype of orgies and child-eating, which had originated in the second century.

THE KNIGHTS TEMPLAR

Jerusalem was captured in 1099 during the First Crusade and it became a sacred place, which many pilgrims visited. In 1118 a fellowship was founded for the military protection of the pilgrims from attack by Moslems. It was based on the Order of the Hospital of St John of Jerusalem, which provided alms and medical care to pilgrims. The new military monastic order vowed chastity, obedience and self-denial as a fraternity of warriors pledged to fight for the King of Heaven. They were first called the "Poor Fellow-Soldiers of Christ of the Temple of Solomon" because their headquarters were a wing of a palace that had once been Solomon's Temple, but soon they became known simply as the Knights Templar.

The Knights Templar, who were backed by the Pope, were committed to struggling against the forces of Islam for the reward of valour in war and salvation. They also, however, entered into financial transactions and cultivated secrecy; their headquarters were used as safe deposits for crown jewels and public monies, as well as for banking and trade.

In 1187 the Templars were massacred by Saladin, but those remaining soon regained their power and wealth, and in 1244 they regained Jerusalem by negotiation. However, the same year they were almost wiped out by the Egyptian army. The Mongols under Genghis Khan and the Egyptians under Baybars kept up the pressure on the

The looting of Jerusalem after it was captured by the Christians in 1099.

King Philip IV accuses the Knights Templar of heresy. From a fourteenth-century illustration.

Knights Templar and by 1303 they had been driven out of the Holy Land. They were finally branded as heretics by King Philip IV of France, who sought to remove them altogether so that he could become Roman emperor and reconquer the Holy Land to establish a federation of nations. This was the beginning of the end for the Templars.

It was held by their accusers that the Knights conducted secret rituals during which an initiate was taken behind an altar and shown a crucifix. The initiate had to deny Christ three times and spit three times on the crucifix. After stripping naked, he was kissed three times by the leader, once on the base of the spine, once on the navel, and once on the mouth, and he was told that he must agree to commit sodomy if requested. These were the charges by which the Knights Templar were tried and with which the fellowship was suppressed. However, like the charges of heresy that were brought against the Waldensians and the Cathars, they had absolutely no foundation.

THE LEGALITIES OF WITCH HUNTING

The stereotype of a witch as a human being who was usually a woman, but could sometimes be a man, or even a child, bound to the Devil by a pact as his assistant, developed as a by-product of the campaign of the Inquisition against heretics. The fully developed stereotype of the witch as someone who specialized in the cannibalistic killing of babies to gain supernatural power, and who attended Sabbaths, was first officially sanctioned by the Church in the fifteenth century. Trial records show accounts of Sabbaths and nocturnal flying from 1420 onwards.

... called on the Devil, who, in the presence of the judges ... seized him and lifted him four to five feet from the ground, and let him drop onto the tiled floor like a bag of wool ...; whereupon, being picked up by two guards he was found to be black and blue all over, frothing at the mouth and suffering grievously in his body. Questioned as to the cause of his levitation and the sudden illness or change in him, he replied that it was the Devil on whom he had called to remove him from the hands of Justice, who having made an effort to do this, could not do it, because he had taken the judiciall oath, and the Devil had no more power over him.

A judge interrogating prisoners. From a fifteenth-century manuscript.

Witchcraft was not just an ordinary crime, it was thought to be the most noxious of all crimes because it represented those who were working against God and good society. This very essence of false religion had to be eradicated, and it was the judge's or magistrate's responsibility to act on the authority of God and the monarch, who ruled by divine right, to put witches to death. To this end, judges and magistrates were seen to have great power over the Devil and his assistant demons, as James VI of Scotland wrote in his *Daemonologie*: "For where God beginnes justlie to strike by his lawfull Lieutennentes, it is not in the Devilles power to defraude or bereave him of the office, or effect of his powerfull and revenging Scepter".

The Devil was seen to lose his power in the presence of judges, as in the case of Jean de Bonnevaux, who in 1599 was tried for witchcraft at Montmorillon in Poitou. While in court, it is reported that de Bonnevaux:

Thus, the primary task of the judge was to maintain true religion and this entailed the destruction of magic and witchcraft. The defeat of witches represented a victory for the authority and the supernatural power of God. People were formally and legally tried for crimes of witchcraft and they were frequently sentenced to death. Between the thirteenth and the sixteenth centuries in Europe there were changes to the legal system that had a direct effect on the people who were accused of witchcraft.

The secular and ecclesiastical courts of continental Europe adopted a new system of criminal procedure called the "inquisitional" legal system, which was different from the "accusatorial" system of trying a suspected criminal. The latter arrangement involved a judge presiding over a contest between two private parties, the outcome of which was left to God to decide. By contrast, under the inquisitional system the judge and court actively investigated whether or not the defendant was guilty from the evidence and facts given.

TORTURE OF SUSPECTS

By the time witch hunting began, England was the only country in Europe that had not adopted at least some of the features of the inquisitional procedure into its legal system. Torture was often used as a means to get an accused person to confess to crimes of witchcraft, and it greatly increased the numbers convicted. Various methods were used, ranging from sleep deprivation to the use of certain instruments of torture. The instruments comprised two types: those of distension – such as the strappado, a pulley that raised the person off the floor by his or her arms, and the rack – and instruments of compression – thumb screws, leg screws and head clamps.

In Germany many courts used a "witches' chair", which was heated by a fire below. In Scotland, according to a pamphlet called Newes from Scotland published in 1591, a witch suspected of treason against the king, "was put to the most severe and cruell paine in the world, called the bootes", and "his legges were crushte and beaten togeather as small as might bee, and the bones and flesh so bruised, that the bloud and marrowe sputed forth in great abundance".

There were strict rules in existence governing the use of torture, but in practice they were relaxed, flouted or

A suspected witch being ducked into the river in a witches' chair.

completely disregarded by the accusers. The effect of torture was to help spread the concept of witchcraft; the inevitable production of confessions under torture

confirmed the inquisitors' most bizzare fantasies, and it also gave the inquisitors names of alleged accomplices of witches.

TRIAL BY ORDEAL

Suspected witches often had to undergo other ordeals that were intended to provide additional evidence of guilt. "Swimming the witch" was widely practised in England and other parts of Europe; it involved tying the witch's wrists to her ankles and throwing her into water. If she sank she was innocent, but if she floated it was confirmation that she was a witch.

The commonest ordeal in Scotland was pricking for the Devil's mark to find a spot where the witch didn't feel pain – this marked the place where the Devil had consummated their pact. In cases of possession the possessed person was taken into the presence of the accused witch and if they had a fit the witch was guilty. Thus ordinary people, mostly old, poor women, were put through a legal system fuelled by fantasies created by the Christian Church and were cruelly persecuted and tortured by "tests" that were manifestly absurd.

Mary Sutton was suspected of witchcraft in 1612, and is here being "swum" to establish her innocence or guilt.

Witch hunters

In the early modern period, the legal system of witch hunting led to the rise of professional people who dedicated themselves to the persecution of women they saw as a threat to society. Witches were seen as real and not imaginary, and published works helped to synthesize ideas about diabolic witchcraft into the recognizable, sexualized and cannibalistic stereotype. Heinrich Kramer and Jacob Sprenger, authors of the witch hunting manual the *Malleus Maleficarum*, Jean Bodin, author of *De la démonomanie des sorciers*, and the self-styled Witchfinder General, Matthew Hopkins, were all well known for their zealous campaigns against witches. Kramer and Sprenger were inquisitors from the Dominican monastic order who were determined to eradicate heretics, who they claimed were most often women. Bodin, a French philosopher and judge, saw the universe as an organic unity ruled over by God. This natural order was broken by witches with their evil ways, and they therefore had to be eradicated to secure social and spiritual harmony. Why Matthew Hopkins felt called to engage in a personal crusade to elimate witches in his native East Anglia is unclear.

judicial proceedings against witches, and when they met resistance from local ecclesiastical and secular authorities, they obtained a papal bull from Pope Innocent VIII which allowed them to continue. The bull accused witches of all manner of abominations:

It has indeed lately come to Our ears, not without afflicting Us with bitter sorrow, that in some parts of Northern Germany, as well as in the provinces, townships, territories, districts, and dioceses of Mainz, Cologne, Trèves, Salzburg, and Bremen, many persons of both sexes, unmindful of their own salvation and straying from the Catholic Faith, have abandoned themselves to devils, incubi and succubi, and by their incantations, spells, conjurations, and other accursed charms and crafts, enormities and horrid offences, have slain infants yet in the mother's womb, as also the offspring of cattle, have blasted the produce of the earth, the grapes of the vine, the fruits of trees, nay, men and women, beasts of burthen, herd-beasts, as well as animals of other

KRAMER AND SPRENGER

These two Dominican inquisitors are well known for publishing a manual for inquisitors called the *Malleus Maleficarum* (sometimes known as "The Witches' Hammer"), which became a seminal text at the time, and a valuable source on contemporary thought ever since.

Heinrich Kramer was a trained theologian and was appointed inquisitor for southern Germany in 1474, while Jacob Sprenger, a professor of theology at the University of Cologne, became an inquisitor for Rhineland in 1470. Together they agreed that women were more likely to be heretical than men because they were more subject to superstition and credulity, more impressionable than men, and were also insatiable with carnal lust, unlike men. The two inquisitors were involved in

"Women are naturally more impressionable", an idea that has continued through the years, as can be seen in this painting from 1832, which perpetuates early modern ideas of women and their susceptability to Satan, in the supposedly more enlightened nineteenth century.

kinds, with terrible and piteous pains and sore diseases, both internal and external; they hinder men from performing the sexual act and women from conceiving, whence husbands cannot know their wives nor wives receive their husbands; over and above this, they blasphemously renounce that Faith which is theirs by the Sacrament of Baptism, and at the instigation of the Enemy of Mankind they do not shrink from committing the foulest abominations and filthiest excesses to the deadly peril of their own souls, whereby they outrage the Divine Majesty and are a cause of scandal and danger to very many.

THE MALLEUS MALEFICARUM

First published in 1486, the *Malleus Maleficarum* was not the first manual giving advice for those involved in judging witches. It was similar to the *Directorium Inquisitorum* by Nicholas Eymerich, which was published a century earlier in 1376, but it was significant because it played a major role in bringing together many ideas about witchcraft and presenting them as a single concept. *Malleus Maleficarum* educated the population about witches and introduced the idea of diabolic witchcraft to a large audience: it was this that played a vital part in witch hunting.

Before the *Malleus Maleficarum* ordinary people did not share the same world-view as the educated elite; their beliefs concerned magic, maleficence, night-flying witches and metamorphosis, but in general they did not feature the Devil. Nevertheless, notions of diabolic witchcraft did filter through from time to time.

Kramer and Sprenger's *Malleus Maleficarum* contributed to the creation of a composite stereotype of diabolic witchcraft; it synthesized ideas about witchcraft and gave them theological support, even though it referred to the Sabbath only in passing, and did not discuss the obscene kiss or the Devil's mark. Perhaps its greatest contribution was the introduction of a sexual element into the stereotype of the witch by strengthening the association of women with witchcraft. It has much to say about wicked women – "All wickedness is but little to the

The Malleus Maleficarum *increased the association of women with witchcraft. After all, it was Eve who had tempted Adam with the apple from the tree of knowledge and caused their expulsion from the Garden of Eden.*

wickedness of a woman" – and it states that the word "woman" is used to mean the "lust of the flesh", and that women are subject to superstition and credulity. Because Eve, the first temptress, was formed from the rib of a man, women are defective, imperfect and always deceive. Having "defective intelligence" they are more prone to renounce the faith and:

… through their second defect of inordinate affections and passions they search for, brood over, and inflict various vengeances, either by witchcraft, or by some other means. Wherefore it is no wonder that so great a number of witches exist in this sex.

Women are "quicker to waver in their faith", "naturally more impressionable", "more ready to receive the influence of

a disembodied spirit". They possess weak memories, are undisciplined, have slippery tongues that make them unable to conceal their knowledge of evil arts, and they vindicate themselves by witchcraft. Women are naturally more carnal than men, and "All witchcraft comes from carnal lust, which is in women insatiable".

The *Malleus Maleficarum* was a practical handbook offering legal advice on how to bring witches to trial. To start the trial proceedings, a notice was to be fixed to the walls of the parish church or town hall and instructions were given as to the wording,

WHEREAS we, the Vicar of such and such Ordinary (or the Judge of such and such county), do endeavour with all our might

and strive with our whole heart to preserve the Christian people entrusted to us in unity and the happiness of the Catholic faith and to keep them far removed from every plague of abominable heresy …

Therefore we the aforesaid Judge to whose office it belongs, to the glory and honour of the worshipful name of JESUS Christ and for the exaltation of the Holy Orthodox Faith, and for the putting down of the abomination of heresy, especially in all witches in general and in each one severally of whatever condition …

Malleus Maleficarum gave information on the initiation of proceedings against an alleged witch, the arrest, treatment of witnesses, defence, use of torture and

A ninteenth-century depiction of the torture of a suspected witch. The conflict between the male world of authority and the female is obvious, as is the artistic addition of female nakedness.

The frontispiece from the Compendium Malificarum *printed by Francesco Guazzo.*

sentencing. It gave a presiding judge specific advice on how to treat the accused, for example he was warned not to touch a witch, especially not with his bare hands, and always to carry salt that had been consecrated on Palm Sunday together with some Blessed Herbs enclosed in Blessed Wax and worn around the neck. A witch should be led backwards into the presence of the judge and his assessors, and he must cross himself and approach her manfully and "with God's help the power of that old Serpent will be broken".

The aim of the *Malleus Maleficarum* was to seek out and punish heretics – those who, while professing the Catholic faith, still held to their error. One sure way of detecting a heretic was if they practised any kind of witchcraft, even people who denied the reality of witchcraft were seen to be heretics. Witchcraft was not imaginary or unreal but a bodily contract with the Devil; women who thought they were riding at night with a goddess were really, so said the inquisitors, riding with the Devil.

It appears that the impact of the *Malleus Maleficarum* was limited: the Spanish Inquisition, for example, was sceptical about its value. Pope Innocent VIII did not sanction the work, even though he did encourage Kramer and Sprenger to hunt witches (they attached the papal bull to the front of the book to make it look as if it had official approval).

JEAN BODIN

In 1580 the French philosopher and judge Jean Bodin published *De la dèmonomanie des sorciers*, which was to become the *Malleus Maleficarum* of the next 100 years. It was a very influential work which fused the judge's or inquisitor's fantasies and obsessions with charges against the accused: Bodin based his belief in the reality of a witch cult on the uniformity of witches' confessions. By extracting confessions, usually under torture, to the activities that he believed the witch had engaged in, the inquisitor received confirmation of his suspicions, and so the beliefs acquired validity.

THEOLOGICAL JUSTIFICATION

Bodin believed in the mystical authority of the divine right of monarchs. He saw the universe as an organic unity regulated by harmonious laws and ruled over by God. The monarch was God's divine representative on earth; those who spoke evil against the monarch spoke evil against God. Bodin saw the magistrate as a person responsible for the creation of harmonic justice in a godly society. Witches broke natural and divine laws – by infanticide, cannibalism, killing by poisoning or charms, blighting crops, slaughtering animals, creating sterility and famine – and had to be punished to appease divine anger.

His condemnation of witches was anchored in the Jewish tradition, and their punishment was supported by texts in the Old Testament: the first rationale for punishments is to appease divine anger (*Numbers* 25); but it is also to obtain God's blessing on a land (*Deuteronomy* 13), to deter other malefactors (*Deuteronomy* 13), to prevent the "infection" of the good (*Deuteronomy* 15,19), to diminish the number of the evil (*Leviticus* 12,14), and to punish the actual crime (*Deuteronomy* 19).

Jean Bodin, French philosopher, judge and witch hunter.

Bodin claimed that the most powerful magic in the world would not work against the officials of the law, and that it was impossible to kill judges. He asserted that witchcraft utilized evil spirits, though these were not evil of themselves but ultimately vehicles for the good because they served God's design; like sewers and cesspools that are necessary even in a palace. Humans have free will and the harmony of the world is sustained by the friendly rivalry between good and evil. His call for the eradication of witches stemmed from his belief that French society was dangerously out of harmony: the bad was much stronger than the good, and he therefore wrote *De la dèmonomanie des sorciers* to deal with the situation.

Various unpleasant instruments of torture from a woodcut of c.1513.

MATTHEW HOPKINS

This man is a mysterious figure, and not much is known about his early life except that his family came from East Anglia and that he lived in the village of Manningtree in Essex, England. It appears that he may have gained some of his education in Holland, and worked as a clerk for a shipowner in Mistley, Essex. He must have been aware of local witch legends and traditions, among them that of sea witches, and it is possible that he was affected by a fear of witches through his work.

SEA WITCHES

There was a widespread fear of witches among seafarers and those connected with the sea. Astrologers were consulted by insurance brokers in cases of mysterious disappearances of ships. In a number of witch trials evidence was taken concerning the bewitchment of ships and captains. One account tells of a woman who lent an old woman some money, taking a brass kettle for security, while awaiting passage from Amsterdam to England. The old woman was unable to repay the debt but demanded the return of the kettle. When the request was refused, the old woman cursed the ship. A bad storm hit the ship and the crew saw an old woman sitting on top of the mainmast. The captain urged the woman to let him throw the kettle into the sea. When this was done, "the witch dismount her selfe from the mast, goes aboard the brasse kettle, and in a moment sails out of sight". After this, the air cleared, the wind grew calm, and the storm came to a stop.

WITCHFINDER GENERAL

For nearly three years – from the beginning of 1645 to August 1647, when he

Two witches, one female and one male, use their powers to create a storm at sea, and succeed in wrecking a ship.

Matthew Hopkins, the self-styled Witchfinder General, shown with two of his accused together with their familiars, or "imps", all of whom have names. From a seventeenth-century engraving.

died – there is documented proof of Hopkins' activities as the self-styled Witchfinder General. His witch hunting extended all over East Anglia, but Essex was the centre of his campaign to eliminate witches. From 1645, Essex witch trials bore an increasing resemblance to the more sensational descriptions of legal proceedings in France or Germany. Hopkins started his campaign on his own but later employed searchers. John Stearne, a Puritan "given to declamatory speeches full of the horrors of hell-fire and brimstone", and Mary "Goodwife" Phillips, a midwife, joined his team.

IMPS AND FAMILIARS

Witches in Essex were not generally thought to fly to Sabbaths, or to have sexual perversions. Instead, the focus of the witch-hunting process was on witches' marks and familiars or imps. The body of

A witch sits surrounded by devils. The witch hunters would search for the marks left by devils such as these. This illustration is from the title page of the seventeenth-century Daemonolatria *by Nicholas Remy.*

a quarter of an hour, after which it was wiped off with a cloth. This woman was more fortunate: she was aquitted.

Hopkins himself allegedly had an encounter with a familiar. He wrote a pamphlet called *The Discovery of Witches: in Answer to Severall Queries, lately Delivered to the Judges of Assize for Norfolk county*, printed in 1647. In it he described how the familiar came into his yard at night, "a black thing, proportioned like a cat oneley it was thrice as big, sitting on a strawberry ned, and fixing the eyes on this Informant; and when he [Hopkins] went towards it, it leapt over the pale ... but ran quite through the yard, with his greyhound after it ... and the said greyhound returned again to this Informant, shaking and trembling exceedingly".

Thus the witch hunters Kramer, Sprenger, Bodin and Hopkins carried out their crusade against ordinary people. Their misogynistic legacy remains in popular stereotyped images of witches as old evil hags. The Christian Church, therefore, played a part in the persecution of many innocent people in the name of a battle against an evil that had never existed except in the often perverse minds of the persecutors.

The Essex witch Joan Prentis sits with her familiars. In the background is a reminder of the penalty of witchcraft.

an accused person was searched for the Devil's marks, which were usually found. The woman was then "watched" or kept awake for a minimum of 24 hours, strapped naked and cross-legged to a stool or table, while her accusers waited for the appearance of her familiars or imps. A woman called Joyce Bonds confessed to having "two imps in the likeness of mice, which came into her bed and sucked her body". Apparently, she used these imps to kill a neighbour's lambs, and she was hanged for the crime. Another woman, who was named Binkes and lived in Haverhill, was reported by Stearne as having a fly for an imp. She denied being a witch and requested to see the rector of her parish, saying that "the Lord would shew an example upon her and that if she had any imps, that they would come out whilst he was there". Apparently the imp appeared while the rector was there, and Stearne claimed that it fastened itself on her body for about

THE REFORMATION

The years between 1520 and 1650, a period later known as the Reformation, divided Christian Europe into Catholics and Protestants. A series of individual movements rather than one coherent organization, it was to have a profound effect on European religious life. The Reformation intensified witchcraft prosecutions and both Catholic and Protestant churches were determined to impose their views and practices in campaigns that were aimed at discrediting folk beliefs in magic. By doing this, the Church would take its rightful place as the sole spiritual and moral influence in the lives of ordinary men and women.

John Wyclif denied that the Eucharist actually transformed into the body and blood of Christ.

John Wyclif appearing before the Prelates at St Paul's to answer the charge of heresy in 1377.

Beliefs about witchcraft took on a specific character during the Reformation, and they were an important part of the reformers' thought. The Reformation, which lasted from 1520 to 1650, divided European Christianity into Catholic and Protestant traditions, and led to many wars and conflicts, most notably the Thirty Years War (1618–48). It was a series of parallel movements that sought to purify society and promote individual morality, rather than a single movement with a coherent organization or a clearly defined set of objectives.

JOHN WYCLIF AND THE LOLLARDS

There had been attacks on the Catholic Church before the Reformation when John Wyclif (c.1330–84), one-time master of Balliol College, Oxford, England, had rejected the notion of papal supremacy, and denounced the wealth of the Church, and denied that the Eucharist bread and wine actually transformed into the body and blood of Christ.

In 1395 the Lollards, Wyclif's followers, were also bitterly critical of what they saw as the Church's involvement with magic in the Eucharist. In their *Twelve Conclusions* they stated:

That exorcisms and hallowings, made in the Church, of wine, bread, and wax, water, salt and oil and incense, the stone of the altar, upon vestments, mitre, cross, and pilgrims' staves, be the very practice of necromancy, rather than of the holy theology. This conclusion is proved thus. For by such exorcisms creatures be charged to be of higher virtue than their own kind, and we see nothing of change in no such creature that is so charmed, but by false belief, the which is the principle of the devil's craft.

In short, false belief was the work of the Devil.

In the fifteenth century many people suffered deep religious unease owing to the hardships that they had had to endure through famine, war and disease. An obsession with death and sin had intensified Christian religious fervour, and more and more people turned to the Virgin Mary and the saints to save their souls. Many placed great faith in the power of relics and indulgences to gain them salvation.

The Pope selling indulgences so that people could be absolved of their sins. From a sixteenth-century woodcut.

The Protestant reformer Martin Luther, who described the Church's sale of indulgences as scandalous.

MARTIN LUTHER

The Reformation began because the Protestant reformers saw the Church as full of false beliefs. Reformers such as Martin Luther (1483–1546) and John Calvin (1509–64) broke with Rome and the papacy in a bid to restore the Church to what they saw as its earlier Christian purity. The dispute was provoked by the sale of indulgences, whereby people could pay to be absolved of their sins. On 31 October 1517 Luther posted up on the church door at Wittenberg, where he was a member of the university, 95 theses in which he contested the worth of indulgences and described their sale as scandalous. Luther, an Augustinian monk, believed that only faith could make people righteous, and that the Holy Scripture was the only source of true faith. He was against the cult of the Virgin Mary and the saints and thought that they should not be worshipped. Luther called for a change in the role of the clergy, relaxing the rule on celibacy and allowing priests to marry. Above all, he stressed the role of the individual conscience in the formation of a direct relationship with God.

The Protestant Reformation led to a reform movement within Catholicism known as the Counter-Reformation, which had the aim of reforming the Church from its worst excesses and eliminating corruption without changing its main structure. These changes, which were authorized by the Council of Trent from 1545 to 1563, claimed that tradition as well as Holy Scripture was a source of revelation.

A portrait of Jean Calvin, a Protestant reformer who broke with Rome in a bid to restore Christian purity.

A sixteenth-century woodcut caricature of Luther's opponents.

WITCH HUNTS INTENSIFY

Did the Reformation cause witch hunting? It has been claimed that the Reformation was a catalyst for witch hunting, but there is no direct relationship between the ideas and events that caused the break-up of European Christianity and the persecution of witches. However, the Reformation did intensify witchcraft prosecutions. The incidence and severity of campaigns mounted against witches depended on a complex mixture of social and political circumstances, which cut across different religious beliefs. According to the historian Brian Levack, witch hunting was most severe in countries or regions where there were large religious minorities, or where the people of one state were of one religion and those nearby were of another. Witch hunting took place in Protestant and Catholic lands but was at its most intense in regions that had a mixed population of Protestants and Catholics, such as Germany, Switzerland, France, Poland and Scotland. Spain and Italy, although they did not avoid witch hunts completely, had fewer "witch panics" because they remained largely

A Protestant caricature of Pope Alexander VI as the Devil. From a sixteenth-century woodcut.

Catholic. The historian Stuart Clark has claimed that beliefs in witchcraft were at the heart of the reforming process. He has argued that although there were differences between witch hunting in Protestant and Catholic regions, both Catholic and Protestant Churches were determined to impose the fundamentals of Christian belief on ordinary people; they vigorously campaigned to discredit popular beliefs in magic, calling them superstition. A Christian was forbidden to observe magical practices, such as:

… casting holy water upon his bed … bearing about him holy bread, or St John's Gospel … ringing of holy bells; or blessing with the holy candle, to the intent thereby to be discharged of the burden of sin, or to drive away devils, or to put away dreams and fantasies; or … putting trust and confidence of health and salvation in the same ceremonies.

How were beliefs in witches part of Reformation thought? During the Reformation there was an increased awareness of the Devil. Protestant reformers, especially Luther and Calvin, adopted the traditional late medieval view of the Devil, and a war was waged against Satan, both internally (by resisting temptation) and externally (by the prosecution of witches and other heretics). The importance of leading a moral life was seen to be an absolute priority: the individual was considered responsible for his or her own salvation. This had a psychological effect. Feelings of guilt could be transferred to another person in the shape of a witch who personified evil. Many witchcraft accusations were made against those who had come asking for charity. To refuse charity caused guilt, but by branding the person a witch, and therefore morally unworthy, the action was justified. It has also been suggested that when priests felt guilty about lapses in their sexual chastity they projected their guilt on to women, and so the witch also came to represent women's uncontrollable sexuality.

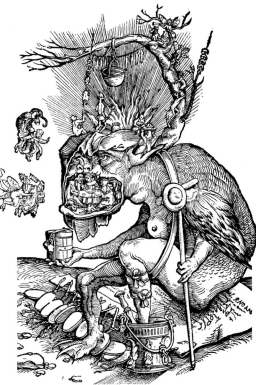

A sixteenth-century anti-Catholic caricature of monks and nuns feasting in the mouth of the Devil, who is sitting on a letter of indulgence.

PROTESTANT ATTITUDES

Stuart Clark argues that the nature of everyday misfortunes lies at the very heart of Protestant attitudes to witchcraft. Protestant theologians argued that to blame afflictions only on witches was a kind of hypocrisy, which undervalued misfortune as a punishment for sin, or as a test of faith. To apply counter-witchcraft, or to seek the services of cunning men or women – so-called "white witches" – was equally bad and was viewed as a form of idolatry, which ignored the need for repentance; it also attributed the power that was rightfully God's to magicians. Protestant demonologists concentrated their attack against superstition on cunning men and women and frequently saw them as more harmful than maleficent witches. According to an account in a book called *A Discourse of the Damned Art of Witchcraft* by William Perkins, published in 1608:

by Witches we understand not those onely which kill and torment: but all Diviners, Charmers, Juglers, all Wizzards, commonly called wise men and wise women; yea, whosoever doe any thing (knowing what they doe) which cannot be effected by nature or art; and in the same number we reckon all good Witches, which doe no hurt, but good, which doe not spoile and destroy, but save and deliver.

The attack against magic and witches served to unite the different factions of Christianity.

Luther writes his 95 theses against indulgences on the church door at Wittenberg in this contemporary allegorical woodcut.

THE GEOGRAPHY OF WITCH HUNTS

Witch hunting varied in intensity, not only in different countries and regions but also at different periods of time. It started, grew, peaked and then declined at varying times in diverse places. The ways and methods of prosecution, conviction and execution of witches also varied greatly in different regions but it is possible to see broad patterns. The majority of witchcraft prosecutions took place in Germany, France, Switzerland and the Low Countries. In the early years, most prosecutions occurred in France, especially in the east, while in later years more people were taken to court in Germany, particularly in the south and west of the country.

A condemned witch is taken to be burnt during the Bamberg witch trials in Bavaria.

The period from 1580 to 1650 was when witch hunting was at its peak. From the 1550s to the 1570s there was an increase in individual witch-trials and small hunts, while in the 1580s and 1590s there was a period of mass trials and large hunts. The process reached its high point between 1610 and 1630. The 1580s were particularly bad in Switzerland and the Low Countries; the 1590s in France, the Low Countries and Scotland; the 1600s in the Jura region and in parts of Germany; the 1610s in Spain; the 1620s and 1630s in Germany; the 1640s in England; the 1660s in Scotland; and the late 1660s and early 1670s in Sweden and Finland. Western and southern European countries (except Portugal) were the first to adopt the ideas of a diabolic witch as constructed by the demonologists. Persecution was only possible where there was a definite image of a witch who was a threat to good Christian society. Thus the spread of the witch hunt depended on the rise of demonology. The areas that were the first to take up the prosecution of witches were also the first to end such trials, with the emergence of ideas that were sceptical about such beliefs.

Early explanations for witch persecutions saw magic and superstition as part of the backwardness and primitivism of

La Murqui, the noted witchfinder of the French Basque country, indicates marks that prove a pact with Satan.

rural folk. The historian Hugh Trevor-Roper thought that the mountains were the home of sorcery, witchcraft and primitive religious forms, which had to be won back to "sound religion". His explanation for what he called the "witch craze" was in terms of the superstition of mountain peasants and concerned what he saw as "disturbances of a psychotic nature" and the "mental rubbish of peasant credulity and feminine hysteria". How could an advanced and civilized society like Europe, which was undergoing a scientific revolution at the same time, unleash a persecution based on the delirious notion of witchcraft?

POLITICAL OR RELIGIOUS PERSECUTION?

The witch persecutions were a single, unified phenomenon that coincided not only with the Reformation and the Counter-Reformation, but also with the growth of the modern nation state, and with new attitudes to science. They occurred at a dynamic time during which the educated elite of the cities and towns came to impose their beliefs on the ordinary people of rural areas.

Village beliefs about ordinary maleficent magic and witchcraft that concerned conflict between neighbours became diabolized by those who controlled the churches, schools and law courts of the emerging nation states. It has been said by some that witch hunting was a political rather than a religious activity, whereby the views of the educated elite, developed in the towns and cities, were imposed on the people who lived in the countryside. European witch trials had two main themes: popular beliefs in malevolent and harmful magic, and elite ideas about a diabolical Christian conspiracy. A precondition for the spread of witch persecutions was that elite ideas filtered down to the lower strata of society.

In rural areas, legal prosecutions reflected the inevitable social tensions of village life, while in urban centres it was sorcery inspired by political life. People such as plague-spreaders, who were thought to be capable of distilling the essence of the plague and infecting parts of the community, were accused of

The alleged activities of witches from the North Berwick coven in England in 1591. One of their number takes down the words of the Devil, while others boil a cauldron to create a storm and sink a ship at sea.

collectively worshipping the Devil and were prosecuted as witches.

The Reformation and the Counter-Reformation encouraged witchcraft prosecutions in the late sixteenth and early seventeenth centuries but during the earlier years, with the disintegration of medieval Christianity and the theological controversy involved, there were distractions from witch hunting. Also, the task of developing a specifically Protestant demonology took time to work out. After much work, finally the Protestants rejected the work of the Catholic Inquisition and drastically changed the legal procedure by moving witchcraft trials to secular courts. Therefore, coinciding as they did with a period of political and religious upheaval in the Reformation, the Counter-Reformation and the rise of the modern nation state, the witch hunts and the way they were prosecuted, represent a response to considerable social change.

The insides of the Justice Chamber at Valenciennes, northern France, during the period of the witchcraft trials.

WITCH HUNTS IN SWITZERLAND AND FRANCE

The first witch trials occurred in the French and Swiss Alps in the fifteenth century. According to the historian Norman Cohn, the early accounts of the witch trials in France in the thirteenth and fourteenth centuries were forgeries. The stereotype of the witch as someone who flew at night to Sabbaths was not sanctioned by the Church until the fifteenth century when trials occurred in the mountainous areas of the French and Swiss Alps as a result of the persecution of a group of Waldensian heretics. In 1428 the peasant communities of the Swiss canton of Valais, under the guidance of the Bishop of Sion, declared that anyone accused of witchcraft by more than two people should be arrested and made to confess. On the basis of their confession they were condemned to the flames. A witch hunt began at the same time in the Val d'Anniviers and the Val d' Hèrens, two valleys south of the Rhône. This was the first time that the stereotype of the witch that would come to inspire the great witch hunt appeared.

In 1453 a sensational witch trial took place in Evreux, Normandy. Guillaume

The witch Guillemette Babin in front of the inquisitors. Jean Bodin was responsible for her capture and trial in 1564, at which she was condemned and burned to death.

Adeline, a doctor of theology and former Paris professor, was accused of writing a compact with Satan binding him to preach sermons against the reality of the Sabbaths. This was allegedly supposed to have the effect that judges would be discouraged from prosecuting those who went to Sabbaths, thus allowing more members to frequent such gatherings. Adeline confessed to a compact with Satan. He said that he had flown on a broomstick to the Sabbaths and had found there a demon called Monseigneur, who changed himself into a he-goat, and whom Adeline kissed under his tail as homage. Perhaps because of his position, Adeline was sentenced to perpetual imprisonment rather than death. Adeline was supposed to have belonged to a sect of Waldensians, but Cohn notes that by this time the term was generally used as a synonym for "witches".

The northern and eastern regions and parts of the south-west of France – the peripheral areas – were the most heavily affected by witchcraft. The prosecution of witches may have been part of a general disciplinary programme for controlling rebellious outlying regions. Courts in these far-flung places had great independence from central government, but when a central monarchy was

Joan of Arc, convicted of heresy and sorcery rather than witchcraft, was burnt at the stake in Rouen in 1431. From a contemporary manuscript.

The burning of witches in Paris.

established in the sixteenth and seventeenth centuries, there were fewer witch executions.

JOAN OF ARC

One famous case was that of Joan of Arc, who was tried for heresy and sorcery and burnt at Rouen in 1431. In 1429 this young peasant girl introduced herself to Charles, the Dauphin of France, as his God-given saviour, telling him that she could change his fortune in the war against the English. She said that a voice from God had told her to raise the siege of Orléans to help Charles recover his kingdom and drive the English out of France. From the age of 12, Joan had seen visions, heard the voices of the Archangel Michael, Catherine of Alexandria and Margaret of Antioch, and made prophecies according to what they had to say. The Duke of Bedford, who commanded the English forces at the siege of Orléans, attributed English losses to the unlawful supernatural forces deployed by Joan of Arc, and called her a "disciple of the Fiend" who used false enchantment and sorcery.

Shakespeare described the two views of Joan in *Henry VI*, part 1 – as a French patron saint:

> *No longer on St Denis will we cry,*
> *But Joan la Pucelle shall be*
> *France's saint.*

And as a heretic:

> *Coward of France! how much he*
> *[the Dauphin] wrongs his fame...*
> *To join with witches and the help of hell.*

Joan was brought before the Inquisition by the English for heresy and for her idolatry and the "cult and veneration" of her saints, which was said to be part of a pact with the Devil. The tribunal was composed mainly of ecclesiastics and lawyers, sometimes numbering more than 70 men. She was taken to the cemetery of St Ouen in Rouen and placed on a scaffold, surrounded by cardinals, bishops and various earls, dukes and officials, while passages from John's Gospel, including

A nineteenth-century portrayal of Joan of Arc being led to her death in Rouen in 1431.

the saying that "the withered branch must be thrown in the fire else the tree cannot flourish", were shouted. There is much controversy surrounding what happened, but Joan signed a document of recantation and was condemned to lifelong imprisonment, on bread and water and in solitary confinement, because the Inquisition could not condemn to death a heretic, only a relapsed heretic. When Joan withdrew her declaration, saying that she was still hearing voices, the way was open for her inquisitors to put an end to what they saw as her communication with evil spirits. When she went to the stake she wore over her shaven head a tall mitre that was inscribed with her crimes and the names of her malign spirits – Belial, Satan and Behemoth.

Gilles de Rais

Some years after Joan of Arc's exploits and execution, one of her comrades in arms, Gilles de Rais, was accused by the state of, among other things, being "possessed by the Evil One", and of killing 140 children under this satanic influence. Gilles admitted to the childrens' murders but insisted that he acted in accordance with his own imagination and was not inspired by the Devil, an important distinction in those times.

Gilles confessed to killing the children and begged the mercy of the court and the forgiveness of their parents. In 1440 he was found guilty of both crimes, that of murder and also of diabolical inspiration, and was sentenced to be hanged and then burnt. His execution took place nine years after Joan's death.

The notorious Gilles de Rais, whose story remains somewhat of a mystery. He was one of the most famous people to be accused of working under Satanic influences.

WITCH HUNTS IN GERMANY

The first major witch hunt in Germany was the Ravensburger persecution of 1484 which inspired Heinrich Kramer and Jacob Sprenger to compose the *Malleus Maleficarum*, the infamous witch hunters' manual.

The main areas of witch hunting were in the south and west of the country, and Würzburg, Bamberg, Eichstött, Württemberg and Ellwangen were all the sites of famous witch hunts. A large witchcraft persecution occurred in 1563, in the small Lutheran territory of Wiesensteig: it claimed the lives of 63 women. Local German courts exercised a great deal of autonomy in the trials of witches and in Ellwangen, a small Catholic region in south-west Germany, almost 400 individuals were condemned to death between 1611 and 1618 without any appeal to a higher court. However, although local German courts did not

The notorious German witchfinder Konrad von Marburg sends another victum to the torture chamber and the stake.

The "Malefitz Haus" constructed at Bamberg specifically for the interrogation and torture of suspected witches.

usually have dealings with imperial tribunals or with supervision by imperial judicial authorities, they were required to consult with the universities for help with the complexities of criminal procedure in witchcraft cases. Before sentencing was carried out, reports were sent to the law faculty of the nearest university so that the advice of academics could be sought. As the universities were the centres for the development

and spread of demonological theory, this process usually resulted in more prosecutions.

THE CASE OF ANNA EBELER

In Augsburg in January 1669, a lying-in maid called Anna Ebeler was accused of murdering her employer by giving her a bowl of soup. Instead of restoring her strength after childbirth the soup had allegedly increased her fever, and she had become delirious and died. As news of the death spread, other women accused Ebeler of poisoning their young children. One child had lost its baby flesh and had become thin and dried out. A second had been unable to suckle from its mother (although it could suck from other women) and had died in agony. Another had died after becoming covered in pustules and blisters, and its seven-year-old brother had suffered from aches and pains and had visions caused by sorcery. His mother had had headaches and all the household had suffered from strange growths on their bodies. One woman had found her baby covered with blisters

and red patches and the mother's menstruation had stopped. Anna Ebeler confessed at the end of the second of her six interrogations, when torture was threatened. She was executed and her body was burnt on 23 March 1669.

Augsburg did not have a witch craze and did not execute a witch before 1625. According to the historian Lyndal Roper, cases came singly, with one or two every few years after 1650. Anna Ebeler was one of 18 witches executed in Augsburg, and Roper says that a dominant theme of the witch trials in this part of Germany was their connection with motherhood: relations between mothers formed the basis of most of the witchcraft accusations in the town. Accusations were typically brought by mothers soon after giving birth against lying-in maids, not midwives. The food the witch gave the mother was said to be sprinkled with white or black diabolic powders, or she administered poisoned soups, and these influenced the mother's milk. The witch perverted the mother's capacity to nourish.

One grandmother was interrogated three times and tortured because her young grandson suspected witchcraft when he felt ill after drinking an aniseed water tonic she had given him. In another case a woman was accused of reversing the flow of maternal fluids by sucking the infant dry and feeding on it. Its mother described how "its little breasts had been sucked out so that milk had been pressed out from the child's little teats … and from this time on the child had lost weight so that it looked as if hardly a pound of flesh remained on it".

Roper is interested in viewing witchcraft accusations as reflecting psychic tensions of maternal depression, anger or envy, or invoking deeply ambivalent emotions from the mother's early life, which might be projected on to the lying-in maid during the six-week period of convalescence after childbirth. However, it was dangerous to antagonize a lying-in maid, and one woman is said to have repeated the following threatening rhyme on her departure:

My dear little treasure, now
you are well recovered
Look master and mistress
Now I depart from the child
Whatever may happen to him now
I will not be held to blame.

A midwife assisting a woman in labour. In the background, astrologers are predicting the future of the child.

The frontispiece for a tract against witchcraft in 1591 shows an affair with the Devil, flying witches and a child being used to make a potion.

Despite 24 hours of torture, Herr Lirtzen, Burgomaster of Rheinbach in 1631, refused to confess to witchcraft but was burnt anyway.

WITCH HUNTS IN BRITAIN AND IRELAND

Compared with other parts of Europe, witch hunting in Britain was restrained and mild, although in Scotland it was more intense and illegal torture was used. In England there was a belated and incomplete reception of the stereotype of the witch, and courts were more lenient, using torture only sparingly. At first witchcraft was seen to be a hostile act rather than heresy, and no reference was made to a diabolical contract with the Devil. A distinction between maleficent witchcraft and less harmful forms, such as divination, was made, and penalties for the latter were much lighter. Few British hunts could be compared in size or intensity with those that occurred in Germany. The total number of British trials probably did not exceed 5,000, and the number of executions has been estimated as less than 2,500.

The main difference between Britain and Ireland and continental Europe was that the notion of diabolic Sabbath meetings of witches and the Devil was largely absent in England and Ireland, although towards the end of the sixteenth century continental demonology and Devil-related evidence did start to make an appearance in British courts. Many English cases centred on the witch's use of familiars, as in the well-known trial of the Chelmsford witches.

THE CHELMSFORD WITCHES

The Witchcraft Bill was passed under Queen Elizabeth I in 1563, and at Chelmsford three women were charged with acts of witchcraft in 1566. Two of these were Elizabeth Francis and Agnes Waterhouse. Elizabeth Francis was accused of bewitching a child and making it ill. She admitted to learning witchcraft from her grandmother, who was named Mother Eve, at the age of 12, and to having a "familiar", a white spotted cat called Sathan, which bewitched people for her. The cat had helped her to become rich by obtaining goods and sheep; it had also helped her obtain a lover, but when he refused to marry her

The English witch Anne Turner who was executed at Tyburn, London, in 1615. From a contemporary print.

the cat had killed him by witchcraft. On the advice of the cat she had become pregnant by a man called Christopher Francis, whom she had later married. She was sentenced to a year in prison for these offences, but she appeared before the same court on two further occasions. When questioned, she confessed to allowing Sathan to kill three of Father Kersey's hogs, to drown Widow Goodday's cow and to kill three geese owned by a neighbour.

Agnes Waterhouse was the first woman to be hanged for witchcraft in Chelmsford, England, in 1566.

Christian Bowman being burned at the stake in the Old Bailey in the eighteenth century.

... [she] willed him to kill a hog of her own, which he did; and she gave him for his labour a chicken, which he first required of her, and a drop of her blood, and this she gave him at all times when he did anything for her, by pricking her hand or face and putting the blood to his mouth, which he sucked, and forthwith would lie down in his pot again, wherein she kept him ...

She also admitted attempting to bewitch another neighbour and to kill her husband.

It was also said that Agnes Waterhouse turned her familiar into a toad, which she kept in a pot. Agnes was charged, alongside Elizabeth Francis, with acts of witchcraft and was hanged in 1566. Elizabeth was hanged soon afterwards.

Agnes's daughter Joan, aged 18, also confessed to witchcraft. When her mother was out, she had gone to a neighbour's child and asked for bread and cheese. When denied the food, she called on the familiar Sathan, who had emerged from her mother's shoe under the bed in the likeness of a great dog. It was alleged that Joan made the dog haunt the child, but officials found her not guilty of bewitching the child.

SCOTLAND

In Scotland the officially appointed witch pricker was a key figure in gathering evidence against a witch. His role was to examine the suspect for any unusual bodily marks and then test them by pricking to find out whether she could feel it. The idea behind this practice was that the Devil would consummate a pact by nipping the witch, and that this left a permanent mark, which did not bleed and did not feel pain. John Kincaid, the most famous pricker, tested Jonet Paiston and reported that:

She did nather find the preins [pin] when it was put into any of the said marks nor did they blood when they were taken out again: and when shoe was asked quhair shoe thocht the preins were put in, schoe pointed at a pairt of hir body distant from the place quhair the priens were put in, they being lang priens of thrie inches or theirabouts in length.

IRELAND

European ideas did not penetrate Ireland either, and witchcraft in Ireland was primarily a crime of maleficium rather than Devil-worship. Even so, there were few witch trials, and those that were held were carried out by English or Scottish Protestant settlers. The best-known case happened in 1661 and concerns Florence Newton, "the witch of Youghal", who, when refused a piece of beef from the household of John Pyne, went away cursing. A short while afterwards she kissed one of Pyne's female servants, and when the servant started having fits and vomiting, she accused Newton of witchcraft. Newton was arrested and while in prison supposedly kissed a man through a gate and caused his death. What happened to Florence Newton after her arrest is not known,

Judith Philips, a cunning woman, fortune-teller and swindler, who was sentenced to be whipped through the City of London on 14 February 1594.

but the witchcraft of which she was accused bore very little relation to European ideas of collective diabolical gatherings of witches.

The execution of Catherine Cawches and her two daughters at St Peter's Port, Guernsey, in 1700.

WITCH HUNTS IN SCANDINAVIA

Witch hunting in Scandinavia was more intense than in Britain; in the same period of activity, the total number of prosecutions was approximately 5,000, resulting in between 1,700 and 2,000 executions. Although the figures are similar to those of Britain, the population of Scandinavian countries was only about 40 per cent of Britain's.

Scandinavian witch hunting was not based on a complete concept of witchcraft, and even when the demonological aspects of collective Devil-worship do appear, they lack the distinctive features of those in German, French and Swiss cases. In addition, there was a reluctance in Scandinavia to use torture on the accused witches to obtain confessions or the names of their accomplices.

Nevertheless, large witch hunts did take place in certain areas. Denmark was the first Scandinavian country to engage in witch hunting, and here the

A Norwegian "huldre" who appears to be an innocent milkmaid but is in reality a witch who can lead the unwary into all kinds of trouble.

Lutheran clergy took the initiative in spreading the idea of witchcraft. In the 1540s the Lutheran bishop of Sealand urged the prosecution of witches, claiming that those with Catholic tendencies were to blame.

NORWAY

The most famous case of Norwegian witchcraft also concerned Lutherans and was focused on Anna Pedersdotter Absalon, the wife of Lutheran minister Absalon Pedersen Beyer, a humanist scholar. A group opposing the Lutheran destruction of holy images attacked the minister's wife, since she made an easier target than the clergy themselves. This followed a pattern common in Germany, where political factions used charges of witchcraft against their opponents' wives to advance their own political careers.

Anna was cleared in 1575 but the case was reopened in 1590 when additional

A sixteenth-century Scandinavian depiction of witches calling up monsters while ordinary people lie asleep.

charges were made. In the second trial she was accused of putting a man into a coma because he had refused to pay for a weaving frame, inflicting sickness on a man who had refused her wine, beer and vinegar, and of causing the death of a four-year-old boy by giving him a bewitched biscuit.

In addition to these accusations came others that included aspects of diabolism: Anna's servant testified that she had turned her into a horse and had ridden her to a Sabbath that was taking place on a mountain called Lyderhorn, where a number of witches plotted to summon up a storm that would wreck all ships arriving in Bergen. On subsequent occasions, they had schemed to burn the town and cause flooding. This Sabbath had been dispersed by a man in white who forbade it in God's name. This time Anna was not so lucky and she was burnt as a witch. Hans Wiers-Jenssen wrote a play about the case (*Anne Pedersdotter*), and a film, called *Day of Wrath*, was made in Denmark in 1943.

SWEDEN

Witch hunting in Sweden was similar to that in Norway. There was an increase in the intensity of persecutions in the three towns of Stockholm, Jønkøping and Vadstena during the period 1490–1614, and there was also a large panic in the late seventeenth century. During the 1600s, isolated but specific references were made to the witches' Sabbaths and they were connected with the Blåkulla or "Blue Hill". A writer of the time claimed that the Blåkulla was used by Nordic witches for their meetings to practise the Devil's arts. Between 1520 and 1699 more than 1,000 people were accused of sorcery and witchcraft: the exact number is unknown because some of the court records were destroyed by fire. In the 1670s the number of cases reached a peak, and during the year 1675/76, at least 157 witches were accused, 41 of whom were sentenced to death.

Swedish witches gather for a Sabbath on the Blokula in a seventeenth-century portrayal.

FINLAND

In Finland, unlike other parts of Europe, witchcraft was not primarily associated with women. Out of 641 people known to have been accused, only around half were female. As late as the sixteenth century, 60 per cent of those accused and 75 per cent of those found guilty were men. However, as soon as the number of trials increased, the percentage of women also went up, surpassing that of men in the 1650s. As soon as the witch hunt had peaked the number of women began to decrease again and the number of men accused increased. The reason for this is that in Finland a sorcerer tended to be a man and, in Finnish folk traditions and religion, supernatural powers were associated with men rather than women.

It is thought that the European stereotype of the diabolical witch as female broke down the Finnish male stereotype. In Iceland too, the typical witch was male, and of the 120 witch trials that took place only ten involved women; out of 22 burnt, only one of them was a woman.

Finnish witches were usually men rather than women, and here some male witches sell favourable winds to sailors. From a woodcut of 1555.

WITCH HUNTS IN EASTERN EUROPE

Witch hunting in Eastern Europe was similar to that in other parts of Europe in the manner in which it relieved social, psychological and religious tensions but, like Scandanavia, it was also different because its foundations were not based so securely on demonological theory. As elsewhere, in order to extend and consolidate its control on ordinary people, the Christian Church in Eastern Europe launched an attack on pagan folk beliefs and versions of Christianity that did not meet with its approval.

HUNGARY

Hungarian witch persecution records show that legal measures against maleficium started with the legislation of the Hungarian kings István (St Stephen) (1000–38), Ladislas I (1077–95) and Kálman (1095–1116). Over the following four centuries, witchcraft charges were dealt with by hot-iron ordeals, at feudal courts and by town juries. A regular prosecution of witches started only in the sixteenth century, intensifying by the end of that century and becoming a mass witch hunt in the final part of the seventeenth century. It peaked in the first half of the eighteenth century, but was finally stopped by the intervention of Empress Maria Theresa and prohibited in 1768.

The historian Gábor Klaniczay points out that the foundation of demonological theory, which was seen to be so important to the explosion of witch hunting in sixteenth- and seventeenth-century Europe, was "almost completely lacking in Hungary". Witchcraft accusations relieved social, psychological and religious tensions through the process of magical revenge, which was practised both among nobles and in the village. The possibility of accusing and denouncing someone as a witch gave power to all members of the community. Klaniczay notes that in 1728 a poor wise woman accused an ex-judge of being the head of a coven; he was arrested, tortured and condemned to death by burning.

The Empress Maria Theresa (1717–80) – a merciful monarch who intervened and stopped witch persecutions in Hungary.

Children of 9 to 11 years old, and many kitchen maids from 14 to 16 years old, also accused people of being witches.

TRANSYLVANIA

Transylvania was already notorious in Europe as a dark and sinister country, ruled by psychopathically cruel princes such as Vlad the Impaler, also known as the notorious Dracula. These kings had fierce military reputations but were also associated with the occult, and the kind of inspired wickedness so out of the ordinary that it is associated with extra-human forces. In later years, Transylvanian princes of the sixteenth and seventeenth centuries accused the families of their defeated political enemies of witchcraft. Sigismund Báthory blamed the mother of Boldizsár Báthory, whom he had murdered, for his impotence. After Gábor Bethlen had taken power from Gábor Báthory, who was murdered in 1612, he accused Anna Báthory, the sister of the dead man, of witchcraft with two other noble women of her entourage. Between 1679 and 1686 Prince Mihály Apafy accused about 20 people of witchcraft in the large trial of the wife of his exiled rival Pál Béldi. She was accused of causing the prince's wife to suffer serious illnesses as revenge for their defeat.

ESTONIA

According to the historian Maia Madar, the earliest records of how many witches and heretics were burnt in Estonia date from the fourteenth century, but it is difficult to tell how many witch trials were held because of the lack of documentation and the loss of court records. At the provincial Synod of Riga, the clergy of Livonia threatened all soothsayers, sorcerers, and practitioners of the "Jewish superstition" with excommunication in 1428.

In 1519 witchcraft was defined as a capital crime, and people were ordered to watch out for sorcerers, witches or heretics and "those who were not true Christians but worshipped at sacred groves, stones and trees". Those who used the services of soothsayers and sorcerers regarding illnesses or misfortune, or followed their advice about cattle, or worshipped thunderstorms, were to be burned as heretics. The majority of those sentenced to death were burnt at the stake, but execution by sword was considered a lighter punishment where a person confessed voluntarily or there was no evidence of a pact with the Devil. In one case, a court ordered that a person named Tattra Santi Michel should have his head cut off before being burned:

... on the basis of his testimony, [that] it cannot be positively established that he entered into an agreement with the Devil. However, in his youth, his father gave him

Like witches, Dracula came to hold a particular fascination for many people in later centuries.

to an evil spirit, and he has twice met the Devil in the guise of a dog. He has learned formulas to bewitch and to heal ... The hangman is ordered to cut off his head and then burn him to ashes.

The bewitching of a person's lord carried a death penalty, and a particularly barbaric execution was carried out in 1642 when Willakasz Jürgen was convicted for having murdered the Count of Audru with the Devil's help.

Below: Vlad the Impaler, Prince of Wallachia 1431-76. Associated with evil and the occult, he was the inspiration for Bram Stoker's novel about Dracula.

WITCH HUNTS IN NEW ENGLAND

The first New England colonists crossed the Atlantic in 1620 and founded the settlement of Plymouth. Their exodus from England was prompted by Puritan religious zeal and the hope of founding a new society based on their spiritual ideals; their flight was an escape from what they saw as the corrupt religious culture of their country of origin.

Life in New England was similar to that in Europe: Protestant religion co-existed with magical beliefs and practices. However, one important difference was the absence of a general organizing structure like the Church of England; instead, small autonomous self-governing bodies of clergy and congregations worked together co-operatively, if not always harmoniously. Magic was condemned by Puritan ministers as blasphemous and diabolical but the courts were ill-equipped to deal with cases of witchcraft. This was because a witch was defined, according to the Bible, as "any man or woman [who] hath or consulteth with a familiar spirit", and most cases brought to court concerned maleficium – cursing or causing harm – rather than communication with familiars. Evidence rarely resulted in a conviction, and out of 61 prosecutions in the seventeenth century only 15 resulted in conviction and execution.

THE SALEM WITCH TRIALS

The one exception was the Salem witch hunt, which erupted in 1692, when formal charges of witchcraft were brought against 156 people from 24 towns and villages in the County of Essex, Massachusetts. A special court was set up to deal with the crisis, and the final toll was 19 deaths by hanging and one fatality that occurred under interrogation. Salem acquired the nickname of "Witch City".

The witch panic started when several girls in Salem Village experienced "fits" and "distempers". Samuel Parris, the minister at Salem Village and the father and uncle of two of the girls, instructed

The pilgrims land at Plymouth in the new land of America on 11 December 1620. Their arrival is watched by hidden Native American Indians.

A suspected witch is arrested in Salem by zealous pilgrims in traditional dress.

them to name their tormentors. The girls accused three women: Tituba, a Caribbean slave in the Parris household; a homeless and destitute woman named Sarah Good; and Sarah Osborne, a resident of a nearby village. Some time later, the girls denounced others. John Hale, an observer of the time, wrote the following account:

These Children were bitten and pinched by invisible agents: their arms, necks and backs turned this way and that way, and returned back again, so as it was impossible for them to do of themselves, and beyond the power of any Epileptick Fits, or natural Disease to effect. Sometimes they were taken dumb, their mouths stopped, their throats choked, their limbs wracked and tormented so as might move a heart of stone to sympathise with them.

Accused witches were brought to a specially appointed court, which was allowed to administer torture to obtain confessions. Hundreds of people became accusers in the 1690s but the girls were the focus of public interest, and they were brought to the courtroom to see if they would be attacked by the accused. The court assumed the guilt of the accused until it was convinced otherwise, and leading questions and bullying were common, as demonstrated by John Hathorne's examination of Sarah Good:

Hathorne: *Sarah Good, what evil spirit have you familiarity with?*
Good: *None.*
Hathorne: *Have you made no contract with the Devil?*
Good: *No.*
Hathorne: *Why doe you hurt these children?*
Good: *I doe not hurt them. I scorn it.*
Hathorne: *Who doe you imploy then to doe it?*
Good: *I imploy nobody.*
Hathorne: *What creature do you imploy then?*
Good: *No creature but I am falsely accused.*

Cotton Mather, Puritan minister involved in the Salem witch trials and founder of Yale College.

Cotton Mather argued in *The Wonders of the Invisible World*, published in 1693, that the threat that faced the New Englanders was an assault by a witch conspiracy, just one part of a diabolical offensive against New England: "... such

A view of Salem, the town in which a frenzy of witch hunting erupted in 1692.

is the descent of the Devil at this day upon our selves, that I may truly tell you, the Walls of the whole World are broken down!". Many confessions were made, which suggests that there was religious anxiety among the New Englanders. Several claimed that the fear of damnation played a role in their recruitment to the Devil's service; one woman confessed to signing a covenant with the Devil after he promised to pardon her sins; another thought that she would be saved if she became a witch. However, there was hardly any evidence and the whole episode may have been a reaction to the threat of Quaker evangelism, which had started in 1656 with the arrival of missionaries.

Accused witches were brought to court to face their accusers. Here a girl is bewitched, thus proving the accused guilty.

THE ENDING OF WITCH HUNTS

Eventually the witch-hunts came to an end and witchcraft ceased to be a crime. People still believed in witches and magic but they were no longer prosecuted and put to death for supposedly practising it. The emergence of modern rationalism and the rise of science, dispelling so called superstition, has been held to be responsible for a different and "rational" way of viewing the world. However, ideas about magic did not disappear, they just went underground and would emerge in secret societies such as the Rosicrucians and Freemasons.

Jane Wenham, who, in 1712, was the last person in England to be convicted of witchcraft.

During the seventeenth and eighteenth centuries there was an increasing reluctance to prosecute witches; many who were tried were acquitted and many convictions were reversed on appeal. Prosecutions and executions for the crime of witchcraft declined and eventually came to an end with the repeal of the witchcraft laws. In 1782 the last officially sanctioned execution was carried out, after which witchcraft ceased to be a crime. This did not stop people naming family members and neighbours as witches, but they could no longer be prosecuted and the accusers had to be careful to avoid prosecution themselves.

The reduction and eventual end of witch hunting occurred at different times in the various regions of Europe. In some areas, such as the Dutch Republic, it declined well before the sixteenth century, while in Poland, for example, it did not finish until the middle of the eighteenth century. In Scotland an initial reduction in the number of prosecutions was followed by more than 50 years of trials. By contrast, in colonial Massachusetts the witch hunts came to a complete end a few years after the courts discouraged prosecutions. Legislation declaring that witchcraft was no longer a crime was passed at different stages. In Hungary and Prussia the decriminalization of witchcraft was responsible for the ending of witch hunting, but in Britain and Denmark legislation was not passed until the witch trials had stopped.

Why did the witch hunts end? It has often been suggested that the reason was human progress: the emergence of modern rationalism during the period known as the Enlightenment, the rise of science and the accompanying dispelling of ignorance and superstition.

Even though witchcraft was no longer a crime, magic was still a preoccupation in society, and was reflected in its literature. Here Faustus makes his pact with the Devil.

However, more recent studies of the witch hunts have pointed to the fact that long after the end of the witch-trials people continued to think in terms of witchcraft, since it formed a useful means of dealing with problems and explaining any misfortune. Witchcraft was also a means of power by which it was possible to damage the position of another person by accusations and counter-threats of bewitchment.

In 1895 in the Irish village of Ballyvadlea, near Clonmel, the 26-year-old Bridget Cleary was beaten and burned to death by her husband, in the presence of her family and friends, for being a fairy changeling. They assumed that the real Bridget had been abducted by fairies. Fairies and witches were associated with misfortune, and in the case of Bridget Cleary, were thought to be responsible for her illness. When Bridget was taken ill a doctor was called in and he diagnosed bronchial catarrh and nervous excitement. A herb doctor was also consulted on the advice of a neighbour, and he claimed that Bridget was a changeling, prescribing a milky drink containing herbs. The drink was forced on to a protesting Bridget while she was repeatedly asked her identity: was she Bridget Boland, wife of Micheal Cleary? She affirmed that she was. On the advice of the neighbour who had recommended the herbalist, she was held over the turf fire and again asked her identity, the idea being that the changeling would leave the house via the chimney. The following evening the procedure was repeated but it had fatal consequences: this time she was covered in lamp oil and Bridget died of her burns. She was buried in a nearby swamp. A court case resulted in 20 years of hard labour for Bridget's husband, six months for her father and two male cousins, and the acquittal of the herbalist and a female cousin.

A belief in a magical world-view did not simply disappear overnight or fade away completely. Rather, ideas, beliefs and philosophies went underground to re-emerge at certain points in time, as they continue to do today in the occult subculture, and also in the various movements that seek to revive a pagan past, such as modern witchcraft. Modern witches do not take on the diabolic stereotype as constructed by the demonologists of the Christian Church, but rather seek to create a pre-Christian pagan alternative, largely modelled on the beliefs and practices of the village wise woman and cunning folk.

Magic and witchcraft was still seen as having the capacity to entice or ensnare, as in this nineteenth-century print.

The witches' Sabbath appears to have an enduring power to fascinate, as in this depiction by Goya painted in 1821–23.

EXPLANATIONS OF THE WITCH HUNTS

The tendency to blame others for misfortune is widespread: the anthropologist Bronislaw Malinowski called it a human universal. Social, political, economic and religious upheaval breed an atmosphere of confusion and uncertainty, a climate of fear in which particular groups or individuals – be they, for example, heretics, witches or Jews – are singled out and labelled the enemy.

THE CHURCH VERSUS WOMEN?

Why were the majority (but not all, as the example of Finland shows) of those accused during the European witch hunts women? Some scholars have suggested that this was because of a patriarchal Christian ideology, which was imposed on ordinary people; that it was a construction that served male supremacy. However, the interesting German case of Anna Ebeler and other cases of conflict between mothers and their lying-in nurses show how witchcraft accusations could involve very deep antagonisms between women.

A simple patriarchal explanation – that men were oppressing and persecuting women – does not address the complexity of the phenomenon of witch hunting. It seems probable that the Christianized ideas of the educated elites of the town were imposed on the country folk of the peripheral areas, and that these went hand in hand with certain patriarchal ideas and values.

THE GODDESS UNDER ATTACK?

Other scholars have gone further and suggested that witch persecutions were part of an organized patriarchal repression of both women and earth-venerating pagan religions, which worshipped a goddess. This hypothesis is based mainly on the evidence of prehistoric cave paintings, pottery remains, carvings and figurines, which suggest the association between women and fertility. However, they do not prove the existence of a belief system founded on the worship of a goddess, and any such interpretation is speculative.

A drawing from the nineteenth century showing a witches' celebration on the first day of May.

WITCH HUNTS IN MODERN TIMES

The persecution of groups of people is not just a phenomenon of the past, and there have been parallel witch hunts throughout history that we can contrast and compare with those of the fiftheenth and sixteenth centuries in Europe. The case of McCarthyism in the United States, in the period 1950–4, demonstrates many of the characteristics similar to those of the early modern witch persecutions.

During the 1950s, Communism was seen to be a threat to America and her allies and there was a widespread fear of government infiltration by the "Reds".

Senator Joe McCarthy, whose motive appears to have been political ambition rather than patriotism, made a number of attacks against what he claimed were "enemies of the people" and accused 205 people working in the State Department of being members of the Communist Party. A Senate Committee was set up to deal with these accusations and McCarthy sought to find proof to back up his claims. To no avail. Out of approximately 81 cases investigated, the Committee found not one of the accused to be a Communist. Undeterred, McCarthy continued his search for Communists in government, using both legal and illegal means, and another Committee was set up to investigate his claims. This Committee also failed to find evidence, yet McCarthyism continued, largely due to the newspapers, which played up his accusations in big headlines, and to a general reluctance to speak out against him for fear of being branded a Communist. Finally, in 1954, a number of Senators took a stand against him and the tide of McCarthyism was turned, but not before a number of people's careers had been damaged by their being unfairly labelled as Communists. McCarthy became dejected and died three years later.

SATANIC RITUALS

Witch hunts to find those who are believed to be enemies of the state can be vicious, but the arguments and the passions involved are reasonably clear cut and well defined. Far more damaging and frightening are the campaigns against those who are accused of satanic rituals. In recent times there have been methodically conducted witch hunts over the suspicion of satanic ritual abuse in America and Britain.

Accusations and prosecutions in both countries led to the convictions of alleged abusers. The evidence was the testimonies of young children who were subjected to suggestive questioning by social workers, therapists and prosecutors. There were accusations of incest and sexual abuse, conducted during organized rituals to worship Satan, made

The interior of the room where Senator McCarthy's committee sat in judgement against members of society who were deemed to be guilty of the crime of communism.

against the parents of children in Orkney, Rochdale, London and Nottingham in Great Britain, as well as in Edenton, North Carolina, and elsewhere in the United States. Around the same time, parallel accusations were levelled against parents by grown children who claimed that they had been sexually abused in their childhoods but had repressed their memories. These memories may have only been "recovered" and become conscious after a visit to a therapist who had prompted the suggestion, or through the reading of a book on the subject.

HISTORICAL LINKS

These modern day manifestations of witch hunts show how the same social pressures that were evident centuries ago still persist. Belief systems or political ideologies are declared by the establishment to be threats to society. These perceived threats are dealt with in many different ways, but it is possible to make some generalizations. It is also possible to see how the same mistakes are made throughout history, as minorities are persecuted by the state.

The anti communist committee caused huge unrest in the United States, and was rigorously campaigned and demonstrated against by a wide section of society.

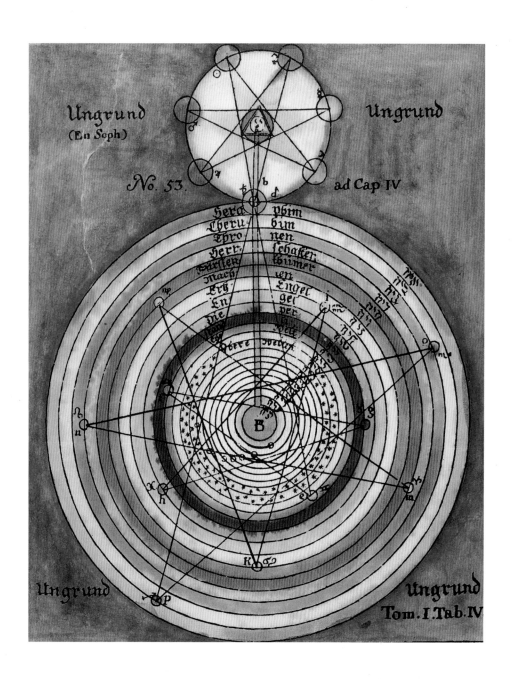

Ungrund
(En Soph)

Ungrund

No. 53.   ad Cap IV

Ungrund

Ungrund

Tom. I. Tab. IV

MODERN MAGIC

Magic today has had a bad press – it is either associated with the work of the Devil, or it is reduced to conjuring tricks and sleight of hand. Magic is seen to be separate from religion, but the way that we view magic in the West has been shaped by Christianity, which has branded it evil. Magic is neither good nor evil in itself and it can be used in a variety of ways depending on who is practising it. During the seventeenth century magic was increasingly seen to be irrational when compared to science. At this time, those who practised the occult arts went underground, and many secret societies – such as the Rosicrucians and Freemasons – were formed. Magical practices today reflect this history.

HOW MAGIC SURVIVED

Since the earliest times, human beings have sought to communicate with, and control, the world around them. Ideas about what we now call magic probably developed naturally from people living together in social groups – through intimate relationships, giving birth to children, mourning the death of a clan or tribe member – and also from the shaman's spiritual link with the animals that were hunted. The idea that there is a subtle, invisible essence that comes from all beings – rocks, stones, plants, fungi and animals as well as human beings – is a basic principle of magical belief. People in different cultures from all around the world have attempted to tap into and control this essence or force.

In many spiritual traditions the human body is seen to be made up of a spirit body (which may be called a soul, an etheric body or an aura) as well as a physical body. The spirit body is often viewed as a life-force. It is thought to be subject to damage, leakage or disease, or even psychic vampirism. It is said that a person's spiritual development can be determined by the condition of their spirit body. A halo – the light that appears around a saint's head – marks advancement. The spiritual aura of the Buddha was said to extend for 320 km (200 miles).

Magicians seek to work directly with the spirit body and use it to link up with the hidden energies of all manner of beings in the cosmos: from the earth energies of trees, through techniques of visualization to invoke gods and goddesses, to wider planetary influences, of the sun and the moon, for example. Each of the magical tradition works in a different way.

The ways that magicians work today have been influenced by ideas from the past. Modern magical ideas were born in the Renaissance. "Renaissance" means rebirth, and the magicians of the time focused on uniting the individual soul with God in terms of what is now called Neoplatonism. The work most influential to Renaissance magicians was the *Corpus*

Halos are not confined to Christianity – the spiritual aura of the Buddha surrounded his body as well as his head.

Hermeticum, a composite of individual writings by various unknown authors, which was probably of Greek origin and not, as was believed in the Renaissance, the work of an Egyptian priest called Hermes Trismegistus. The works are philosophical and concern magical and astrological ways of making talismans to draw down the powers of the stars, and record the means by which individual souls can find divine knowledge without the aid of a personal god or saviour. Magicians need to try and understand the hidden forces in nature: of external phenomena and within themselves.

Alchemy was highly popular during the fourteenth to the seventeenth centuries, as shown in Shakespeare's Sonnet 33:

> *Full many a glorious*
> *morning have I seen*
> *Flatter the mountain tips*
> *with sovereign eye,*
> *Kissing with golden face*
> *the meadows green,*
> *Gilding pale streams with*
> *heavenly alchemy.*

The halo that surrounds the heads of the Christian saints is a sign of their special holiness.

The sonnet suggests a mystical, alchemical link between the natural elements of mountain, meadows and streams.

Alchemy became the greatest passion of the age, combining the search for the philosopher's stone, which was believed would hold the power to transmute base metals into gold, with an internal (esoteric) spiritual quest. Alchemy was viewed as an art that would lead to transmutation. It was considered an embryonic science – a protochemistry; early alchemists used laboratories for their experiments and study, and made a number of discoveries that contributed to the development of chemistry.

Alchemists conducted experiments with metals and other substances and interpreted their results using astrology, cabbalism and herbalism, frequently employing the language of mystical Christian symbolism.

This was also a time when great store was set by divination. One famous diviner was Nostradamus (1503–66). Born Michel de Notredame, he came from a Jewish family in St Rémy-en-Provence and graduated as a doctor of medicine in Montpellier. He worked with plague victims in Marseilles and Avignon, but he refused to bleed his patients, as was the usual procedure. On a couple of occasions he had to flee the area because the Inquisition thought he was a wizard.

Nostradamus' prophecies were composed with the aid of magical, astrological and cabbalistic books and were published in two parts, in 1555 and 1568. Both Napoleon Bonapart and Adolf Hitler, in their respective centuries, believed that their careers had been foreseen in Nostradamus' predictions, and it is also said that he predicted the French Revolution of 1789.

During the seventeenth century, the rise of scientific rationalism and Protestantism drove magic underground. Scientific rationalism was a mechanistic philosophy that viewed the world as a machine. As Protestantism grew, it attempted to take out of religious practice what it viewed as magical elements – for example the Catholic dependence on the powers of saints'

A contemporary portrait of Nostradamus, whose prophecies are still read avidly today.

A painting from the late fifteenth century of an alchemy master preparing ingredients.

relics. During this period, these two developments in thought meant that people who practised magic did so in secret, and tended to be attracted to underground societies such as the Rosicrucians or the Freemasons.

Left: Conjurors were an accepted part of everyday life between the fourteenth and seventeenth centuries.

Neoplatonism

The philosophy of Neoplatonism originated with Plotinus (c.AD205–270). It was a synthesis of earlier philosophical thought and religious beliefs, combining alchemy and magic to provide not only an image of the universe and the human place within it, but also a method of spiritual salvation. The 'One' as a deity is the source of all goodness and reality. The One is the source from which everything flows, and the gradual dispersion of the original unity results in multiplicity and matter (which is sometimes equated with evil). Human imperfection, which is due to a flaw or the Fall,

stems from the soul's remoteness from the One. The soul is longing to return to completeness, but as the One is beyond description and cannot be reached through rational thinking, it has to be approached through ecstatic contemplative absorption. The soul has many levels: the highest is intellectual thought, and the lowest is the animating principle of the material universe. All humans have all aspects of soul within them and have to choose whether to wake the higher elements or remain immersed in the concerns of the material body.

THE MYTH OF ATLANTIS

The kings of Atlantis were said to be descended from the sons of Poseidon, the sea god.

hose who continued to work with magic, despite the movement against it, attempted to create meaning by looking for significant connections between things, and this frequently involved the use of myths. A myth is a sacred story that is shared by a group of people who find their most important meanings in it. In Western cultures mythology is often equated with fairy stories, the "unreal" or even falsehood, and contrasted with history, which is associated with the truth. However, myth has played an important part in magic by explaining how the world came to be formed, and by marking out significant relationships with ancestors and other beings. The myth of Atlantis is especially important to Western magicians. It is said to be a sunken continent that occupied most of the area of the Atlantic Ocean, and is the place from which the peoples of Europe arose.

THE ORIGINS

The myth of Atlantis has a very important position in Western magic. The name "Atlantis" conjures up visions of a wonderful land of beauty and plenty, a utopian society where peace and justice reigned; a golden country lying in the midst of a wide blue sea. The legend concerns the story of an ancient island civilization, in conflict with Athens and Egypt, which vanished in a day and a night due to spiritual disaster. It was Plato (c.428–347BC) who first wrote about the myth in *Timaeus*, telling how a mighty power had once come out of the Atlantic Ocean. The size and position of lost Atlantis was revealed to the Athenian statesman and poet Solon by an Egyptian priest in about 590BC. The priest described Atlantis as a kingdom that had been much larger than Libya and Asia Minor put together, which had, some 9,000 years before, been situated beyond the Pillars of Hercules at the western end of the Mediterranean Sea. Its armies had once conquered most of the countries of the Mediterranean:

The idea of the lost land of Atlantis came from Classical Greece, where students of philosophy would discuss utopian societies and ideal states, which were governed by democratic principles or benign dictators.

Now in this island of Atlantis there was a great and wonderful empire which had rule over the whole island and several others ... This vast power, gathered into one, endeavoured to subdue ... the whole of the region ... She was pre-eminent in courage and military skill, and was the leader of the Hellenes. And when the rest fell off from her, being compelled to stand alone, after having undergone the very extremity of dangers, she defeated and triumphed over the invaders, and preserved from slavery those who were not yet subjugated, and generously liberated all the rest of us who dwelt within the pillars. But afterwards there occurred violent earthquakes and floods; and in a single day and night of misfortune all your warlike men in a body sank into the earth, and the island of Atlantis in like manner disappeared in the depths of the sea.

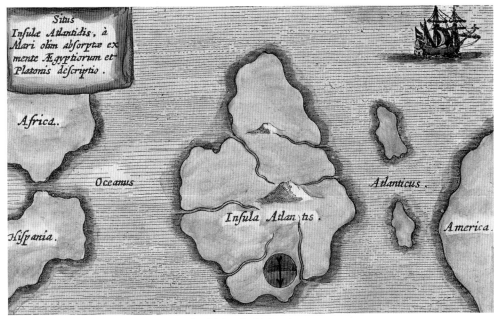

A seventeenth-century map of the imagined island of Atlantis.

Ya-uli, an Atlantean high priest, according to theosophists Besant and Leadbeater.

In *Critias*, Plato describes how, after the Creation, the gods divided up the world:

Athena acquired Greece, and set up the first Athenian state, and the sea-god Poseidon received Atlantis. Poseidon divided the island between his sons to rule, and it was these kings and their descendants who built the city of Atlantis. The kings met every fifth or sixth year to discuss affairs of state after sacrificing a bull during an elaborate ceremony. For a long time the Atlanteans were virtuous but gradually they became corrupt and greedy, and Zeus decided to punish them. The gods were called to a meeting but there ....

Plato's dialogue ends in mid-sentence, so nothing more is known.

THE GOLDEN AGE

The enthusiasm among magicians for the legend of Atlantis indicates a nostalgia for a lost world and a primal state of wholeness before humans lost contact with their spiritual source. The myth forms an ideal vision of a golden age, a time in the past where there was complete social and spiritual harmony: a Garden of Eden before the Fall, when humans were in touch with divinity.

Many modern magicians search for ways to reconnect with this ideal state of existence and, at the same time, work with their internal spiritual selves. Some claim to be in telepathic communication with the erstwhile inhabitants of Atlantis; others have memories of previous incarnations spent on the island. A profusion of books appears each year on Atlantis and a popular theme among Atlantists is that the civilizations of the New and Old Worlds shared a common cultural origin that sprang from it. This would explain common myths, symbols and even language.

Atlantis and the occult

Atlantis is seen to be the home of the initiates of a secret occult tradition, which has been passed on through various sects and secret magical societies, from the Templars, the Rosicrucians, the Freemasons and various occult schools. Some of these schools have claimed to have reconstructed the entire history of Atlantis by means of spirit messages. Edgar Cayce, a well-known American psychic Christian, born in 1877, was disturbed to find out that in trance he had delivered the history of humanity dating back to Atlantis. In a science-fiction like epic, he said that Atlantis had been inhabited by a technological civilization, based on the power of crystals.

An Atlantean pyramid, as imagined in 1923 by Manly P. Hall.

THE TAROT

The methods used to reconnect with the spiritual world are various, but one that is central to many magical practices is the set of cards called the tarot. The origin of cartomancy, or divination by cards, is unknown. The practice was established in Italy, France and Germany by the late fourteenth century and has been attributed to the Knights Templars or the Gypsies, but both are unlikely. Evidence suggests that the idea of playing cards came from China, Korea or India but that the designs of the tarot came from Europe.

The tarot consists of 78 cards, and these are made up of 56 cards of the lesser arcana, and 22 cards of the greater arcana. The lesser arcana is divided into four suits: batons, cups, swords and coins. Each suit has four court cards – King, Queen, Knight and Page – and ten numbered cards. The greater arcana depicts certain symbols and images that are numbered in sequence and range from the Fool (who is unnumbered or zero) to the World (number 21). The images on the cards represent the total energies of the universe, and some magicians say that they concern

Examples of four of the Tarot cards from the Waite-Coleman Tarot deck.

initiation into the mysteries. They represent the stages of a life journey and, by solving the riddle that each card presents, they offer an opportunity for spiritual development. The tarot is said to speak in symbols, the language of the unconscious, and, when approached in the right manner, to open doors into the hidden reaches of the soul.

The French occultist Eliphas Lévi (1810–75), whose first work on magic, *Dogme et Rituel de la Haute Magie*, was published in 1855, linked the tarot to the esoteric system of the cabbala and the

The magician Eliphas Lévi, who first linked the tarot to the esoteric system of the cabbala.

A.E Waite, the co-producer with Pamela Coleman Smith of an extremely popular tarot deck.

22 letters of the Hebrew alphabet. He also connected the four suits of the lesser arcana to the four elements, and to the four letters of the divine name of God. This had a great influence on later occultists. Lévi was also largely responsible for the revival of interest in the nineteenth-century theory of astral light as a fluid force that permeated everything, and which the magician must learn to control.

The Hermetic Order of the Golden Dawn adopted Lévi's system but assigned the cards in a slightly different way; they also linked the 22 cards of the greater arcana with the 22 paths of the cabbala, and added the signs of the zodiac and the planets to combine various systems into one.

TAROT DECKS

The three most important tarot decks of the modern era are those of the Golden Dawn, A. E. Waite and Aleister Crowley. The magician A. E. Waite and the artist Pamela Coleman Smith produced an extremely popular version of the tarot pack in 1910. In 1944, Aleister Crowley (1875–1947), an ex-Golden Dawn member, published *The Book of Thoth*, and directed the artist Lady Freida Harris to illustrate a pack according to this interpretation. All three decks were dependent on a set of tarot papers called Book T, which were issued to members of the inner lodge of the Hermetic Order of the Golden Dawn. These papers suggested that the key to the tarot was found in the cabbala and that the tarot was an external symbol of the underlying pattern of the cosmos. The book includes lines from the Revelation of Saint John the Divine and suggests that the tarot is the book referred to in this work, and that only those who have been initiated into the secret mysteries can fully understand the tarot. It begins:

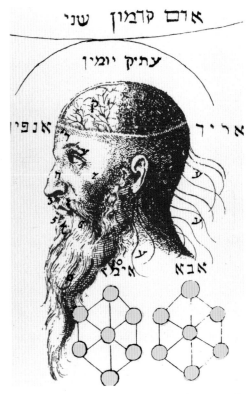

Hru the Great Angel is Set over the operations of the Secret Wisdom What thou seest write in a Book, and send it unto the Seven Abodes that are in Assiah. And I saw in the right hand of Him that sat upon the Throne a book sealed with Seven Seals. And I saw a strong Angel proclaiming with a loud voice. Who is worthy to open the Books and to loose the seals thereof?

Only an initiate is worthy of loosening the seals and understanding the true mysteries of the tarot.

Tarot cards are used today in many forms of divination. Said to reach the deepest parts of a person's subconscious, they can give personal and spiritual insight.

The cabbala was originally an esoteric aspect of Judaism; today it is interpreted more widely.

The cabbala

The cabbala, originally the inner and mystical aspect of Judaism, provides a framework for many magical systems – such as the tarot, astrology and alchemy – and is thought to represent every force manifested in the universe. Essentially a form of Neoplatonism, Godhead is seen to be brought down to humanity via the spheres (sephiroth) of the Tree of Life. In cabbalistic cosmology, Creation, like the descent of pure light, works downwards from AYIN (God transcendent) to EN SOF (immanent God) through to AYIN SOF OR (limitless light), which becomes manifest in the ten spheres of the cabbala. The relationships of the spheres represent the whole of existence – they are both attributes of God and aspects of human experience – and offer human beings the means of attaining spiritual oneness with the Ultimate.

The Tree of Life is used as a framework for meditation (on the qualities of a particular sphere, for example), or for "pathworking", an active meditation that engages the imagination, while in a state of trance, on the pathways interlinking the spheres. Cabbalistic magical training concerns training the mind through visualization – the creation of images using the imagination.

Tarot cards are often used to represent the energies and attributes of a particular path on the Tree of Life. Thus by working on the Tree of Life a magician is said to be able to reach deeper and unknown parts of his or her subconsciousness; this is said to lead to greater self understanding and also spiritual revelation. The Tree of Life represents an inner "map" of the cosmos and a way of uniting with God.

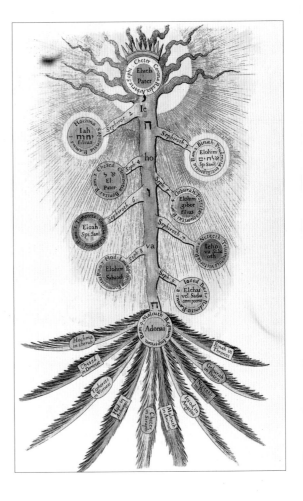

There are many interpretations of the cabbalistic Tree of Life. This one is from Kircher's Oedipus Aegyptiacus, *1652. More modern ones have distinct pathways linking the spheres to aid meditation.*

MAGICAL SOCIETIES

The word "occult" conveys the ideas of secrecy and hidden knowledge; a central component of magical organizations in the past was the transmission of esoteric wisdom through initiation rites. During the seventeenth century there was a fascination with secret societies and it was at this time that Rosicrucianism and Freemasonry were established. Rosicrucianism was founded on myths and allegories that were based on the restoration of a divine state through inner experience. The Rosicruicians used alchemy and cabbala to achieve this divine state. In similar fashion, the spiritual aspects of Freemasonry are concerned with making contact with a divine source through the symbolism of the Temple of Solomon. The nineteenth-century Theosophical Society was based on the idea that there was an ancient spiritual science concerned with the mysteries of the interaction between human beings and God. Likewise, the later nineteenth-century Hermetic Order of the Golden Dawn – a synthesis of the practices and traditions of Rosicrucianism, Freemasonry and Theosophy – was also focused on a mystical union with divinity. All these magical societies sought a higher spiritual knowledge or experience as a means of uniting with God.

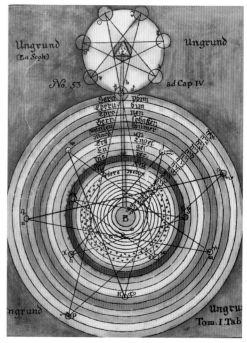

A Rosicrucian diagram of the spiritual realm in relation to the descent of the reincarnating soul.

THE ROSICRUCIANS

The years 1614 and 1615 saw the publication of two short pamphlets, the *Fama* and the *Confessio*, which became known as the Rosicrucian manifestos. They were utopian myths about bringing humanity back to its divine state before the Fall, and made the stirring announcement of the dawn of a new enlightenment. Their message was framed in an allegory in which the central message was a spiritual opening to divine inner experience. According to this allegory, a Rosicrucian brother had discovered a large brass nail during building alterations. When the nail was removed it revealed a door behind, on which was written the words *"POST CCXX ANOS PATEBO"* ("After 120 years I shall reopen"). When the door was eventually opened,

... there appeared to our sight a Vault of Seven Sides ... although the Sun never shined in that Vault, nevertheless it was enlightened with another Sun ... and was situated in the upper part in the centre of the

ceiling. In the midst ... was a round altar, covered with a plate of brass, and thereon this engraven "I have made this Tomb a compendium of the Universe". Round the brim were the words "Jesus is all things to me". In the middle were four figures, enclosed in circles, whose circumscription was (1) Nowhere a Vacuum (2) The Burden of the Law (3) The Liberty of the Gospel (4) The Untouched Glory of God. Now as we had not yet seen the body of our careful and wise Father, we therefore removed the altar aside; then we lifted up a strong plate of brass and found a fair and worthy body, whole and unconsumed ... In his hand he held the book T, the which next unto our Bible is our greatest treasure.

Behind the walls of the tomb the brethren found books, magical mirrors, bells and even "ever-burning lamps". The first two manifestos were connected with a third publication, *The Chymical*

Wedding of Christian Rosencreutz, written in 1616 by Johann Valentin Andreae. This concerned another allegory, this time based on the mystic marriage of the soul. By setting forth an alternative to the Jesuit Order, the Rosicrucians promised

The Rosicrucian Rosy Cross as depicted by the nineteenth-century Hermetic Order of the Golden Dawn.

a prophetic return to a state of paradise through the use of alchemy, cabbala and evangelical piety. Their aim was to promote a programme of research and reform of the sciences.

FREEMASONRY

The origins of Freemasonry are unclear; it has been linked with Rosicrucianism and the Knights Templar, but nothing is known for certain.

The history of Freemasonry is entwined with the Hermetic and cabbalistic traditions, which were studied in England during the second half of the sixteenth century. In 1717 the Grand Lodge was formed, this used a system of symbolism based on the society of stonemasons called the Operative Mason's Craft, together with ideas from the Western mystical tradition. In ancient Greek culture, much effort had been made to capture the gods' characters in stone structures, and this decorative architecture influenced the Roman architect Vitruvius, who wanted to capture the spiritual essence of building to demonstrate that the human being and the building were constructed according to the same plan. The mystical tradition that Vitruvius discovered was handed down through the medieval guilds of stonemasons, and preserved by a small group within the trade.

In the view of Freemasons, the complete human being is made up of a body, a psyche or soul, a spirit and a contact with his divine source. The human psyche contains four levels, which reflect the larger four-level structure described above. In specific terms, Freemasonry represents the psyche with the Temple of Solomon, which it describes as a three-storey temple within which one can be conscious of the presence of divinity.

Freemasonry consists of three basic degrees: Entered Apprentice; Fellow Craft; and Master Mason; as well as "higher" or "side" degrees of the *Rose Croix*. In addition there is the Knight of the Pelican and Eagle and Sovereign, Prince Rose Croix of Heredom, Grand

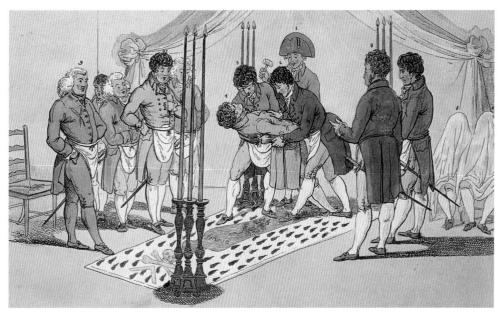

A nineteenth-century depiction of a Freemasonry initiation.

The ceremonies and symbols of Freemasonry as shown in the frontispiece to a nineteenth-century book on its history.

Elected Knight Kadosh and Knight of Black and White Eagle. There are also many offices within a lodge such as Worshipful Master Deacons and Wardens, which are positions rather than levels of initiation. In Britain, Masonry was responsible for keeping alive the occult tradition from the sixteenth to the nineteenth century. Freemasonry has had an important influence on contemporary magical practices, mainly the Hermetic Order of the Golden Dawn.

THE THEOSOPHICAL SOCIETY

The nineteenth century was an age of independent spiritual teachers in a time of declining established religion, when many people were looking to find a single key to solve the mysteries of the universe. Among these was Emanuel Swedenborg (1688–1772), who developed a theory of correspondences and a view of the universe as a harmonious whole, which was only temporarily disturbed by sin. This was coupled with a belief in the accessibility of the spiritual world together with a trust in the reality of a new political and religious dispensation that would bring together the various orders of science and religion and would combine them with the imagination.

The theory of magnetism propounded by Anton Mesmer (1734–1815) was also popular. This was based on the notion that the human body was surrounded by a magnetic force, which a healer could detect for therapeutic purposes. The movement that became know as spiritualism also attracted many people who believed that the spirits of the dead could be channelled by mediums who had special psychic powers.

HELENA BLAVATSKY

This was the climate of ideas from which the Theosophical Society emerged. It was founded by Helena Petrovna Blavatsky (1831–91) and Henry Steel Olcott (1832–1907) in 1875, and it played a major part in spreading occult ideas at the turn of the nineteenth century. At its inception its objectives were to form a universal brotherhood of humanity without distinction of race, creed, sex, caste or colour; to encourage the study of comparative religion, philosophy and science; and to investigate unexplained laws of nature and the powers latent in humans. These last two objectives were later developed by HPB, as she was popularly known, in *Isis Unveiled*, subtitled "A Master-Key to the Mysteries of Ancient and Modern Science and Theology" (1877), in which she attempted to integrate science and religion. At this stage the theosophical doctrine was still in its formative stages, but was being structured around the idea that there was an ancient, secret spiritual

Anton Mesmer, the Austrian physician who popularized the idea that the human body was surrounded by a magnetic force, a belief that still holds sway in many different natural therapies.

Helena Blavatsky, a co-founder and prominent personality of the Theosophical Society.

science known to a brotherhood of adepts who would transmit it to select individuals. Blavatsky claimed that science was called "magic" in the far-off days and explored the primary force of nature's mysteries within a universe of cyclic phenomena. These mysteries were in essence the interaction between God and humanity.

The core of Blavatsky's theosophy was that "Man must know himself" and that ordinary religion was just dogma with no scientific foundation. Science, too, was unsatisfactory because it ignored the unseen being. For Blavatsky, the whole was constituted of both the visible and the invisible, the facts of nature being grasped from within the human body as well as without. She was an adamant anti-Darwinian, believing in the spiritual evolution of the psyche rather than the physical evolution of primates. The role of theosophy was to investigate universal religious wisdom by means of science.

Blavatsky claimed that her cosmology was based on her contact with a brotherhood of Himalayan masters whom she

Henry Steel Olcott, co-founder of the Theosophical Society.

Annie Besant, a leading Theosophist and a supporter of rights for women, as a young woman, c.1868.

Madame Blavatsky with the emblem of the Theosophical Society above her head. At the centre of the emblem is the six-pointed star of the Seal of Solomon, a sign of the macrocosm, surmounted by a crowned swastica, a symbol of light and life, and surrounded by an ouroboros, a snake biting its own tail and representing cyclicity. The Egyptian ankh to the left symbolizes life, while the square topped by a triangle represents human beings: the triangle signifies the spiritual element, while the square portrays the material dimension.

of women's rights and a socialist, took a maternal charge of Krishnamurti. Eventually turning from Theosophy, Krishnamurti developed his own spiritual teachings on finding truth within and liberation from organized religion. The Theosophical Society has had a major influence on modern Western magic, particularly on Samuel Liddell "MacGregor" Mathers and William Westcott, who were founders of the Hermetic Order of the Golden Dawn. The Society was also responsible for introducing Eastern ideas about reincarnation to Western occultism.

called the "Great White Brotherhood". The masters formed a "cosmic radio" to link humans with the chiefs of the divine hierarchy, which ruled the cosmos.

Blavatsky published *The Secret Doctrine* in 1888 and sought to explain universal creation as a scheme by which the primal unity of an unmanifest divine being filtered down into consciously evolving beings. The spirit was attempting, through a series of rebirths and by moving through the cosmos from planet to planet, to recover from a fall from divine grace. According to Blavatsky's view, a lord of the world originally came from Venus with several helpers who were, in descending order of authority:

Buddha; Mahachshan; Manu (who had an assistant Master Morya or "M"); and Maitreya (who had an assistant Master Koot Hoomi or "KH"). The two assistants Master Morya and Master Koot Hoomi were Blavatsky's masters and probably played a vital role in the founding of the Theosophical Society.

In 1909 a leading Theosophist Charles Leadbeater "discovered" a young Indian boy named Jiddu Krishnamurti who he thought to physically be the avatar – the incarnation of divine consciousness on earth – of Maitreya, and the new Messiah and World Teacher. Annie Besant, a leading free-thinker advocate

Annie Besant with Krishnamurti, the Theosophical Society's chosen World Leader, who later disassociated himself from the organization.

THE GOLDEN DAWN

The creation of the magical society called the Hermetic Order of the Golden Dawn in the late nineteenth century marked an important milestone in the history of Western magic. It was primarily a synthesis of a number of occult traditions, and brought the mystical union with the divine to the forefront of modern magic by combining Hermeticism (which suggested that divine powers are latent within human beings, who may recover them by learning their own true natures) with a study of cabbala (through which humans can achieve union with God by the study of the Tree of life).

The Golden Dawn resembled the Societas Rosicruciana and Freemasonry with its structure of initiations, elaborate ceremonies and use of occult symbolism. Like theosophy it offered leading roles to women, and a number of well-known women played a leading part – such as the actress Florence Farr, the Irish nationalist Maud Gonne, Moina Bergson, sister of the philosopher Henri Bergson, and wife of the founding member Samuel "MacGregor" Mathers, and Annie Horniman, the tea heiress. The society also attracted the eminent Irish poet William Butler Yeats, who had joined the Theosophical Society as an art student in the 1880s.

THE FOUNDING MEMBERS

The Hermetic Order of the Golden Dawn was founded in London in 1888 by three members of the Societas Rosicruciana in Anglia, a Masonic-Rosicrucian body formed by Robert Wentworth Little in 1865 and based on the Rosicrucian legend of Christian Rosencreutz. They were called William Wynn Westcott (1848–1915), a doctor, coroner, Mason and

William Butler Yeats, the Irish poet, dramatist and member of the Hermetic Order of the Golden Dawn.

Left: The Irish nationalist Maud Gonne, a member of the Golden Dawn.

Above: Annie Horniman inherited a large fortune from her father's tea business; she was a theatre manager and founder of the repertory system, as well as a member of the Golden Dawn.

member of the Theosophical Society, William Robert Woodman (1828–91), a doctor, Mason, cabbala enthusiast and Supreme Magus of the Societas Rosicruciana, and Samuel Liddell "MacGregor" Mathers (1854–1918), a Mason who "spent almost half a lifetime in the British Museum in London and the Arsenal library in Paris, delving into magical and alchemical texts". Mathers, a particularly colourful and flamboyant character who assumed the title of Count MacGregor of Glenstrae, was

Dr William Wynn Westcott, co-founder along with Samuel Mathers and William Woodman of the Hermetic Order of the Golden Dawn.

Samuel Liddell "MacGregor" Mathers was mainly responsible for bringing together various magical systems into the Hermetic Order of the Golden Dawn. A lover of ceremony, he is here shown performing the Rites of Isis.

responsible for constructing a coherent magical system from the various elements of Masonic symbolism, cabbala, tarot, astrology, numerology and ritual magic. A fourth founder member, who died soon after the establishment of the Order, was the Rev. A. F. A. Woodford, a country vicar, who had acquired some manuscripts in cypher from the mystic and would-be magician Fred Hockley. He sent them to Westcott to decode and they proved to be a skeletal

description, in English, of five hitherto unknown rituals of a Rosicrucian nature which the writer had witnessed – presumably in Germany, as the manuscript also contained the address of a certain Anna Sprengel of Nuremburg, allegedly a high-grade Rosicrucian. Westcott asked Mathers for his co-operation in working up the bare bones of the system into a coherent whole suitable for "lodge-work", and to this Mathers agreed.

EARLY SPIRITUAL LINKS

In October 1887 Westcott wrote to Fraulein Sprengel asking for occult teaching. This was given in a correspondence course and honorary grades were conferred upon Westcott, Mathers and Woodman. A charter was given for the establishment of a Golden Dawn Temple to work the grades in the cypher manuscript. Temples were set up in London, Weston-super-Mare, Bradford, Edinburgh and Paris. In 1891 the correspondence with Anna Sprengel stopped: a communication from Germany informed Westcott that his correspondent was dead and that no further information would be given to the English students; if they wished to establish a link with the Secret Chiefs of the Order they must do it themselves.

Mathers and Westcott were both friends of Madame Blavatsky and, while she lived, there was a friendly alliance between the Theosophical Society and the Golden Dawn. The roots of the two societies are deeply intertwined and the two organizations saw themselves as an élite, secretly working towards humanity's evolution. In 1892 Blavatsky died; Mathers claimed to have established links with the Secret Chiefs and supplied rituals for a Golden Dawn Second Order: the Red Rose and the Cross of Gold, based on the legend of Christian Rosencreutz. These rituals were adopted and a "Vault of the Adepts" became the controlling force behind the Temples of the Golden Dawn in the Order.

Mathers based his system on Eliphas Lévi's system of magic, which itself drew on Mesmer's theories that the planets influenced human beings

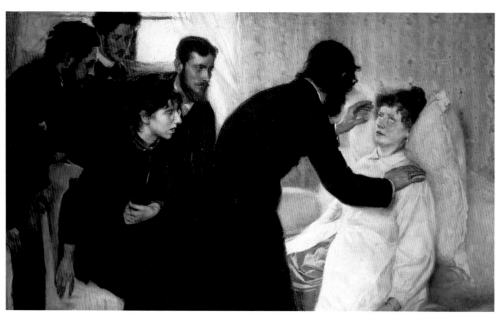

Mesmer's theories of magnetism, as a universal fluid that could be controlled by human will, were extremely popular in the nineteenth century. Here a physician attempts a cure through hypnotism.

through the fluid of animal magnetism. Mesmer claimed to have discovered that animal magnetism, as a universal medium, could be directly controlled by the human will. This became a basis of modern magical theory.

Lévi identified animal magnetism as the "astral light", which, like a magnet, had opposite poles that carried good and evil, and responded to the human will.

He said, "To direct the magnetic forces is then to destroy or create forms; to produce all appearance, or to destroy bodies; it is to exercise the mighty powers of Nature".

ORGANIZED MAGIC

Eclectic in nature, the Golden Dawn used many deity forms including Hebrew, Christian and classical, and

Symbols of the Hermetic Order of the Golden Dawn

Samuel "MacGregor" Mathers, a co-founder of the Golden Dawn, was fond of saying "There is no part of me that is not of the Gods". He paraphrased this from the Book of the Dead. Mathers and other Golden Dawn members used god forms from various cultures as currents or potencies of energies, which could be tapped during ritual. These energies were embodied in the design of wands, banners and badges such as these.

The Order of the Pectoral, with signs of the zodiac. The swastika, as an emblem of light and life, was a spiritual sign before it was adopted by the Nazis.

Pectoral Cross with Hebrew characters showing Judaeo-Christian influences, particularly through Rosicrucianism.

A symbol used in the Hermes Lodge of the Stella Matutina. The triangle represents the number three, symbolizing the highest realm of the spiritual world.

these reflected the spiritual interests of its various members. Mathers declared, in true theosophical fashion, that the order respected the truths of all religions, and he created a flexible system of magic, which could be used in many different ways.

Mathers loved the ornate trappings and highly organized aspects of ceremonial magic, and he ran the Golden Dawn like a military organization. But in 1900 his imperious behaviour eventually caused a rebellion among the other members. Mathers had accused Westcott of forging the foundation documents, and the other members of the Golden Dawn claimed that Mathers had put the authority of the order under question. This infuriated Mathers who decided to curse them all; according to one account, he took a packet of dried peas, rattled them violently in a sieve, and called on the demonic forces of Beelzebub and Seth-Typhon to avenge his opponents.

REBELLIONS AND SCHISMS

Further disagreements splintered the Golden Dawn, and the poet William Butler Yeats took control of the rebel faction for a time. The Christian mystic A. E. Waite took command of the London temple. Born in Brooklyn, New York, Waite was brought up a Roman Catholic, but became interested in spiritualism and theosophy before he joined the Golden Dawn in 1891. He wrote a number of books and is perhaps best known for designing the most widely used modern tarot pack, illustrated by Pamela Coleman Smith.

The Golden Dawn eventually fragmented into four daughter organizations: the Isis-Urania Temple, a Christian mystical organization run by Waite and others; the Stella Matutina run by R. W. Felkin and J. W. Brodie-Innes; the Alpha et Omega run by Brodie-Innes and Mathers; and the pagan A.A. headed by Aleister Crowley.

Aleister Crowley wearing a robe of the Golden Dawn. Note the Rosy Cross on his chest.

Below: Samuel Mathers and Mina Mathers, his wife, dressed as priest and priestess.

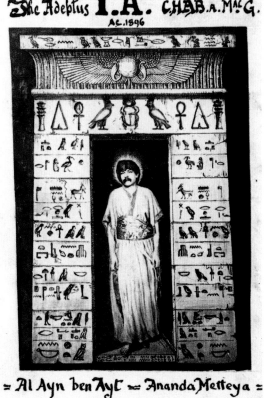

A "certificate" of initiation into the Golden Dawn showing that Alan Bennett, a disciple of Aleister Crowley, was initiated by Samuel Mathers.

ALEISTER CROWLEY

Aleister Crowley, a one-time member of the Golden Dawn, is perhaps the most notorious occultist of the twentieth century and is famous for being a "black magician". He is one of the few people whose reputation extends outside the world of magic and witchcraft. Crowley, the self-styled "beast", was a controversial figure and courted publicity of the worst kind, but he was a talented magician and his ideas about magic remain influential today. He developed a system of magical anarchism – his declared creed was: "do what thou wilt shall be the whole of the law" – and his ideas have also shaped the development and organization of modern witchcraft.

"The beast" – Aleister Crowley.

Edward Alexander Crowley was brought up a strict member of the Plymouth Brethren, but he decided to rebel, and as he explains in his autohagiography, at the age of 12 years he "simply went over to Satan's side". Crowley eventually developed his own theology, which was based on personal communication with the Devil against the forces of good, which had "constantly oppressed" him. Thus, Crowley's magical work is a direct rebellion against Christianity

THE BOOK OF LAW
Crowley joined the Golden Dawn in 1898 after leaving Cambridge. In April 1904, Crowley "received" The Book of the Law from an intelligence named Aiwass, mediated through his clairvoyant wife Rose Kelly. From this he developed the religion of Thelema. Thelema (which means "the will" in Greek) was said by Crowley to represent a new aeon, which would release humankind from its obsession with fear and its consciousness of sin. Crowley's brand of magic was based on Lévi's theories, which made the human being the centre of the universe. Lévi's view of magic emphasized finding the "True Will", which is the magician's magical identity – his or her "true self". Drawing on these ideas, Crowley claimed that each individual should be the centre of his or her own universe.

Aleister Crowley's writing on magic is widely regarded by magicians as

brilliant; his excessive, publicity-seeking behaviour, on the other hand, is often deplored (except by his direct followers, the Thelemites) as giving magic a "bad name". In Crowley's scheme of things, the knowledge of the will is the basis of a magician's empowerment, and the evolution of what he termed the Aeon of Horus is the aeon of individualism. Crowley's aim was the emancipation of humankind by the announcement of an "unconditional truth", which was "appropriate for the present evolutionary stage". This truth was to create an interpretation of the cosmos from an egocentric and practical viewpoint.

Thelema was a new cosmology and set of ethics for the Aeon of Horus. This marked a new stage evolving from the previous stage of the worship of the Father, which had followed on from the worship of the Mother. The Aeon of Horus was thus the aeon of the Child, which would, according to Crowley, destroy the Christian formula of the "Dying God" by offering complete moral independence, in this way releasing humankind from fear and the consequences of sin. Humanity was to govern itself, and self-sacrifice was viewed as

Aleister Crowley in Golden Dawn robes.

romantic folly, the sacrifice of the strong to the weak was, according to this view, against the principles of evolution.

Do What Thou Wilt

From these ideas Crowley developed the maxim "Do what thou wilt shall be the whole of the law", meaning that every person had the right to fulfil their own will and in so doing had the forces of the universe behind them. He defined the magician as one who knows the "Science and Art of causing Change to occur in conformity with Will". He believed that magic was the science of understanding the self and its conditions, and was the art of putting that knowledge into practical action.

Thus Crowley's religion of Thelema was based on the idea that the individual was a star within its own galaxy. "In a galaxy each star has its own magnitude, characteristics and direction, and the celestial harmony is best maintained by its attending to its own business."

The certificate acknowledging Aleister Crowley as a member of the High Order of the Freemasons of the 33rd Rite in Scotland.

A self-portrait. Note that the medal around his neck is inscribed 666, denoting the beast from the Book of Revelations in the Christian Bible.

Crowley's version of magic puts the magician as human being in control of his or her will firmly at the centre of magical practices and thus in control of the universe; this creates a sharp break from ideas of theosophical spiritual evolutionism and the Christian notion of union with God as expounded by some members of the Hermetic Order of the Golden Dawn.

LIBERATION PHILOSOPHY

Aleister Crowley was a controversial figure, but there is no doubt that he was extremely influential in the shaping of modern magic. Crowley's major philosophical influence was through a liberation philosophy that focused on recreating a powerful magical self, and his impact stemmed from his connection of themes of human evolution (the Aeon of Horus) with modernism (the development of the self through the will). He is also identified as playing a part in the creation of modern witchcraft as a nature religion, although how much he actually contributed is contested. His poem, *Hymn to Pan*, written in 1929, displays classical themes combined with a focus on nature:

Thrill with the lissome lust of the light,
O man! My man!
Come careering out of the night
Of Pan! Io Pan!
Io Pan! Io Pan! Come over the sea
From Sicily and from Arcady!
Roaming as Bacchus, with fauns and pards
And nymphs and satyrs for thy guards,
On a milk-white ass, come over the sea
To me, to me,
Come with Apollo in bridal dress
(Shepherdess and pythoness)
Come with Artemis, silken shod,
And wash thy white thigh, beautiful God,
In the moon of the woods, on the
marble mount,
The dimpled dawn of the amber fount!
Dip the purple of passionate prayer
In the crimson shrine, the scarlet snare,
The soul that startles in eyes of blue
To watch thy wantoness weeping through
The tangled grove, the gnarl'd bole
Of the living tree that is spirit and soul
And body and brain – come over the sea,
(Io Pan! Io Pan!)
Devil or god, to me, to me,
My man! my man! ...

ORDO TEMPLI ORIENTIS

Crowley was influenced by Eastern schools of thought such as Buddhism and Tantrism, and joined the Ordo Templi Orientis in 1912, becoming its leader in 1922. The Ordo Templi Orientis (OTO) had been founded at the beginning of the twentieth century

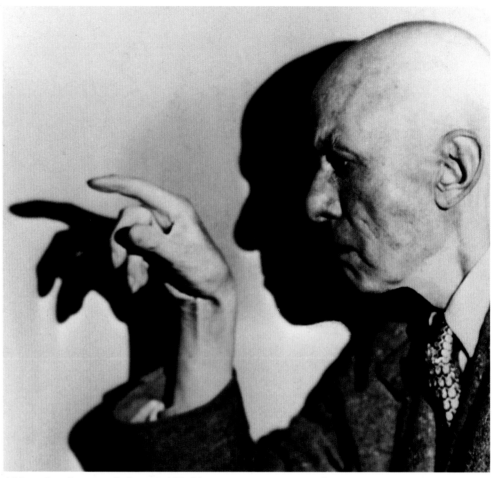

Aleister Crowley towards the end of his life.

A card from the tarot deck designed by Crowley and painted by Frieda Harris in 1941.

by Karl Kellner, a German Mason and occultist. It is claimed that it was the product of the German occult revival, which was sparked off by the opening of the Berlin branch of the Theosophical Society in 1884. The OTO was a modern form of Templarism, drawing on the Knights Templars movement, which had been suppressed in the fourteenth century on the grounds of heresy, sodomy and bestiality. Kellner is said to have been initiated into the use of "the sexual Current" by an Arab called Soliman ben Aifa and two Indian Tantrics, Bhima Sen Pratap and Shri Mahatma Agamya Paramahamsa. He was also influenced by a group of French followers of the American occultist P. B. Randolph. The OTO made grand claims that it possessed the key that would open up all Masonic and Hermetic secrets through the teaching of sexual magic. Reuss invited Crowley to rewrite the OTO rituals, and it has been suggested that Crowley saw the OTO as the first great

"The Resurrection of Zoroaster", a drawing by Austin Osman Spare, 1905.

"Blood on the Moon" by Austin Osman Spare, 1955.

A symbolic painting for Crowley's Temple of the A.A., the Order of the Silver Star.

magical order to accept the Law of Thelema, and by doing so to slough off the techniques of ceremonial magic and to revive pagan elements of ecstasy and wonder as the keys to the "Mysteries of Man".

AUSTIN OSMAN SPARE (1886–1956)

Austin Osman Spare was a pupil of Crowley, and he was also the protègè of a Mrs Patterson, who was said to be a hereditary witch descended from a line of witches from Salem, Massachusetts. Spare developed a method of "atavistic resurgence" – the evocation of beings from the primitive depths of the mind, which could make themselves known through visions and art. His magical philosophy was based on the power of

the will to influence the subconscious mind, and he believed that it was possible to instruct the subconscious mind through the creation of personal symbols known as sigils. A sigil could be implanted into the unconscious by making the mind blank at the time of a magical act, at sexual orgasm, or through self-hypnosis. Spare's "Cult of the Zos and the Kia" – or Zos Kia Cultus – was informed by his contact with Mrs Patterson and was based on the idea that it was possible to retrace earlier existences. After locating the first personality (Zos) it could be trans-cended and merged with the void (which he called Kia) through sexual union. Spare's magical ideas have formed an important part of chaos magic practice. Chaos magic is the ultimate expression of liberation philosophy in magical practices.

DION FORTUNE

Considered one of the leading occultists of her time, Dion Fortune was perhaps one of the first occult writers to approach magic and hermetic concepts using the precepts of psychology, in particular of Jung and Freud. Her role was a significant one and the written material she left behind is still used today, valued in particular for its rich source for rituals, and its pagan themes. Dion Fortune also succeeded in bringing about a renewal of interest in British myths and legends, and their importance in the country's historical inheritance. She was also instrumental in emphasising the importance of balance between male and female elements in magic.

A rare photograph of the young Dion Fortune. The picture was taken in 1911, at the beginning of her studies at Warwick Horticultural College.

Dion Fortune was born Violet Mary Firth on 6 December 1890 to a wealthy family in the steel business. She adapted the family motto, "Deo, non Fortuna", to create her magical name. A leading magician of her time, Dion Fortune had been initiated into the Hermetic Order of the Golden Dawn in 1919 but, according to her biographer Alan Richardson, she disliked the idea of pouring the "regenerative spiritual force of the East into the group-soul of the British Empire". Being a staunch British nationalist, Dion Fortune also reacted against the Eastern influence in theosophy and turned instead to a mystical Christianity and what she saw as the indigenous British mythology of King Arthur and the Holy Grail.

Acting on these convictions, in 1923 she formed a Christian Mystic Lodge of the Theosophical Society with the aim of interpreting Christianity in terms of theosophy and vice versa, but she eventually rejected the ideas of the Theosophical Society in 1928 and went on to develop her own magical society.

A pupil of the occultist Theodore Moriarty, who taught that the "Christ Principle" had first been propounded in Atlantis and was manifested through Horus, Mithras, Quetzalcoatl and Buddha, Dion Fortune began to form her own magical contacts. During the winter of 1923–4 she contacted the people she referred to as her secret chiefs, and in 1927 she left the Hermetic Order of the Golden Dawn to found the Fraternity of the Inner Light (still in existence today as the Society of the Inner Light).

Fortune's secret chiefs included a trinity of masters, with Melchisedec of Salem as the source. These three chiefs sent out three distinct "rays" of wisdom, which were defined as the following: the Hermetic, which was concerned with philosophy and ritual; the Orphic or Green Ray, which was devoted to earth mysteries; and the Mystic Ray, concerned with the mysteries of the Son.

From 1926 Dion Fortune published a number of books on magical cosmology,

For Dion Fortune the Knights of the Round Table represented a chivalric era that could be magically tapped into.

The death of King Arthur and his passage to another plane was central to his mystic significance.

cabbala and practical magic, as well as many novels with an occult theme, the most famous being *The Sea Priestess*, first published in 1938.

THE INFLUENCE OF CARL JUNG

Carl Gustav Jung created an individual practice of spiritual rebirth, and he has been called a prophet by spiritual seekers; it has also been claimed that Jungian psychology has helped to legitimize modern paganism, and indeed his psychology has had a major influence on modern magic, primarily through the work of Dion Fortune. Carl Gustav Jung was the founder of analytical psychology. His methods included using the active imagination and amplifying dream and fantasy images; he thought that people from every society were predisposed to form what he called archetypal images – certain symbols that were found cross-culturally in mythology, fairy tales and religious iconography. During the period 1914–18 Jung experienced a psychological breakdown, and for the rest of his life he sought explanations for what had

The ideas of Swiss psychologist Carl Gustav Jung had a profound influence on the magical work of Dion Fortune.

happened to him, trying to understand the images and symbols that had arisen from his unconscious. Jung attempted to liberate the unconscious and developed what has since turned out to be a form of spiritual cult based on trying to understand the mystical process of "inner reality", which will hopefully produce a new secret wisdom. Jung took the idea of the unconscious seriously and developed techniques for encouraging dissociation – freeing the mind from its usual patterns of conscious thought – so that the unconscious could regulate actions.

Much of Carl Jung's theory stemmed from a powerful dream that he once had of a house with two different floors: he took the upper storey to represent his consciousness and the ground floor to symbolize his unconsciousness. From the ground floor was a stairway leading down to a cellar, the cellar led in turn to a cave. This is how he described the dream:

I was in a house I did not know, which had two storeys. It was "my house". I found myself in the upper storey where there was a kind of salon furnished with fine pieces in rococo style ... It occurred to me that I did not know what the lower floor looked like. Descending the stairs, I reached the ground floor. There everything was much older ... The furnishings were medieval; the floors were of red brick. Everywhere it was rather dark ... Beyond it, I discovered a stone stairway that led down into the cellar. Descending again, I found myself in a beautifully vaulted room, which looked exceedingly ancient ... I knew that the walls dated from Roman times ... I looked more closely at the floor. It was of stone slabs, and in one of these I discovered a ring. When I pulled it, the stone slab lifted, again I saw a stairway of narrow stone steps leading down into the depths ... I descended, and entered a low cave cut into the rock. Thick dust lay on the floor, and in the dust were scattered bones

Much of Dion Fortune's work focused on the magical power of the Goddess as the feminine aspect of a cosmic polarity. Isis, as the sea priestess in one of her novels, was especially important.

emphasis on integrating the contra sexual other. In other words, a woman must get in touch with her "masculine" psychic self and a man his "feminine" to achieve psychic harmony.

THE HARMONIOUS UNION

In her magical novels, Dion Fortune utilizes Jung's notions of animus and anima as masculine and feminine forces, whereby a woman develops her masculinity and a man his femininity.

In *The Sea Preistess*, sea priestesses and priests came from the mythical island of Atlantis – which was for Fortune, as for many occultists, the home of divine wisdom – and engaged in selective breeding rites to pass on magical lore. The work focused on the magical power of the Goddess, as the feminine part of a polarity underpinning the cosmos, and, according to the historian Ronald Hutton, drew on three influences: her reading of D. H. Lawrence; her husband Thomas Penry Evans' interest in the god Pan; and the interest shown in

and broken pottery, like the remains of a primitve culture. I discovered two human skulls, obviously very old and half disintegrated. Then I awoke.

Interpreting this house as an image of his psyche, Jung saw his consciousness as represented by the salon; the ground floor as his first level of unconsciousness; while the cave represented the world of the primitive human within himself, an area that he thought was scarcely reached by consciousness.

Jung's main theme was of the evolution of consciousness. The first stage of this process was through contacting the "world of memories", which led to a rebirth through the realm of the under-world, the ancestors and the dead. He said that his psychoanalytic techniques were like an archaeological excavation and involved using the active imagination to contact the ancestral past.

The unconscious, for Jung, consisted of all the forgotten material from an individual's own past and the inherited behavioural traces of the "human spirit". Contact with what he called the "collective unconscious" – symbolized by gods – led to access to wisdom and universal human experience. Jung also developed notions of what he called the animus and the anima. The animus was

the masculine aspect of a woman's psyche, while the anima was the corresponding feminine part of a man's psyche. His psychology put much

Dion Fortune pictured with her husband on the left, and an unknown friend on the right.

Inside the Temple of the Grail by W. Hauschild. The Grail represented a source of spiritual wisdom for Dion Fortune.

the Great Mother and women's mysteries by Charles Seymour, her magical partner. As Isis, goddess of nature and the fertility of the land, the sea priestess draws her partner, the Lord of the Sun into magical union:

Isis of Nature awaiteth the coming of her Lord the Sun. She calls him. She draws him from the place of the dead, the Kingdom of Amenti, where all things are forgotten. And he comes to her in his boat called Millions of Years, and the earth grows green with the springing grain. For the desire of Osiris answereth unto the call of Isis. And so it will ever be in the hearts of men, for thus the gods have formed them.

At the beginning of World War Two, Dion Fortune became involved in a number of magical operations against Germany. Seeing Britain as being under threat from the forces of evil, she organized a magical meditation group from the Society of the Inner Light to confront the evils of Hitler's Nazi forces. Fortune wrote weekly letters to her students between 1939 and 1942, and every Sunday morning from 12.15 until 12.30 members were asked to meditate on the forces of good overcoming evil.

FORTUNE'S LEGACY

Dion Fortune's work has greatly influenced modern magic, especially the practices, rituals and ceremonies of witchcraft, which is focused on the Goddess. Her ideas and the words she wrote have influenced many different aspects of magic, and she is respected by diverse groups of people.

Dion Fortune's work has also brought a renewed focus on British mythology – especially that of King Arthur – that has revitalized links with historical traditions, and she has also helped to bring about an emphasis on the spiritual harmony of balancing feminine and masculine aspects of the psyche in magical practice.

Dion Fortune and her Society of the Inner Light fought a spiritual Battle of Britain to protect the country from invasion by Hitler's forces.

WITCHCRAFT TODAY

Modern witchcraft, or Wicca as it is also known, is a form of spirituality that seeks harmony with nature. Usually celebrating eight seasonal festivals, witches honour nature – both within their bodies, which are seen as sacred, and the wider environment. Combining a positive view of women and an ecological awareness, this new form of religion seeks a holistic way of experiencing and understanding the world. This modern definition of witchcraft is very different to that of the early modern era, when witches were viewed as evil by the Christian church. This chapter examines the different strands of witchcraft that are practised today, and highlights the various influences and personalities involved in the movement.

TODAY'S WITCHES

Modern witchcraft is a far cry from the witchcraft imagined and created by the Christian Church during the witch hunts of the early modern period in Europe. Rather than being in league with the Devil and practising evil acts, today's witches are seeking a relationship with nature and the changing seasons of the natural world, experienced within themselves as an intuitive understanding. Reclaiming the word "witch" not as an anti-social person who is seen to have magical powers in small-scale communities, but rather as the cunning woman or man of the European village, they attune themselves with the powers of nature. All of nature – the land, mountains, lakes – as well as the past, as seen through ancient cultures, is viewed as sacred.

Modern witches relate to what they see as a time when people were more in contact with nature and the natural environment. Here, at Trethevey in Cornwall, England, offerings have been left near prehistoric rock carvings.

Thus the witchcraft that is becoming increasingly popular today is not the witchcraft practised in small indigenous societies around the world, nor the diabolic type of witchcraft imagined by the Christian church during the European witch hunts. It is a witchcraft that is a form of spirituality: modern witchcraft is a religious practice that venerates nature. It was created in the 1950s using the structure of Western high magic ritual to worship the natural forces inherent in nature personified as various gods and goddesses. This form of witchcraft is not part of an ancient pre-Christian paganism, but instead draws on many sources from the Western magic tradition as well as some of the craft magic of the country cunning folk.

Modern witchcraft is gaining many new members who are disenchanted with mainstream religions; which are increasingly seen by many as being out of touch with direct spiritual experience. People are also attracted to witchcraft because it views women and sexuality as sacred, and this marks an important distinction between this new form of religion and more orthodox faiths, which frequently hold that women are in some ways inferior or less spiritual than men.

Another reason for its appeal is that as ecological awareness increases, modern witchcraft, as part of a wider group of pagan practices, offers a spirituality which is in tune with the natural world – it seeks harmony with nature, rather than its domination or control.

Witchcraft is just one spiritual path within a group of magical practices

A modern witches' altar showing a pentangle, a five-sided star symbolic of the union of the five senses of the human body – sight, hearing, smell, taste and touch – and of the four elements – fire, air, earth and water – and of the spirit.

commonly referred to as paganism. The term "pagan" comes from the Latin *paganus*, meaning "rustic", and was first used to distinguish unfavourably those who did not belong to the dominant urban faith of Christianity. More recently, historians have debated the origins of the word, and it has been suggested that it originally referred to non-military civilians – those not enrolled in the army of God. Another suggestion was that the word *pagani* was used to designate followers of an older religion when the earlier, non-military meaning had ceased to have relevance. However, by the end of the nineteenth century, "pagan" had a clear association with the countryside and the natural world, and this is largely because of its association with the Romantic movement.

Romanticism was one of a range of alternative political visions in the nineteenth century. Drawing on Renaissance theories of the connections or correspondences between the material world and the creative imagination, nature was seen as visible spirit; Romanticism involved a heightened sensitivity to the natural world. The Romantic movement was a reaction against the Enlightenment's celebration of reason, progress and notions of a common humanity and universal truth. By contrast, Romanticism valued the individual, the relative and the internal; it explored different levels of consciousness, the supernatural and mythic interpretations of the world. Wild woods, once seen as a threat to the forces of civilization, now offered the opportunity of solitude, contemplation and oneness with nature. The experience of nature became a spiritual act: nature was not only beautiful, but was uplifting and morally healing. This was particularly well expressed in the works of poets such as Wordsworth, Coleridge, Blake, Byron and Keats.

Inspired by the spirit of the Romantic movement and by his knowledge of Western magic and folklore, Gerald Gardner, the founder of the modern witchcraft movement, crafted a new religion based on the creation of a sacred ceremonial circle in which gods,

The land is imbued with history and mythology as here in Cornwall, England, where the Inner Ward of Tintagel Castle, the legendary birth place of King Arthur, may be seen above the wizard Merlin's Cave.

goddesses and the spirits of nature could be invoked. This religion of witchcraft would come to take a prominent place in the spiritual and cultural history of Western Europe, the United States, Australia and other parts of the world.

Modern witchcraft is a new religion – its roots cannot be traced back to an ancient pre-Christian pagan tradition. It draws its inspiration from the past, and although often archaeologically and historically inaccurate in its claims, it nevertheless is in tune with a different, more holistic way of understanding the world, one that would probably have been understood by our ancestors.

The traditional European view of natural springs as sacred places survives today at "clootie wells", where rags are tied to nearby trees as offerings to the spirit of the place.

GERALD GARDNER

The founder of modern witchcraft, Gerald Gardner claimed that he had been initiated into a witch coven in the New Forest, England, in 1939, by a woman named "Old Dorothy". Whether this is true or not remains unclear. However, Gardner was deeply influenced by the work of Margaret Murray who stated that the victims of the early modern witch hunts were practitioners of a surviving paganism which she described as the "Old Religion". Murray's ideas have since been disproved – modern witchcraft is not a form of the ancient paganism practised in pre-Christian times – but her influence on the birth of a new religion created by Gardner is enormous. In 1951, the repeal of the Witchcraft and Vagrancy Acts provided Gardner with the opportunity of promoting and publicizing his witch religion.

Gerald Gardner, thought by many to be the founder of modern witchcraft.

The form that modern witchcraft has taken is largely due to the imagination and creative flair of Gerald Gardner (1884–1964). He united paganism with the figure of the witch; he was what the historian Ronald Hutton calls the originator of a countercultural religion based on a nature goddess and a horned god. Gardner argued that witchcraft was an ancient, pre-Christian, pagan mystery tradition.

THE BEGINNINGS

Gardner had a keen interest in magic and at various times in his life was involved in Freemasonry, spiritualism, Buddhism and other, magical practices. He put many magical ideas and practices in his book *Witchcraft Today*. It was published in 1954, after the repeal of the laws against witchcraft in Britain, and it became the foundation text of modern witchcraft. Gardner was helped by his friend Ross Nichols (then leader of the Ancient Druid Order, and later the founder of the Order of Bards, Ovates and Druids) in the creation of a series of rituals, that were conducted within a purified circle, and the aim of which was to contain and channel the magical powers released from the participants' bodies.

At one time an owner/manager of tea and rubber plantations in Ceylon, North Borneo and Malaya, Gardner later became an inspector in the Malay customs service. He retired to London in 1936 at the age of 52, then moved to the New Forest in 1938. It was there that he joined the Rosicrucian Theatre in Christchurch, and was, so he says, initiated into a surviving coven by a mysterious woman

A modern witchcraft Yule altar with decorations that represent the seasonal festival.

named "Old Dorothy". He worked with this coven until the late 1940s, forming a magical partnership with a woman called "Dafo". In 1947 they created a company to buy a plot of land near a naturist club in St Albans in Hertfordshire, England, and there erected a reconstruction of a sixteenth-century witch's cottage. This cottage, which had cabbalistic symbols painted on the inside, provided the focus for a working coven, which was run by Gerald Gardner and Dafo in the early 1950s.

MARGARET MURRAY

Gardner was greatly influenced by the Egyptologist Margaret Murray. In 1921 she had published a book called *The Witch-Cult in Western Europe* in which she stated that the victims of the early modern witch hunts were practitioners of a surviving pagan religion. Murray claimed that an incarnate deity, in the form of a god, had been worshipped but that this may have been because the god superseded the Mother Goddess; she said that the position of the chief woman was obscure, but that the worship of a female deity had probably been supplanted by that of the male. The witch-craft rites varied with the seasons, but "The greater number of the ceremonies appear to have been practised for the purpose of securing fertility", and a marriage took place, usually once a year.

In her autobiography, Murray describes how ancient religion was her pet subject and that during World War I she researched witchcraft as she was prevented from working in Egypt. She explains how she started:

"I started with the usual idea that witches were all old women suffering from illusions about the Devil and that their persecutors were wickedly prejudiced and perjured. I worked only from contemporary records, and when I suddenly realised that the so-called Devil was simply a disguised man I was startled, almost alarmed, by the way the recorded facts fell into place, and showed that the witches were members of an old, primitive form of religion and the records had been made by members of a new and persecuting form."

A modern representation of a wicker man, a contemporary link with supposed pagan celebrations of the past.

Giving the impression that there was a fairly uniform surviving pagan religion in Western Europe, Murray's work focused on the notion that witchcraft centred on fertility. The horned god represented the generative powers of nature and was personified by a male

A portrait of Margaret Murray, Egyptologist and influential anthropologist.

person during coven rituals. Sabbaths were held four times a year at All Hallows, Candlemas, May Day and Lammas during which there was much feasting, sacrifice of animals and children, processional dances and ritualized sexual intercourse to promote fertility. Homage was paid to the horned god.

Murray even claimed that Joan of Arc and her contemporary, Gilles de Rais, had been members of this ancient pre-Christian religion. In fact Murray had constructed this pre-Christian pagan religion, and simply ignored evidence that did not support her view. She wrote a second book, which was titled *The God of the Witches*, in 1933. In this, she celebrated what she described as the "Old Religion" and linked in folk tales and customs.

GARDNER'S PRACTICAL MAGIC

The historian Ronald Hutton points out four lines of influence on Murray: first, Jules Michelet's *La Sorcière* (1862), which portrayed the pagan witch religion led by women as democratic and nature-loving. (Michelet also claimed

The god Pan is thought to be a manifestation of the ancient horned god in modern witchcraft, largely because of the work of the Egyptologist, Margaret Murray.

that the Renaissance had been caused by the natural wisdom of the witch religion working its way upwards to artists and writers). Second, Charles Godfrey Leland's *Aradia* (1899), which was directly inspired by Michelet and which purported to be the gospel of the Italian branch of Michelet's witch religion. Third, James Frazer's theory of evolution, which suggested that surviving folk customs could be the fossils of old religions. Finally, Murray's association with the Folklore Society. It was Murray's work that gave Gardner the idea of a fertility religion, but how did he put together a practical system for working magic?

Aidan Kelly has made a detailed study of modern witchcraft using his experience of studying the origins of Christianity as a historical problem. He could not discover any "ancient" material in Gerald Gardner's *Book of Shadows* (part of the witch's magical paraphernalia in which ritual details are recorded), and claims that the only magic that Gardner could find out about was high magic, which was inherently Judaeo-Christian and "too complex". Folk magic was too practical for Gardner's purposes:

methods of curing warts, or a knowledge of herbs and charms, do not offer a system or theological structure for working magic, so Gardner had to incorporate elements of high magic. Ronald Hutton says that there are four direct links between ancient paganism and Wicca, or modern witchcraft, and these are: high magic; the knowledge of the use of plants and herbs and spells; folk rites and customs to honour or manipulate the powers of nature; and finally, the literature and art of the ancient world. If Wicca is seen as a form of ritual magic – rather than an age-old paganism – then it has a distinguished and very long pedigree.

CROWLEY'S INFLUENCE

As an initiate of Aleister Crowley's Ordo Templi Orientis (OTO), Gardner was also deeply influenced by Crowley's ideas and, according to one view, hired him to write witchcraft rituals for him. One version of events claims that Crowley was pleased to do this because he saw witchcraft as a "popularized form of his own creed". However, Ronald Hutton claims that there is no evidence for this and points to the fact that Aleister Crowley's writings about witchcraft were brief.

A Secret Wicca ritual that is based on the work of Gardner, with the dramatic addition of lights and theatrical effects.

The historian Gordon Melton claims that Gardner was influenced by high magic as described in Crowley's *Magick* (1929) and *The Book of the Law* (1936). Hutton argues that Gardner was initiated into all the degrees of the OTO and, in addition, that he was held to be Crowley's heir as head of the OTO but that he could not find enough people interested in joining it. Hutton further argues that Gardner had sympathies for both high magic and medieval witchcraft (through a reading of Margaret Murray) and that he "crossed the line" from one to the other, finally devoting himself to witchcraft. From 1947 to 1953 he was writing and devising rituals, which were either copied from existing rituals or were newly created.

VENERATION OF THE GODDESS

Modern witchcraft is a religion that venerates women, the earth, the dark and nature, all of which have been denigrated by Christianity and by Western cultures generally. In *Witchcraft Today*, Gardner links death and rebirth with the myth of the Goddess. When the Goddess journeyed to the nether lands to solve all mysteries she encountered Death:

The guardians of the portals challenged her. "Strip off thy garments, lay aside thy jewels, for nought may ye bring with you into this our land." So she laid down her garments and her jewels and was bound as are all who enter the realms of Death, the mighty one. Such was her beauty that Death himself knelt and kissed her feet, saying: "Blessed be thy feet that have brought thee in these ways ... " [Death] taught her all the mysteries, and they loved and were one; and he taught her all the magics. For there are three great events in the life of man – love, death and resurrection in the new body – and magic controls them all.

The god of Death falls in love with the Goddess and teaches her that he provides rest and peace, and that if humans love they will be reborn among their loved ones at the same time and in the same place. The myth of the

Goddess often forms part of an initiation ritual into witchcraft.

Gardner wrote another ritual called "Drawing Down the Moon", a term taken from ancient Greece. As Hutton notes, Gardner put his own creative spin on the ancient tradition that saw the malign power of Thessalian witches as so great that the most powerful of them could pluck the moon from the sky and bring it to earth. By contrast Gardner created a ritual whereby the Goddess could be drawn down into the body of the high priestess in a positive and beneficial way which united human being and deity. When invoked into the body of the high priestess the Goddess was thought to speak through her.

A short time later, Doreen Valiente would make her own contribution to Wicca, both as Gardner's high priestess and by rewriting his rituals to provide some of the most poetic expressions of modern witchcraft. She is particularly well known for revising what is known as "The Charge" – the words spoken by an invoked goddess.

It is no coincidence that modern witchcraft is becoming popular at a time of rapid social change. It often seems to address people's needs in ways that

A sacred altar to the Goddess, piled with offerings of Maiden dolls.

honour both women and nature, both of which have been devalued by a rationalistic, male-dominated society whose main religious traditions reflect this. Only in recent years have matters substantially changed, for example by allowing the ordination of women in the Church of England.

Many established and folk religions throughout the world have viewed women as inferior or less spiritual than men, modern witchcraft offers an alternative space where women and men can relate to each other in a more equal manner.

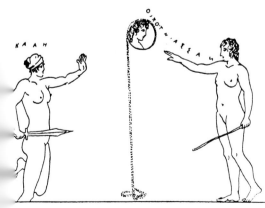

An illustration from a second-century BC Greek vase showing a female magician "drawing down the moon"; this provided the inspiration for the modern witchcraft ritual.

A modern witchcraft ritual representing the balancing of masculinity and femininity: the priestess inserts the athame, or ritual knife, which is a symbol of masculinity, into a chalice – a symbol of femininity, held by the priest.

THE GODDESS

Women in modern witchcraft are celebrated as the embodiment of the Goddess, and witchcraft is believed by some to have originated in matriarchal times. Others see early agricultural societies in neolithic Europe as matrifocal – focused on women – peaceful and living in harmony with nature until they were invaded by cultures with violent patriarchal religions. There is little to support these views, archaeologically or anthropologically, but the association of women with both nature and peace is a strong one and it shapes contemporary witchcraft practice today.

Diana, a goddess revered and summoned by the followers of magic traditions. In this picture she wears her distinctive moon headress.

In modern witchcraft, or Wicca, the divine is generally represented by two deities – the Goddess and the God – who take different forms including the Great Mother and the Horned God. Modern witchcraft is unique in that it celebrates women as the embodiment of the Goddess, and this is the essence of the craft; in some cases the Goddess is emphasized almost to the exclusion of a god. Gerald Gardner wrote in *Witchcraft Today* that the witches did not know the origin of their practice, but that he thought it was a cult from a matriarchal time when woman was the chief, and only at a later time did a male god become dominant. By acting the part of the Goddess the priestess is thought to be in communion with her. Later writers on modern witchcraft have suggested that Wicca is, by its very nature, concerned with the development and use of "the gift of the Goddess" – the psychic and intuitive faculties of women. "The gift of the God", which represents the linear, logical, and conscious faculties, is important too, but it is the Goddess who must be re-awakened after too much emphasis has been placed on the God of the monotheistic religions of Judaism, Christianity and Islam.

THE GODDESS'S CHARACTER

The Goddess is called by many names and has many different forms but, as described by the poet Robert Graves, she is usually seen as having three dimensions corresponding with the waxing, full and waning moon; these are her maiden, mother and crone aspects and the trinity is linked with the goddesses Artemis (Diana), Selene and Hecate respectively. As Queen of Heaven, the Goddess represents the moon as the source of feminine attributes connected to intuition, emotion and psychic ability. Her divine feminine force is manifested in a polarity with the masculine principle, often portrayed as the Horned God, her son and consort, who has two aspects related to the waxing and the waning year; these two gods are rivals, and are in constant competition with each other for her favours. The union of Goddess and Horned God is described as a sacred marriage, which transcends all difference.

Persephone is an important goddess in modern witchcraft because she descends into the dark of the underworld before returning to the everyday realm. This is thought to confer great knowledge and often forms part of initiation rituals.

Artemis, seen as one aspect of the triple goddess in modern witchcraft, and symbolic of the waxing moon.

THE GODDESS VERSUS THE GOD

Known as the Great Mother, the Goddess is the creatrix whose limitless fertility brings new life; she is identified with Mother Nature: she creates but she also destroys. It has been claimed by many writers that the worship of the Goddess has been ignored or suppressed by patriarchal religions and that early agricultural societies in neolithic Europe were dominated by goddess-worship; they were focused on women and were peaceful, living in harmony with nature until they were invaded by warlike Indo-Europeans and goddess-worship was supplanted by sky-gods. This idea, according to the historian Ronald Hutton, was taken up by a number of archaeologists who assumed that the concept of a universal goddess was a proven fact; this governed the interpretation of archaeological sites, especially those of neolithic Turkey.

On the strength of these ideas, the archaeologist Marija Gimbutas reissued her original 1974 study entitled *The Gods and Goddesses of Old Europe* in 1982 with the revised title of *The Goddesses and*

Diana (centre), goddess of the full moon and an aspect of the triple goddess in modern witchcraft.

Gods of Old Europe. In the earlier edition she had asserted that the great Goddess was a force of regeneration, responsible for the transformation from death to life; she emerges miraculously out of death, and in her body new life begins. She was not the earth, but a human female who could transform herself into living aspects of doe, dog, toad, bee, butterfly, tree or pillar. The preface to the revised edition, and later works by Gimbutas, incorporated ideas influenced by her

Drawing down the moon

In his book, *Witchcraft Today*, Gardner describes an example of a witch rite to cause the sun to be reborn and the summer to return. A circle is cast and purified, and the celebrants are also purified. A ceremony called 'drawing down the moon' is then performed in which the high priestess is regarded as the incarnation of the Goddess. This ritual was later formalized by Wiccans so that the high priest draws down the moon on the high priestess, who stands with her back to the altar, with a wand in her right hand and a scourge in her left, held against her breasts in the 'Osiris position'. The priest kneels before the priestess, and after giving her a ritual kiss, he kneels again before her and invokes the Goddess into her with these words:

I invoke thee and call upon thee,
Mighty Mother of us all, bringer of all
fruitfulness; by seed and root, by bud and stem,
by leaf and flower and fruit, by life and love
do I invoke thee to descend upon the body
of this thy servant and priestess.

During this invocation the high priest touches the high priestess with his right forefinger on her right breast, left breast and womb, and then repeats this, starting on her left breast. Still kneeling, with arms outstretched, he says:

Hail Aradia! From the
Amalthean Horn Pour forth thy store of love;
I lowly bend Before thee, I adore thee to the end,
With loving sacrifice thy shrine adorn.
Thy foot is to my lip [he kisses her right foot],
my prayer upborne Upon the rising
incense smoke; then spend Thine ancient love,
O Mighty One, descend To aid me, who
without thee am forlorn.

The high priestess then draws an invoking pentagram of earth in the air with her wand, and says these words:

Of the Mother darksome and divine
Mine the scourge, and mine the kiss;
The five-point star of love and bliss –
Here I charge you, in this sign.

The priest honours the priestess as the incarnation of the Goddess as she stands in the "Osiris position", wand in the right hand and scourge in the left.

The stag god Cernunnos from Celtic mythology; a manifestation of the horned god for modern witches.

This nineteenth-century romantic representation of Pan portrays him as a sensuous half-human, half-goat god in touch with the forces of nature.

personal radical feminist view. It was in these works that she extended Goddess-worship from her area of specialism – the Balkan countries – to all of Europe, the Near East and the Mediterranean region. The early witch trials were the suppression of Goddess-worship, when women were killed for practising the Old Religion of their foremothers.

The Goddess spirituality movement started in the mid to late 1970s as a form of thealogy (*thea* means female divinity); it is a growing form of spirituality – sometimes called "earth mysteries" or "women's mysteries" – that includes witches, pagans, New Agers and druids, as well as some Jewish and Christian feminists. All use female imagery for celebrating the divine and see the Goddess as primary, all-encompassing and immanent rather than as a distant transcendent spirit. A fluid practice that lacks a sacred text, authority is said to lie within the individual. The celebration of the Goddess celebrates a wholeness of self, and a power to define the self is implicit within many rituals.

Mary Daly, a Catholic theologian and feminist who came to abandon the Christian Church, calling it patriarchal, wrote a book in 1973 called *Beyond God the Father*, in which she wrote about changing the perception of "God" as male, and this proved to be an inspiration for many to turn away from what they saw as male-dominated religions. The Goddess is seen as a symbol of the strength and wholeness of women, as Elinor Gadon writes in her book *The Once and Future Goddess*:

In reclaiming the Goddess, in recovering our full human history as men and women, we can learn other patterns of behavior. We can redress the imbalance between the human species and our natural environment, between men and women, exploring the possibility of living in harmony and justice with all things.

Thus the Goddess is an earth-centred metaphor for the earth as a living organism, and also for an alternative, supposedly more egalitarian, social order.

Many other goddesses, as well as a Great Mother Goddess, are venerated. Some, such as Lilith, embody the dark and death as well as more obvious life-giving and nurturing qualities. Lilith, a hybrid bird-woman, was Adam's first wife, but she refused to lie beneath him, and, uttering the magical name of God, flew away to the wilderness where she gave birth to demons. God sent three angels to bring her back to Eden, but she refused to return. Lilith is perhaps the source of ideas about strix, striga, or striges, the owl-like creatures in classical and European folklore, and later the prototypes of the diabolical witch stereotype created and fostered by the established Christian Church.

THE GOD

The partner of the Goddess is the God. He is sometimes called Cernunnos or Herne, but is more frequently referred to merely as the horned god. The historian Ronald Hutton argues that the cultural forces that brought the modern perception of a single goddess also

An owl mask worn to invoke the goddess Lilith. Demonized by the Christian Church, Lilith is seen by many magicians as the first feminist.

delivered a single god as her consort. He points out that before the nineteenth century many gods had a variety of associations and connections, such as Jupiter (ruler), Neptune (sea), Mercury (commerce, education, communication), Vulcan (industry), and Apollo (poetry, the natural world). For the Romantic movement the god Pan, personified as wild nature, overshadowed them all. He became a major theme in the work of Wordsworth, Keats and Shelley, and represented the English countryside. He later featured in the literary works of Robert Louis Stevenson and in Kenneth Grahame's classic children's story *The Wind in the Willows*.

Hutton observes that Pan became the expression of the natural world as sublime, mysterious, and awe-inspiring but also benevolent and comforting; this was in direct contrast to the industrial and urban environment, and represented a return to the lost innocence of a rural paganism. In witchcraft, Pan became characterized as the horned god, not least through Margaret Murray's work *The God of the Witches*, published in 1933, which was formative in shaping modern ideas about a nature god.

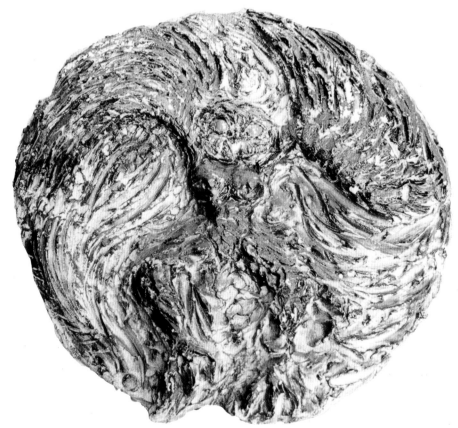

A contemporary owl goddess plaque inspired by a dream of Lilith, the fabled first wife of Adam, who rejected him and his God, and fled from Eden.

Baubo, an ancient Greek figure who perched on a well making Demeter laugh when her daughter Persephone was in the Underworld. She represents the sacrality of women's bodies for many witches today.

CELEBRATING NATURE

Referred to as a "nature religion", modern witchcraft honours the Earth and the body rather than a transcendental spirit. The physical body and all of nature are seen as inherently divine and part of a larger whole, commonly seen to consist of interconnecting energies. Many modern witches take the view that their religion is the Old Religion of the village wise woman and cunning man, who practised herbalism and divining as part of their craft. Most now accept that there is no unbroken tradition that connects their current practices with those of the cunning folk, but modern witches talk about a sense of connectedness with nature, which links them spiritually and mythologically, if not historically, to a view of life where everything is connected through various energies and forces. Many are turning to direct action to protect the environment.

A modern witch celebrates a Winter Solstice ritual in a forest.

Witches today seek a relationship with nature, and conduct rituals to create a place where it is possible to be aware of the wider connecting pattern of the universe. This is often visualized as a web, a sacred force that is the very grounding of existence. Sometimes it is envisaged as a "web of wyrd", as outlined by the psychologist Brian Bates in his books *The Way of Wyrd* (1983) and *The Wisdom of Wyrd* (1996). Human beings are seen to be a part of nature, intimately connected via a web of forces and energies.

In *Witchcraft Today*, Gerald Gardner, the founder of modern witchcraft, said that whereas ceremonial magicians used a circle to keep demons at bay, the witches that he knew worked within a magical circle to contain the power generated from their bodies. He outlined four great festivals that the witches celebrated – November eve (Hallowe'en), February eve, May eve and August eve – which corresponded to the ancient Gaelic fire festivals of Samhaim (1 November), Brigid (1 February), Bealteine or Beltene (1 May) and Lugnasadh (1 August). Gardner wrote that the festivals corresponding to midwinter and midsummer were both said to have been founded in honour of female deities, while the two winter ones were those in which the God took precedence (although "he is not superior but merely her equal").

MODERN RITUALS

Today witches create a circle as sacred space "between the worlds" into which the divine, usually personified as the Goddess and God, manifests. The witchcraft circle is always arranged according to the cardinal points of north, south, east and west. Each cardinal direction has certain attributes, which relate to the natural world. Thus the circle is usually ceremonially opened in the east because the east represents light, the first light of dawn and also

All of nature is seen to be part of a pattern of the universe to modern witches; some visualize this as a "web of wyrd", others as a manifestation of the Goddess.

the spring; it is symbolic of air, intellect and rational thought. The magical tool of the east is the athame (a ritual knife or dagger) or the sword. The south represents fire and the energy of the magical will, the summer, sun and heat. It is symbolized by the wand, a slender branch of wood. The west represents water, the emotions, rivers, oceans, streams and autumn; it is symbolized by the cup or chalice. The west flows and merges while the east separates and canalizes. The north represents the earth, mountains, valleys, winter and the body. The pentacle is its symbol: its five points represent the five senses of the human body and all the elements: earth, air, fire, water and spirit. In the centre of the circle stands a large cauldron representing transformation: of the raw into the cooked and, on the spiritual level, of changes of consciousness within the natural rhythms of nature.

Wicca operates a seasonal myth cycle whereby the processes of nature – conception, birth, maturation and death – are portrayed in dynamic interaction with the Goddess and the God as personifications of the forces and powers

Witchcraft harnesses the power of the mind, using natural objects and visualization techniques.

Many Wiccan rituals are performed outside. Here two initiates are bound into a coven.

of nature. Thus the inner self of the individual witch is linked in with the wider mythological cycle.

The Wiccans Janet and Stewart Farrar, in their book *Eight Sabbats for Witches* (1981), work with what have now become the eight standard seasonal rituals for many pagans: Yule or Winter Solstice (22 December), Imbolg (2 February), Spring Equinox (21 March), Bealtaine (30 April), Midsummer or Summer Solstice (22 June), Lughnasadh (31 July), Autumn Equinox (21 September) and Samhain (31 October).

The Farrars have adapted Gardner's ritual year to reflect what they call a solar theme and a natural-fertility theme. The Goddess does not undergo the experiences but presides over them; she is always there but changes her aspect, while the God dies and is reborn. The solar theme, which dominates the solstices and equinoxes, reflects the concept of a sacrificed and resurrected god: he dies and is reborn at the Winter Solstice, and at the Spring Equinox his waxing power impregnates Mother Earth; he reaches his prime at the Summer Solstice, then his waning powers lead through to the Autumn Equinox and his death and

Creative visualizations may be conducted outside, in the midst of nature, for inspiration.

rebirth at the Winter Solstice to complete the cycle. The natural-fertility theme involves the god of the waxing year, represented by the Oak King, and the god of the waning year, personified as the Holly King – both aspects of the horned god, a natural-fertility figure. According to the Farrars, they are light and dark aspects of each other and compete eternally for the favour of the Great Mother. At Yule the Holly King ends his reign and falls to the Oak King, while at Midsummer the Oak King is replaced by the Holly King.

THE ENVIRONMENT

Increasingly modern witches are looking to ritual sites in nature, and ancient stone monuments, to contact the energies of their ancestors, those that practised the "Old Religion". These sites, which often date from the neolithic, are often viewed as places of female mysteries and the land itself is though of as the Goddess incarnate. Believed to be gateways into the otherworld, a "dreamtime" that enables witches to connect with an inner sacred place within, these places are the locations for healing, divination, and the conducting of life rites such as handfastings (weddings). A Wiccan high priestess, Vivianne Crowley has observed that Wicca has changed its focus from the early days. She says that Gerald Gardner's original stress was on witchcraft as a fertility religion but that a more recent portrayal of witchcraft is as an environmental movement. Crowley notes that Gardner made little mention of nature, being more interested in magical powers and the traditional image of the witch as caster of spells, and points out that it was Doreen Valiente, Gardner's high priestess, who recast the concept of fertility into one that included the mind and the soul. Valiente thought that there was a spiritual as well as a material fertility, and that human life was like a desert without it. Valiente talks not so much

Stone circles are especially sacred to modern witches and other pagans as places where the Earth's energies are particularly potent.

Paganism

Nature is central to modern pagan experience, and Selena Fox, Wiccan high priestess and founder of Circle Sanctuary in the United States, describes this side of paganism:

I am Pagan. I am a part of the whole of Nature. The Rocks, the Animals, the Plants, the Elements, and the Stars are my relatives. Other humans are my sisters and brothers, whatever their races, colors, genders, sexual orientations, ages, nationalities, religions, lifestyles. Planet Earth is my home. I am a part of this large family of Nature, not the master of it. I have my own special part to play and I seek to discover and play that part to the best of my ability. I seek to live in harmony with others in the family of Nature, treating others with respect ...

I am Pagan. Nature Spirituality is my religion and my life's foundation. Nature is my spiritual teacher and holy book. I am part of Nature and

Witchcraft, as a part of modern paganism, views all of nature as sacred.

Nature is part of me. My understanding of Nature's inner mysteries grows as I journey on this spiritual path.

about literal fertility but about finding harmony with nature; she calls the star goddess the soul of nature.

According to Vivianne Crowley, Wicca has changed from a secret fertility cult to a more open movement, with nature high on its agenda. This marks a significant transition whereby Wicca moves out of the darkness of witchery to take the moral high ground of environmentalism. To be at one with nature in one's inner self is no longer enough: radical action to preserve nature is now important. While many witches are content to cast spells to help nature, others are becoming involved in direct action. So witchcraft encompasses many different practices but all are focused on nature, both within and without, rather than a transcendental spirit that is separate from the natural world.

To pagans, Nature is a source of divinity and enchantment, thought to be inhabited by spirits or "the little people".

DOREEN VALIENTE

I f Gerald Gardner was the founder and "father" of modern witchcraft, then Doreen Valiente surely is his female counterpart. It was she who carried on and expanded his work in formulating and defining this relatively new form of paganism. A modest, unassuming woman, she brought a down-to-earth, yet poetic vision to modern witchcraft practice, as well as a greater emphasis on attaining harmony with nature. At the time of her death, on 1 September 1999, she was held in great esteem as the "mother of Wicca" who had contributed to its growth as a religion, to its poetry and to the beauty of its ceremonies and ritual.

Doreen Valiente, photographed in January 1999.

Doreen Valiente, who was initiated by Gerald Gardner in 1953 and eventually became his high priestess, has had a great influence on modern witchcraft in the form of rewriting, changing and adapting Gardner's rituals. Valiente discovered Gardner's witchcraft in 1952 when she read an article on "Witchcraft in Britain" published in a magazine.

The article quoted Cecil Williamson, the owner of a witchcraft museum on the Isle of Man. He was talking about witchcraft as the "Old Religion" and telling how the witches in the New Forest had raised a "cone of power" to stop Hitler from invading Britain. Doreen Valiente, who had been interested in magic for many years, wrote to Williamson for information about contacting witches. Williamson passed her letter to Gardner who, after some correspondence, invited her to Dafo's house in Christchurch. There he gave Valiente a copy of his book *High Magic's Aid* to read for information on the witch cult.

Valiente said that her initiation was virtually identical to that described in *High Magic's Aid* except that it included something called "The Charge" (a ritual utterance from an invoked deity) which she recognized as containing passages from Leland's *Aradia* and parts of Aleister Crowley's writings. When she confronted Gardner with the inclusion of this material, he replied that he had had to supplement the fragmentary material from the old coven.

A REVISED CHARGE

Valiente accepted his challenge to revise the wording of The Charge, removing much of the borrowing from Crowley. It begins with a summons to assemble and adore the Great Mother:

A witch consecrates the salt with her athame on an altar which includes flowers to link with nature as well as magical symbolism in the pentagram and the flame of the candle.

Listen to the words of the Great Mother,
who was of old also called among men,
Artemis, Astarte, Dione, Melusine,
Aphrodite, Cerridwen, Diana,
Arianrhod, Bride, and by
many other names.
At mine Altars the youth of Lacedaemon
in Sparta made due sacrifice.
Whenever ye have need of anything,
once in the month, and better it be
when the moon is full. Then ye shall
assemble in some secret place and
adore the spirit of Me who am
Queen of all Witcheries.
There ye shall assemble, ye who are
fain to learn all sorcery, yet who
have not won its deepest secrets.
To these will I teach things that
are yet unknown ...

A *"Path to Female Empowerment"*, *planted by followers of the Goddess, which illustrates the link between nature and the female.*

A *modern practising witch holding an athame in her right hand and a scourge in her left, in the "Osiris position".*

The priestess representing the goddess identifies herself as the soul of nature:

I who am the beauty of the green earth;
and the White Moon amongst the Stars;
and the mystery of the Waters; and the
desire of the heart of man, I call unto
thy soul: arise and come unto me.
For I am the Soul of nature who giveth
life to the Universe;
From me all things proceed; and unto
me, all things must return.

The source of all knowledge lies within:

And thou who thinkest to seek me,
know that thy seeking and yearning
shall avail thee not unless thou know
the mystery, "That if that which thou
seekest thou findest not within thee,
thou wilt never find it without thee,"
for behold; I have been with thee
from the beginning, and I am that
which is attained at the end of desire.

Valiente went on to become a formative influence in the development of modern witchcraft, writing a number of books that displayed her own distinct interpretation of the "Old Religion". She recast Gardner's concept of witchcraft as a fertility religion into one that included the mind and the soul, saying that there was a spiritual as well as a material fertility, and that this spiritual fertility was found through finding harmony in nature.

In her later work Doreen Valiente came to distance herself from the position taken by Gerald Gardner, critically describing his version of the craft as rather airy-fairy. She then took instead to working with what she called traditional hereditary witchcraft with Robert Cochrane, who claimed to be a genuine hereditary witch from a long and secret tradition.

A *Wiccan initiation.*

ALEX SANDERS

At seven years old, Mr Sanders, in an austere and bloody ritual, was initiated into the cult by his grandmother. As a professional, practising witch, and having had first hand experience with the evils of black witchcraft, which brought him an immense fortune but great personal tragedy, Mr Sanders pledged himself thereafter to the furtherance of witchcraft as a benevolent religion. This is how the cover of Alex Sander's book of teachings on Alexandrian Wicca introduces its author. A composite of Gardnerian witchcraft and high magic from the hermetic tradition, Alexandrian witchcraft is often considered to be the "high church" of witchcraft, borrowing as it does from the Judaeo-Christian tradition and having elaborate and highly ritualized ceremonies

A great showman, Alex Sanders is pictured here with a skull and crossbones.

Gerald Gardner's original formulation of witchcraft was adopted by his followers, who called themselves "Gardnerians", but a later derivative group, whose members came to be known as "Alexandrians", has come to be especially influential in the development of modern witchcraft. Alex Sanders (1926–88), the self-proclaimed "King of the Witches", was its founder. He attracted many followers and boasted that he had 1,623 initiates in 100 covens, but little is known about his early involvement with witchcraft and it seems highly likely that he derived most of his material from Gardnerian sources. Sanders, who was born Orrell Alexander Carter in Birkenhead, England, was the eldest of six children, and claimed that he was initiated into witchcraft by his grandmother Mary Bibby, a cunning woman, when he was seven years old. Sanders said that he discovered her standing naked in the middle of a circle drawn on the kitchen floor. Ordering him to enter the circle and to take off his clothes, she made him bend over and cut his scrotum with a knife saying, "You are one of us now".

Sanders spent much of his early life drifting from one job to another, drinking and having sexual liaisons with men and women. After pledging himself to the "left-hand path" or "black magic" and making a fortune, he decided to use his powers for beneficent purposes such as healing. He met Maxine Morris in the 1960s and initiated her into the craft. The couple were handfasted (married) and Maxine became his high priestess.

PUBLIC WITCHCRAFT

Sanders courted publicity and a film (*Legend of the Witches*), a biography written in 1969 (*King of the Witches*) and his numerous public appearances in the media brought witchcraft into the public eye, much to the dismay of other witches who shunned the association with such a showman. He upset many prominent

Alex Sanders holds a ritual sword during an Alexandrian ritual. Maxine Sanders sits on his right.

figures, including Patricia Crowther, an initiate of Gardnerian witchcraft. In 1966 Sanders' behaviour prompted Pat Crowther and Ray Bone, another leading spokesperson for witchcraft, to make a public denunciation of Sanders, calling him an impostor because he had not been properly initiated into the Gardnerian witchcraft tradition. This forced Sanders to respond with the story about his initiation by his grandmother. He claimed that hers was the authentic craft, and that Gardner and the Gardnerians were following a later and inferior version.

In fact, Sanders based his version of witchcraft on Gardner's model but incorporated more elements of high magic, being greatly influenced by Eliphas Lévi. Some witches refer to Alexandrian witchcraft as "high church", and Gardnerian witchcraft as "low church". Sanders blurred the boundaries between paganism and Christianity and, according to the historian Ronald Hutton, this marks a distinct difference between the two traditions because Gardner was always concerned to mark a clear separation, preferring to depict himself, like Margaret Murray, as a discoverer of a surviving ancient religious tradition. Alex Sanders and

An initiation ceremony. Here the prospective candidate is blindfolded and challenged by the High Priestess and High Priest.

Maxine Morris, by contrast, portrayed themselves through their life stories as "warriors in a constant battle of good magic against bad". Sanders also placed more emphasis on practical magical techniques such as clairvoyance, astral projection, thought-transference and the use of charms and talismans.

In 1969 a reporter named Stewart Farrar interviewed Sanders for an article in the magazine *Reveille*, and Sanders invited him to attend a witch's initiation. Farrar wrote a two-part feature for the magazine and was sufficiently impressed to become involved himself. He was commissioned to write a book, later

Alex Sanders in ritual regalia.

published as *What Witches Do*, and he started attending Sanders' training classes. In the Sanders' coven he met Janet Owen and they later formed a magical partnership – and their own coven – in 1970. They have published many books on witchcraft.

A film portrayal of a witchcraft ceremony inspired by Alex Sanders' work.

Witchcraft paraphernalia; skull, wand, chalice, cord, candle, crystals and divination cards.

RAYMOND BUCKLAND

It was Raymond Buckland who was largely responsible for taking Gardnerian witchcraft to the United States. An Englishman with Romany blood, Buckland moved to America in 1962 and founded Seax-Wica, a Saxon branch of witchcraft which worships four principle deities: Woden, Thunor, Tiw and Frig or Freya. Buckland had established a relationship with Gerald Gardner when he was living on the Isle of Man and running his witchcraft museum. Impressed with Gardner's museum, Buckland set up a similar one in the United States.

In his introduction to Gardner's book *Witchcraft Today*, Raymond Buckland acknowledged his debt to Gardner, saying that all witches owed Gardner a debt of gratitude for learning his original coven's rituals and adapting them, before breaking from the group and starting his own. Buckland explained that his own life paralleled Gardner's: after being initiated into Gardnerian witchcraft by Gardner's then high priestess Monique Wilson, known as the

Lady Olwen, in Perth, Scotland, he felt it necessary after nearly 12 years to leave this tradition to found his own in the early 1970s. He saw the Saxon tradition of Seax-Wica as a more open branch of Wicca, having no oaths of secrecy.

In Gardnerian witchcraft the high priestess, in partnership with her magical working partner the high priest, is overall leader of her coven. She is seen to be the channel and representative of the Goddess and the coven cannot

Raymond Buckland in his magic regalia.

Raymond Buckland acknowledged his debt to Gardner and adapted many of his rituals.

function without her or a female representative. By contrast, in Seax-Wica men and women are seen to be equally important and a high priest can act alone. Buckland's version of Wicca has no degrees of advancement and therefore differs from other forms of modern witchcraft, which usually have three initiation degrees (in Alexandrian Wicca the second and third may be taken together). The first is often an introduction to the Goddess, and a time for understanding the unconscious: a man must find aspects of himself in the Goddess, while a woman must absorb qualities that she has projected elsewhere. The second initiation concerns the descent to the underworld, to face fears and find the self. The third initiation concerns the bringing together of all aspects of the person to discover the wisdom within.

SEAX-WICCA

Buckland's system allows for self-initiation by the performance of a rite of self-dedication, after which the initiate may start their own coven. The self-initiate stands with both arms lifted facing an altar and says:

> Woden and Freya, hear me now!
> I am here a simple pagan
> holding thee in honor.
> Far have I journeyed and long
> have I searched,
> Seeking that which I desire above all things.
> I am of the trees and of the fields.
> I am of the woods and of the springs;
> The streams and the hills.
> I am of thee; and thee of me ...

However, it is preferred that the initiate is introduced and trained in the customary manner, and there are three categories of relative involvement in Seax-Wica. The first is the Theows: those who do not belong to the Saxon craft, but attend the rituals by invitation. This introduction may lead to a request for further involvement and training leading to initiation, when the neophyte is termed a Ceorl. After a period of time – anything from a month to a year depending on the person's spiritual

A Wiccan Samhain (Hallowe'en) ceremony with the high priestess crowning the high priest.

development – the neophyte is initiated and becomes a Gesith, after which there is no further degree of advancement. Buckland claims that this counters any tendency for one person to become too powerful, and helps to stop any egoism developing. Recognizing that it was not

possible for everyone to go through the course of training, Buckland tried to make the craft more accessible to earnest seekers. He started many covens and established the Seax-Wica Seminary correspondence school in Virginia in the early 1970s, later moving to San Diego. He has written many books about witchcraft but has subsequently turned his attention to writing about Gypsies. He notes that the Romany word for "witch" is "shuvihani" (the masculine form is "shuvihano") meaning "wise one", the implication being that the witch is knowledgable in all aspects of the occult. A shuvihani has experience of magical beliefs and practices; she is not considered evil in any way. Many shuvihanis undertake a vision quest similar to the Native American Indians to gain previously unknown knowledge.

Thus Buckland has, as a "poshrat", or half-blood Romany, sought to understand and practise both witchcraft and gypsy magic. Like Alex Sanders he adapted Gardnerian witchcraft to his own ideas and experience. In this sense Wicca has proved to be a flexible set of techniques open to much interpretation.

Wiccan high priest and priestess of the Gardnerian tradition, the foundation for Buckland's own interpretation of witchcraft.

HEREDITARY WITCHCRAFT

While most witches now accept that their religion is a modern recreation of paganism that links back to a past spiritually rather than historically, others reject this and assert that their practices have been handed down through family tradition. Many of the beliefs and practices of hereditary witches can be traced back to the work of Charles Godfrey Leland, and his research on the supposedly secret religion of witches who worshipped the goddess Diana and the god Lucifer.

It is now fairly well estblished that modern witchcraft was formulated in the early 1950s. A significant minority, however, claim that they do belong to an unbroken inherited tradition, that comes to them through their own family rather than any social inheritance. Scholarship on this subject has so far failed to provide any proof to support these claims. Most hereditary witches draw on the work of Margaret Murray and her view that the Old Religion was a fragmented form of pagan religion, which had managed to survive centuries of Christian persecution. Others claim that their traditions stem directly from the Italian witchcraft explored in the writings of Charles Godfrey Leland, especially his book *Aradia: Gospel of the Witches*, published in 1899.

THE COCHRANE COVEN

Robert Cochrane claimed that he was a hereditary witch who was initiated at the age of five, his practice passing through his family. A former blacksmith, he named his coven the Clan of the Tubal Cain after a smith in Hebrew legend. Doreen Valiente was initiated into Gardnerian Wicca in 1953. In a book called *Witchcraft: A Tradition Renewed* (1990) she collaborated with another initiate from Cochrane's coven, Evan John Jones, to put forward the basic ways of working according to this tradition.

An ideal coven structure consisted of 13 members: six men and six women, with the Lady – who directed proceedings, dedicated the circle, led celebrants in, dedicated the cakes and wine, and closed the ritual – as the thirteenth.

Each of the correspondences had an officer associated with it: the north was attended by the "Dark One", the Hag; the south by the Mother aspect of the Goddess; the east by a young man who symbolized light; the west by a male guardian of the gates of the underworld. The rest of the coven was made up of initiates and apprentices, who served an apprenticeship of a year and a day. A "Man in Black" maintained contact between covens; and a "Summoner", while keeping contact with the Man in Black, acted as a record-keeper and also organized such things as transport to ritual sites. Cochrane's coven followed a Gardnerian pattern of rites – celebrating

Lucifer, or the Devil, is another representation of the horned god or Pan, the goat-footed god of nature, life and vitality.

Tradition is an important part of modern magic and much folklore and many beliefs are passed on through museums, such as this witchcraft museum in Cornwall.

the Great Sabbats of Candlemas, May Eve, Lammas, and Hallowe'en, and also the Lesser Sabbats of the equinoxes and solstices – but there were also important differences. They assigned air to the north (earth in Gardnerian Wicca), earth to the south (fire in the Gardnerian tradition) and fire to the east (air in Gardnerian Wicca), while the west was associated with water as in the Gardnerian tradition. Ronald Hutton noted that there was more emphasis upon the God as Lord of Death than in Gardner's tradition, and that the Man in Black or "Magister" functioned as high priest in the role of divine sacrificial king; in this he was supported by the Maid or Lady. The Magister also conducted a rite before the ceremonial consumption of cakes and wine, dipping his knife into a cup of wine in which the moon was reflected by the use of a mirror. Doreen Valiente noted that Cochrane's rituals were more spontaneous and shamanistic, more earthy than those of Gardner, and that this was partly because the coven did not use a Book of Shadows in which to record rituals, leading to more creativity.

A hereditary coven will often work its rituals and celebrations outside.

Charles Leland

Raven Grimassi used the works of Charles Godfrey Leland, particularly *Aradia* (the Italianized name of Herodias, who was portrayed as a villain in the New Testament for her part in the death of John the Baptist) to trace the alleged origins of his craft. Leland wrote that the Italian witch came from a family in which her calling or art had been practised for many generations. In 1886 he had met a woman called Maddelena who claimed to be a witch. She had apparently inherited a collection of family charms and invocations that could heal, break curses and invoke certain spirits. Leland used these and employed her as a research assistant to find out more about the secret religion of the witches. In particular he sought to find the gospel of its body of beliefs, and eventually Maddelena managed to provide him with such a manuscript obtained from oral sources. What Leland considered to be an ancient pagan religion was thus recorded.

A portrait of Charles Godfrey Leland.

The frontispiece of Leland's seminal and highly influential work, Aradia.

Ronald Hutton concluded that Cochrane used a Wiccan framework to develop his own ideas and practices, and called it hereditary witchcraft.

Cochrane's hereditary legacy lives on in a coven named the Regency, which was formed on Hallowe'en in 1966 by two former members of Cochrane's coven. They combined his ideas with those of Ruth Wynn Owen, who also claimed to be a hereditary witch coming from a family with psychic skills whose rituals were similar to Wicca in their veneration of a god and goddess. The hereditary craft spread to America through the work of Joseph Wilson, who developed the "1734 tradition", a special numerological value based on Robert Graves' *The White Goddess* (1948).

RAVEN GRIMASSI

Also claiming to be a hereditary witch in the "Strega Tradition" of old Italy, Raven Grimassi was taught by his mother about the Old Religion. He says that the old faith is based on the belief that spirits inhabit both physical objects and all of nature, and that he learnt that it was possible to call up the fairy folk. This was done by pouring milk, honey and wine into a bowl, putting it under a myrtle bush and then swinging a reed tied to a string in a clockwise circle while whistling. A rustling of the leaves signified that the fairies had come.

DIANA

The old faith focused on deities personified as the great Goddess, represented by Diana, and the horned god, represented by Lucifer. The myth of Diana tells that she was the first to be created and in her were all things. She divided herself into darkness and light: her brother and son Dianus was her other half and was the light, while she was the dark. When Diana saw the beauty of the light she yearned for it and swallowed it up in delight. This desire was the dawn. However, Dianus fled from her and would not yield to her wishes. Diana lamented to the Fathers of the Beginning, to the Mothers and the Spirits, and they told her that to rise she must fall and that therefore she had to become

The goddess Diana is closely associated with the moon in hereditary witchcraft. She is seen here in part of a series of reliefs depicting the planetary symbols and signs of the zodiac.

Diana is always depicted as a beautiful goddess with an essentially feminine aspect.

mortal. So Diana descended to earth with Dianus, where she taught magic and sorcery; thus witches and magicians came to be. Her brother Dianus had a cat, which slept on his bed. One day Diana took the form of a cat like her brother's; she lay with her brother and in the darkness assumed her own form. This is how Diana became the mother of Aradia. Dianus was angry, but Diana sang a spell to keep him silent. She hummed a song like the buzzing of bees and the spinning of a wheel. Like a spinning wheel spinning life, she spun the lives of men. All things are said to be spun from the wheel of Diana, while Dianus turned the wheel.

Grimassi says that the Gardnerian tradition took on elements of Italian witchcraft from the works of Charles Leland: part of the Charge of the Goddess contains elements of Leland's material, and other borrowings are full-moon gatherings, worship of a goddess, ritual celebrations involving cakes and wine and worshipping naked.

Wiccan ritual celebrations may have been inspired by traditions that were handed down by hereditary witchcraft, according to some.

Some hereditary witches say that Gardnerian witches borrowed elements – such as worshipping naked – from their tradition.

FEMINIST WITCHCRAFT

Feminist witchcraft is a later variant of modern witchcraft. It is now primarily associated with the work of Starhawk, an influential figure in feminist witchcraft, and has a strong political dimension. Feminist witches often work with what they term ecstasy, rather than the feminine/masculine polarity, which is central to Gardnerian Wicca. Magical work for social change – to end patriarchal oppression – is also a predominant part of their rituals.

In the 1970s the women's liberation movement produced a general critique of world religions, which, it was said, denied women's experience. Two differing branches of feminist spirituality emerged: those keen to reform orthodox religions and those who looked to pre-Christian goddesses such as those celebrated in modern witchcraft. Ideas of the witch as a freedom fighter against patriarchy were used by American radical feminists. According to Rachel Hasted, writing in the magazine *Trouble and Strife* (1985), the original WITCH (Women Inspired To Commit Herstory) group accepted ready-made "facts" about the witch-craze in Europe and claimed that nine million witches had been burned as revolutionary fighters against patriarchy and class oppression. They drew on the work of Jules Michelet, Joslyn Gage and Margaret Murray. Each of these writers had contributed to the idea that there was an underground movement of women's spirituality, originating from matriarchal times, which had been suppressed.

The French historian Jules Michelet's *La Sorcière* (1862) had interpreted witch hunters' records as a massive peasant rebellion and rejection of Christianity in which pagan priestesses led a doomed peasants' revolt against the oppression of a Christian ruling class. Matilda Joslyn Gage, a radical leader of the US suffrage movement, had argued in *Woman, Church and State* (1893) that witchcraft and the occult were a form of knowledge that was based on the worship of a female deity which had been outlawed by a jealous patriarchy. Margaret Murray's *The Witch-Cult in Western Europe* (1921) had claimed that European witchcraft was an ancient pre-Christian fertility religion, which had survived among the peasantry.

Feminist witchcraft's mythical origins lie in a golden woman-centred age before patriarchal religions came to dominate both women and nature. Judaeo-Christian traditions were seen to have deepened the split, finally establishing a duality between spirit and matter. Women became identified with matter, nature, the body, sexuality, evil and the Devil, and had to be controlled, while the male God was uncontaminated by birth, menstruation and decay and was removed to

Jules Michelet, the French historian who studied the records of the witch hunters.

the realm of the spirit. Feminist witchcraft, in common with Wicca, has a holistic vision of the world: the Goddess is seen to link people with nature; she is seen to be within every human being and her worship involves celebrating life: she is associated with renewal and the regeneration of life.

The origins of Goddess-worship are traced to ancient, peaceful, egalitarian cultures where the change of seasons and lunar and solar cycles were experienced as mystic bonds linking humanity with nature. Much of this feminist reinterpretation of witchcraft is based on the work of the archaeologist Marija Gimbutas, who attributed a single religious system of Goddess-worship to both palaeolithic hunter-gatherers and neolithic farmers and horticulturalists. Gimbutas claimed that when food-gathering gave way to food-producing, leading to a settled way of life, there was no corresponding change in the religious symbolism – the Goddess ruled throughout. According to Gimbutas, this peaceable old European culture was overrun by violent patriarchal invasions between 4300 and 2800BC. The anthropologist Ruby Rohrlich disagrees with this view and

The old stereotype of the witch shown in this illustration has recently been recast by feminists.

points to the earliest civilizations in Sumer, Egypt, India and China, and also the societies of the Incas and the Aztecs, claiming that they gradually transformed themselves from peaceable, women-centred enclaves into warring, stratified cultures. She argues that the changes were made from within rather than by patriarchal invaders from without. Nevertheless, the idea that there was a peaceful, Goddess-focused, pre-patriarchal society is very common among feminist witches.

ZSUZSANNA BUDAPEST (1940–)

In 1971, "women's mysteries" were created in Malibu, USA. According to Zsuzsanna Budapest, a group of women sat around a weatherbeaten old café table eating eggs and potatoes, drinking coffee, talking and fantasizing and laughing, and knowing that they were doing something revolutionary that was going to influence the world. Budapest, who claims that she comes from a long line of witches, and that she is the "last branch of an 800-year-old family tree", says that her mother Masika was the result of an immaculate conception, and was taught all the arts of witchcraft by a very well-known witch from Transylvania.

Spiritual Suffrage

The Susan B. Anthony Coven No.1 was started by Zsuzsanna Budapest on the winter solstice in 1971 in Hollywood. It was named after the suffragist Susan B. Anthony, a leading campaigner for women's suffrage and president of the National American Woman's Suffrage Association. When Anthony was asked what she would do in the afterlife, she reputedly answered "When I die, I shall go neither to heaven nor hell, but stay right here and finish the women's revolution', a comment that inspired Budapest to acknowledge Anthony as an ancestress, whose work should be honoured and continued.

The American feminist Susan B. Anthony.

Budapest was part of a Malibu core group of eight women who created what has been termed the "Dianic tradition" of feminist witchcraft by celebrating rituals together and contributing their experiences to *The Holy Book of Women's Mysteries* (1989). Dianic tradition witches are usually either celibate or lesbian.

This form of witchcraft is based on Wicca and shares its structure: the coven is composed of up to 13; sabbaths are held on the same festivals; the ritual structure is based on a circle and four quarters. Other similarities are the emphasis on feasting and sexuality; witches are supposed to enter the circle "in perfect love and perfect trust"; the naked body is seen to represent truth; and the abiding moral maxim is "Do as thou wilt and harm none". The main differences focus on the central role of politics and an emphasis on democratic working (whereas Gardner's system was based on a hierarchical, initiatory system of three degrees); and the primacy of the Goddess, sometimes to the total exclusion of the God.

Feminist politics have been central to the practice from the start and Budapest speaks of the difficulties of combining religion with politics in the early days. For Budapest, spirituality concerns the struggle to liberate the religious woman inside by the creation of a faith system that will serve women. She has written that in the true beginning, before the Judaeo-Christian Genesis, "the Goddess was revealed to her people as the Soul of the Wild. Called Holy Mother, she was known to be a Virgin who lived in wild places and acted through mysterious powers. Known also as Artemis, She was worshipped in the moonlight, and young nymphs and maidens were called to serve in Her rituals. The Holy Mother, Virgin, Artemis was also called by the name Dia Anna, 'Nurturer Who Does Not Bear Young'."

Women and the earth are seen as especially sacred in feminist and Goddess spirituality. This is a ritual at the Goddess Festival in Glastonbury, England, honouring the powers of nature.

Starhawk leading a spiral dance in America: she is the central figure holding a drum. The spiral dance gathers everyone and engenders a feeling of collectivity and connectedness.

STARHAWK (1951–)

Starhawk (Miriam Simos), the woman who has had the most formative effect on feminist witchcraft, attended her first ritual with the Susan B. Anthony Coven, according to Budapest. Starhawk's background is Jewish and she still sees herself as Jewish but she sought an alternative spirituality because "in Judaism there were no images of powerful women". She also had powerful spiritual experiences, which did not fit Judaism because they "seemed to take place in nature or in the context of sexuality", and in traditional Jewish circles at this time these were not discussed.

THE FAERY TRADITION

In 1975 Starhawk began to study with Victor Anderson and was initiated into the Faery (Feri) tradition as taught by him. Victor Anderson and Gwydion Pendderwen founded the Faery tradition of witchcraft, and it is likely that Anderson was influenced by Margaret Murray's work on fairies. Anderson was allegedly initiated into the craft by witches who called themselves faeries, and he worked in covens with people from southern America and practised a "devotional science", harmonizing with nature, performing magic and engaging in ecstatic dancing. Anderson was also initiated into the Harpy coven in Oregon in 1932. This was eclectic, mixing Huna from Hawaii with varieties of folk magic more common in the rest of the United States. There was an emphasis on practical magic and little concern with worship, theology, ethics or ritual.

According to the Faery tradition, there is a Mother-Father God called the "Drychton" (after the Anglo-Saxon word for "lord" or "ruler") who is the male-female power, being both the God and the Goddess. In the beginning, according to the mythology, the light from the stars bounced off the curved mirror of space in the directions of left and right and produced the other deities: the gods on one side and the goddesses on the other. Above all, the Faery tradition is an ecstatic one – rather than one that is based on fertility, as in Gardner's original formulation of Wicca – and the aim is to become one with the gods. The sexes are seen to be equal and there is no high priestess in overall charge. Later, Alexandrian witchcraft material was incorporated into the tradition.

In her first work, *The Spiral Dance: A rebirth of the ancient religion of the Great Goddess* (1979), Starhawk located the origins of Goddess-religion in peaceful neolithic Europe, which suffered attack from patriarchal Indo-European warrior tribes. Starhawk's view of the history of the "Goddess peoples", which is heavily influenced by the now discredited theories of Margaret Murray, is based on their escape from persecution from waves of invasion by warrior gods, who drove the Goddess peoples out of the

Another performance of the sacred spiral dance, this time in Glastonbury, England. The dance begins with all the participants holding hands and beginning a winding snake-like movement around the room, during which a complex pattern allows everyone to have contact with each other at some point.

fertile lowlands into the hills and high mountains, where they became known as the sidhe, pixies, fair folk or faeries.

Murray had claimed, in *The Witch-Cult in Western Europe* (1921), that witch beliefs were associated with an early European dwarf race, which at one time inhabited Europe and survived in stories of fairies and elves, and that every seven years they made a human sacrifice to their god. According to Murray, fairies gradually became identified with witches. Both fairies and witches were said to cast and break spells, heal, divine for lost objects and the future, "traffick" with the Devil, change shape, fly, levitate and steal unbaptized children.

Starhawk builds up a picture of the faeries based on the ideas of Victor Anderson and Margaret Murray. According to her version, the faeries preserved the pre-Christian, pre-patriarchal Old Religion: they bred cattle in the stony hills and lived in turf-covered round huts. Clan mothers, called Queens of Elphame, led covens, together with a priest, the sacred king, who embodied the dying God who died a mock death at the end of his term of office. They celebrated the eight festivals of the wheel of the year with "wild processions on horseback, singing, chanting, and the lighting of ritual fires". Starhawk writes that the sacred king, or high priest, held office for nine years, after which he underwent a ritual death, abdicated and joined the council of elders.

POLITICS

There is a political thread running through all of Starhawk's writing. She contrasts a peaceful vision of society where all are honoured and live in empathy with the natural world, with a culture based on the dominance of some people over others and the destruction of the environment. In *Dreaming the Dark* (1982) she says that the "burning times", when women were persecuted as witches in Europe, were linked to a stealing of common land, natural resources and knowledge by a culture based on what she calls a "consciousness of estrangement". She contrasts this with the "consciousness of immanence",

The Goddess is worshipped in many guises. Here a "black Madonna" is venerated at the Goddess conference in Glastonbury.

which she claims is found in women, sexuality and magic. In her next book *Truth or Dare* (1990), she focused on ancient Sumerian Mesopotamia, and wrote about a spiritual battle of power between the priestesses of the temple and the king. Initially, she says, these roles were elected and based on an equal relationship, ritually maintained, but eventually the king usurped power: refusing to relinquish his kingship to an elected successor, he passed it on to his sons instead. This changed the relationship with the priestesses of the temple, and relations with women in general, by establishing an oppressive patriarchy with its consciousness of estrangement. In her novels *The Fifth Sacred Thing* (1993), which is set in the

year 2040, and *Walking to Mercury* (1997), which is a fictionalized autobiography, Starhawk finally developed the "fantasy of a living future", which is briefly outlined at the end of *Truth or Dare*. Starhawk's works offer a vision of the future by using the imagination, which is the basis of magic, to envision a different reality.

Moving away from Dianic witchcraft, Starhawk includes men in her version of witchcraft. However, men have to learn how to be non-oppressive and how to discover, or rediscover, the parts of themselves that have been repressed by patriarchy. Starhawk's vision of witchcraft combines political activism and therapeutic techniques within a spiritual system loosely based on Wicca.

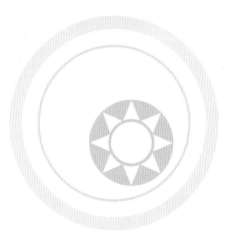

WESTERN MAGIC TODAY

Western magical practices, including modern witchcraft, offer a kaleidoscope of paths or techniques for attaining alternate forms of consciousness. All of these attempt to go beyond ordinary, everyday awareness to achieve a heightened state which some, such as high magicians who practise "Western mysteries", describe as contact with a deity or angels. Others, such as chaos magicians, strive to achieve an altered state of consciousness by deconditioning the self to obtain inner knowledge. Many, but not all, of those who have an interest in Western magic see the world in a spiritual way, and so the link that magic has had with religion in the past is still in evidence.

TODAY'S MAGICIANS

By using a variety of different techniques, magicians learn to see themselves as part of a magical whole – a wider pattern underlying all of life, including the seen and the unseen. There are many different paths – from the various forms of modern witchcraft, where people of either sex work alone or with others, to New Age, which has a very wide variety of different expressions and beliefs. What these different branches of Western magic share is that most followers and practitioners seek communication with what is often termed the "otherworld", a realm of spirit beings, defined or personalized in many ways. A trained magician can move in and out of contact with the otherworld with facility, in much the same way as shamans have done in times past, and still do today.

Who are the people who practise magic today in Western cultures? To call them magicians is likely to conjure up an image of Tolkien's Gandalf striding into the unknown, staff in hand, long robes and hair flowing in the wind. This romantic image has currency among those who practise magic, helping to add glamour and bring mystery into many magical traditions. Alternatively, magicians may be seen as Satanists, evildoers, part of a malevolent cosmic force working against God and the forces of good. Neither of these images are how most modern magicians see themselves, and most would strongly assert that they use magical powers for healing and positive purposes rather than for negative or

Modern Western magic often forms an alternative religious or spiritual practice today, and much of the symbolism remains the same.

destructive ends. There are many magical practices and paths to choose from today. A glance at the noticeboard in a local occult or New Age bookstore will reveal advertisements for courses, groups, healing, astrological consultation and much more; as will any of a number of specialist magazines. It is possible to join a witchcraft coven, train as a high or ceremonial magician in an occult school, become a druid, engage in a whole variety of New Age activities, practise Western forms of shamanism, perform magical rituals within the Northern or Nordic tradition, or become a chaos magician. These magical groups and traditions offer a kaleidoscope of ways of engaging in magic.

A magical world-view is a different way of seeing the world; it is holistic – often viewed as an interconnected web of forces and energies, which may be communicated and worked with, or controlled and directed. Each magical tradition will have a slightly different

White-robed druids celebrating Spring Equinox at Tower Hill, London, by sowing seed and making blessings for new life.

emphasis and way of working. For example, witches may prefer to work outside in nature, while high magicians may work in a specially consecrated temple dedicated to Egyptian deities, and a modern Western shamanic practitioner may go on spirit journeys conducted within a drumming circle. Many modern magical practices have adopted the eight seasonal festivals of the year developed by Gerald Gardner and his druid friend Ross Nichols. These festivals are seen to be the points where the magician links in with the wider forces of the cosmos. This is based on the understanding that the human being, as magician, witch, druid or shaman, is part of a wider pattern of life. This pattern of life includes the unseen as well as the seen.

Some magical practices offer training and a series of graduated initiations as part of a process for opening up awareness of magical forces and energies. By using various different techniques, such as meditation, guided path-workings or visionary journeys, the initiate is encouraged to value and focus on realities that are not always apparent in the everyday, ordinary world. This may mean learning to experience and

feel using intuition as well as using the critical faculties of the mind; it also involves learning to see significant connections between what would previously have been seen as separate events. It concerns coming to value the

Not all magical practices are viewed as spiritual traditions. This Baphomet statue is celebrated by chaos magicians who see magic primarily as a technique for changing consciousness.

Modern witchcraft can be practised in many different ways. People work alone or together and are free to formulate their own rituals.

connections of the whole as part of a spiritual journey that leads into another reality. This reality is often called the "otherworld" and it may be described in terms of spirits, deities and a whole range of other beings that are believed to inhabit this other dimension. Communication with the otherworld is possible through the active imagination, when the mind is in a state of light trance. The otherworld is said to co-exist with the ordinary world, and a trained magician can move in and out of these different forms of awareness with ease.

An important part of many magical practices is being able to see the seen and the unseen. Here, a crystal ball is being used to access the deeper parts of consciousness to gain what is seen to be spiritual truth.

WESTERN MYSTERIES

M odern magic's central ethos is working with the idea of spiritual evolution – the bringing down of higher angelic or elemental forces into the magician. This bringing down is a process that is thought to enable the soul to evolve; an idea which has been at the centre of much religious thought. Practitioners of Western Mysteries often work with esoteric versions of Christianity to seek unity with God. They may also use Egyptian myths, such as that of Isis and Osiris, to access what they see as deep levels of inner knowledge and wisdom in the name of spiritual and divine truth, or the legends and myths of other cultures, such as the British Arthurian legends.

Angels play an important role in Western magical traditions.

High or ceremonial magic, or "Western Mysteries", is a form of European magic distinguished by modern magicians from eastern magical systems. For those magicians who practise the Western Mysteries, all life forms – animals, plants, rocks – are evolving, but human beings are often seen as the supreme carriers of divinity, and they consequently have a responsibility to other life forms.

Magical rituals are frequently based on mythological themes and cycles concerning life and death, such as those of Isis and Osiris, and the descent into the underworld as undergone by Persephone. Each myth is seen to reveal a deeper inner truth. Western Mysteries are a magical form of Neoplatonism whereby the individual soul of the magician seeks reunion with the divine One. This frequently encompasses versions of esoteric Christianity which seek unity with divinity after the Fall, and concerns the mastery of the lower self and baser nature in the spiritual pursuit of the Ultimate Being. This is seen in terms of a union of the magician's soul with the One. It is said that the primordial teachings came from Egypt and were derived from the lost island of Atlantis.

The Western Mysteries are usually taught in occult schools and have initiation schemes whereby the apprentice may progress to a number of different levels or degrees, each of which

Each angel is seen as a being of pure consciousness in profound union with God.

has an appropriate outward insignia – for example, a distinctively coloured robe or girdle. Western Mystery magical work is usually focused on working with Cabbalistic path workings or meditation on certain spheres of the tree of life. Group rituals are conducted in a lodge or a temple dedicated to a deity.

ANGELS

Most Western Mystery schools work with the idea of spiritual evolution and the bringing down of higher angelic forces into the magician to aid the soul's progress. This developed from the Hermetic tradition, which attempted to rise above the deceptions of sense by attunement to the divine mind through the contemplation of the universe. The practice is concerned with raising a fallen human nature in a wider movement of spiritual evolution. According to the high magician David Goddard, from the One, which is beyond understanding or comprehension, comes an overflowing of eternal love that expresses itself in a multitude of beings. The One is a creator and through this overflowing of love comes creation. The One becomes many – the seven great spirits of the Elohim, seven princes, archangels or "lords of flame": the Elohim form a prism through which the One is refracted and through which the One acts. Each angel is a being of pure consciousness and is in profound union with the One, beyond time or space, channelling the divine light without distortion. An angel is a focus of power, wisdom, beauty and love, and they have a teaching function. For David Goddard, Michael helps in matters of achievement and ambition; Gabriel is concerned with psychic development; Samael is invoked for courage or perseverence; Raphael is a specialist in healing and communication; Sachiel helps in financial matters; Asariel rules in mediumship and trancework; Haniel is associated with the devas of nature; Cassiel supervises the energies of the planet; and Uriel transmits the Magical Force. Thus angels can be invoked in times of trouble or consternation to give practical and spiritual insight.

Some modern magicians use Egyptian myths as part of their magical practices.

Angels are called on to help in a whole range of human concerns and dilemmas.

THE ARTHURIAN LEGEND

The mythology of King Arthur and his Knights of the Round Table is important to magicians following the Western Mysteries because, like most other mythologies, they provide a moral and spiritual model on which to base magical practice.

Arthur is a Celtic hero, the son of King Uther Pendragon and the Lady Igraine, and his birth was made possible by the magical workings of Merlin the magician. The earliest written historical record of Arthur is in the *Historia Brittonum* (compiled in the early ninth century) which says that "the warrior Arthur" fought with the kings of the Britons against the Saxons, whom he conquered in 12 battles conducted in the sixth century. Arthur's entry into legend was effected by Geoffrey of Monmouth, who mixed these historical fragments with local traditions and Celtic myth. Consequently, Arthur and Merlin are hybrids, blending historical people with mythological characters.

THE ROMANCE OF ARTHUR

According to legend, Arthur was a fifth-century Christianized British warrior who made a stand against the barbarian Anglo-Saxon invaders from Denmark and Germany when Roman rule collapsed in AD400. Writing in the twelfth century, Geoffrey of Monmouth portrayed Arthur's reign as the climax of the history of the kings of Britain. Drawing on Welsh monastic writing, Breton folklore, poems and legends, he created the realm of Arthur as a piece of literary fiction. Arthur came to preside over a court with complex codes of etiquette and expression: jousts and combats were conducted under strict

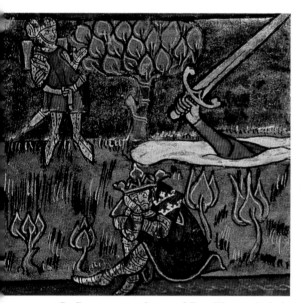

Bedivere returns the sword Excalibur to the lady of the lake, as Arthur dies in the foreground.

moral and ethical rules of behaviour. The language of courtly love was based on the theme of unattainable passion – the beloved was seen to embody the image of the divine and was married to another. Underpinning the whole was a deeper dimension of the spiritual quest: the court was the point of departure for adventures into the otherworld.

The Round Table was set up by Merlin and had places for 150 knights, who were all equal in rank and loyal to King Arthur, who was first among equals. The knights embarked on quests, venturing deep into primeval forests, and these were metaphors for the soul's journey through uncharted

The central magical figure of the Arthurian legends is Merlin. Here, he comes under the enchantment of the Lady Nimue, the female magic figure who inherited his wisdom and who acts as a benign counterbalance to Arthur's sister, the malevolent female sorceress, Morgan le Fey.

worlds. The quest is an archetypal image of a spiritual search for the soul: Jason's quest for the golden fleece and Dante's wanderings in the dark forest to find an earthly paradise are but two examples. The goal of the quest could be a person, such as a maiden in distress, or a divine object such as the Holy Grail.

THE QUEST FOR THE GRAIL

The Grail is a complex symbol with many meanings. Allegedly the cup from the Last Supper used to collect the blood of Christ, it was said to have been brought from Palestine to Britain via Spain and North Africa by Joseph of Arimathea. It is associated with Glastonbury in Somerset, sometimes called the sacred Isle of Avalon, where Joseph of Arimathea founded the first Christian community. The Grail is seen to be a sacred vessel that contains the potentiality of all wisdom, intuition and knowledge; it is also thought to be the source of creativity and inspiration; it is a magical chalice of transformation, a cauldron of rebirth. It is thought to be able to effect a form of spiritual alchemy, bringing about a higher form of consciousness; it is held that it can bring healing; it is also symbolic of the female power of the womb, and of the Goddess. The myth of King Arthur offers magicians a range of heroic patterns or archetypes with which to identify in a personal quest for a higher form of consciousness whereby the ordinary, everyday consciousness is dissolved, purification ensues, and the individual soul is reunited with the One.

AN ETHICAL MODEL

The Arthurian legend and the figures within it are important components of the Western Mysteries for many magicians. This is because the Western Mysteries are a form of Neoplatonism – a philosophical view of the world that gives a view of the universe and explains the human position within it. Above all, it outlines how human beings can achieve salvation by restoring their original divine nature in union with God. Arthurian mythology offers a moral and ethical model for this purpose.

The Grail was allegedly the cup used by Jesus and his disciples at the Last Supper, and then later to collect the blood of Christ during his crucifixion. Once thought of as a mark of spiritual purity, the Grail today represents the potentiality of all wisdom, intuition and creativity for many magicians.

Symbolic of magical transformation, the Grail represents a form of spiritual alchemy to bring about a higher form of consciousness. This twelfth-century depiction shows the cup standing at the centre of the round table, another very potent symbol within the Arthurian legend.

DRUIDRY

The druids are thought to have been Celtic spiritual leaders, but exactly who they were and what they did remains unknown. What information is available comes from Roman sources but pagan Celtic beliefs were intensely localized and few generalizations can be made. It is clear that the druids have been imagined in various ways in different periods, from the Renaissance to the Romantic movement, and more recently in the 1970s as part of the general expansion of spiritualities in Western cultures. Once only associated with men in white robes, celebrating the solstice at Stonehenge, today druidry is interpreted more widely as a spirituality in touch with nature.

Stonehenge is particularly associated with the druids, as this nineteenth-century aquatint shows.

The esoteric origins of modern druidism are located in the Western Mystery mythological tradition. Philip Carr-Gomm, the current chief of the Order of Bards, Ovates and Druids, says that the magicians of Atlantis discovered the secrets of nature and worked in tune with her powers. However, some used their powers for selfish ends and there developed a struggle between good, or white, magic and bad, or black, magic. The battle lines were drawn between those who saw in nature the great divine Mother of men and used her gifts for human welfare, and those who saw nature as a Satanic temptress with cruel power. As catastrophe struck Atlantis, the dark lords were engulfed while the white sages, having greater gifts of foreknowledge, journeyed both east and west. In the west they landed on the shore of America, and in the east, on the shores of Ireland and the western coasts of Britain, and so Druidry spread.

Human sacrifices were said to have been put in wicker-work images and burnt by the Celts, supposedly to promote the fertility of the land.

DRUID FESTIVALS

Today, modern druids celebrate the same eight festivals as witches. In druidism these are called: Samhuinn (31 October–2 November), Winter Solstice or Alban Arthuan (Light of Arthur), Imbolc or Oimelc (2 February), Spring Equinox, Beltane (1 May), Summer Solstice or Alban Heruin (21 or 22 June), Lughnasadh (1 August) and Autumnal Equinox or Alban Elued (21 September). Of these festivals, Samhuinn is the time when "the veil between this world and the World of the Ancestors is drawn aside" and druids prepare to make contact with the spirits of the departed as living spirits of loved ones who hold the "root wisdom of the tribe" as a source of guidance. There is much variety in druid rituals and they differ from group to group. Sometimes members adapt or completely rewrite rituals for their own use. According to Philip Shallcrass, the British Druid Order rituals are based on the story of Lleu Llaw Gyffes in the *Mabinogion*, a collection of supposedly Welsh Celtic myths. According to Ronald Hutton, however, they were popular international tales with their origins in Egypt, India or China, which had spread across Asia and Europe and were mixed with Irish and British myths. They were put in their final form by a courtly entertainer by the late eleventh century, when they were probably not more than a century or two old.

DRUID BELIEF SYSTEMS

Shallcrass points out that there is no central druid theology but that two generalizations about druid beliefs can be made: the first is that there is a belief in a power or energy resident in the earth or in nature, which is often represented as a mother, but it is left to individuals to decide how they wish to look upon this entity; the second is that there is some kind of unified force underlying the manifest world, but again that force is defined by each individual.

Emma Restall-Orr, joint chief with Philip Shallcrass of the British Druid Order, says that druidism includes a whole spectrum of beliefs but that a love of the earth is what holds druids together. Restall-Orr describes druidism as an animistic faith, not a "call of the gods". Communing with nature means learning to grow, to trust and to hear the response of the earth. Nature as deity is drawn down into the ritual circle and this is experienced as joy and love. The internalization of love, joy and inspiration is called "Awen" in modern druidism, and it is the role of bards – as poets and musicians – to encourage the flow of Awen. Ovates, or vates, have a different function: they listen to the voices of the otherworld using various forms of divination such as tree lore and

Modern druids celebrate dawn within the circle at Stonehenge at the Summer Solstice or Alban Heruin. A vigil is held through the night and as dawn breaks a ceremony marks the sun's rising. A further ritual is held at noon.

runes. Ovates are facilitators, healers, "changers of situations", and their role is to interpret signs and ask questions. Tree lore is associated with a symbolic language called Ogham (pronounced o'um), which links a tree with a letter of the alphabet, and runes are a series of symbols often inscribed on wood or stone. They are associated with the Norse god Odin, who hung upside down on the cosmic tree Yggdrasil, and through his suffering came to understand the cosmic meaning of the universe, which he then revealed to humans through the runes. Modern druidism is a quest for a spirituality that connects the individual with the natural world through artistic expression and inspiration.

THE DRUID'S HISTORY

Modern druidism developed from the late eighteenth-century Romantic movement, but this was not the first time that the druids had been "discovered". Stuart Piggott shows that from the Renaissance onwards those steeped in the philosophy and scholarship of the Greek and Roman thinkers had sought to rediscover the beliefs and practices of the druids. In the eighteenth century, when "fashion shifted from classical to

romantic, the druids were quietly waiting to take on a new life in the contemporary modes of Western thought and emotion". The druid story has an evidential basis in archaeology and what can be deduced of ancient Celtic religion from texts and iconography. In searching for the origins of the druids, Piggott has outlined three types of source material. The first is archaeological evidence from graves, ceremonial sites or representations in Celtic or Romano-Celtic art; the second is the writings of Greeks and Romans on the Celts; and the third is the development of ideas about the druids that originated in the antiquarian speculations of the seventeenth and eighteenth centuries, and were used by scholars as well as imaginative writers and artists. Piggott concludes that the combined evidence from all available sources leaves modern knowledge of pagan Celtic religion in a "state of the most rudimentary vagueness".

The Reverend William Stukeley (1687–1765) revived a cult of the druids. Stukeley had visited Stonehenge and believed that druidry was the native religion of the British Isles. He laid out a druidical temple in his garden, complete

Emma Restall-Orr, joint chief of the British Druid Order.

with apple trees and mistletoe. His numerous publications on the Celtic past led to an interest in discovering and recreating a Celtic past.

Ronald Hutton notes that a number of writers between 1760 and 1840 "set out to 'reconstruct' the principles of a noble and natural religion worthy to be associated with prehistoric philosopher-priests". Of note is Edward Williams (1747–1826) who assumed the name Iolo Morgannwg and "revived" the medieval Order of Bards to teach a "prehistoric system of mystical belief". He added ritual, ceremonies, regalia and hierarchy to texts. The first ritual, the "Gorsedd" (the assembly of new Bards), was held on Primrose Hill in London in 1792. Hutton observes that the notion of a home-grown system of very old wisdom akin to those of the East is very important to many people in the British Isles. This has, he argues, resulted in the belief in the importance of national characters, racial identity and folk-memories as a product of the Romantic movement of the late eighteenth century. The Celts have come to represent the

Sacred mistletoe

Mistletoe is often called the 'druid's plant'. Godhead is seen to be located in the oak, and the white berries of the mistletoe are thought by some druids to resemble drops of semen. At the druid Winter Solstice ceremony (Alban Arthuan) the mistletoe is ritualistically taken from the oak tree and laid upon an altar. Mistletoe is seen to bring fertility to the earth through its representation of the semen of the oak god given to the earth goddess, thus fertility is renewed.

A nineteenth-century romantic portrayal of a druid priestess with sacred mistletoe.

emotional, mystical, creative and "feminine", while the Anglo-Saxons have been defined as the embodiment of progress, industry, utilitarianism, science and masculinity.

HISTORICAL EVIDENCE

According to Hutton, the Graeco-Roman writers agreed that the Celtic intellectual elite was divided into bards, druids and vates (only the latter two were religious officials). The druids were more prestigious and were more concerned with philosophy and theology, but according to Julius Caesar they were also teachers, healers and judges. The vates specialized in divination and sacrifice. Hutton points out that the druids were male and that the formal religion of the Celtic peoples was mediated through men, although bards, physicians and women were all depicted as skilled in magic and capable of communing with deities in Irish literature. As far as religious beliefs are concerned, the Graeco-Roman writers tended to agree that the Celts had some sort of theology but it was not recorded

This painting depicts the druids of Angelsey, North Wales, being massacred by the Romans by order of the governor Suetonius Paulinus. It is conveying a specific nationalistic message and was painted during a Celtic revival by the Scots, Irish and Welsh against English imperialism, and also against the rationalism of the Enlightenment.

An arch-druid at the Avebury stone circle in England during the Summer Solstice celebrations. The growing informality of the druid order is shown in the different types of clothing worn.

in any detail. Most of the early Irish and some of the early Welsh tales described a divine otherworld – a version of the mortal world – where people enjoyed eternal life. This otherworld could be entered via certain doors concealed in mounds, islands, hills, lakes or the sea, and some humans could visit and return.

THE MODERN INHERITANCE

A great deal is unknown about the religious beliefs of the ancient druids, but modern druids interpret druidism in terms of worshipping the natural forces of the environment through the creative arts. Gone are the days when druidry was represented by men in white robes. Now it attracts a variety of people interested in a Celtic heritage and wanting to relate to nature.

Druids celebrate the Winter Solstice at Stonehenge. Much controversy and publicity has surrounded the solstice celebrations at Stonehenge. For a number of years rituals were strictly controlled or banned altogether, but at the Summer Solstice in 2000 all restrictions were lifted and many people were able to enjoy being in the midst of the stones as the sun rose over the eastern horizon.

THE NEW AGE

The New Age movement originated in 1971 when it emerged in America as a self-conscious form of spirituality. The New Age was originally world-denying in its search for a new order based on spiritual enlightenment. The Earth was seen to be entering a new cycle of evolution marked by a new human consciousness, which would give birth to a new civilization – the "Age of Aquarius" – which would overcome the present corrupt culture by cataclysm and disaster. The idea of a New Age was an amalgamation of various predictions: those of Nostradamus; the American psychic Edgar Cayce; the Theosophical Society; and the Lucis Trust, Rudolf Steiner's anthroposophy. These prophecies were founded in the spiritual traditions of the Maya, Aztecs and Hopi people, and also the Judaeo-Christian belief in the second coming of Christ. When the anticipated apocalypse did not arrive there was a "turn inward" and nature became a source of revelation rather than something that obscured real spirit.

New Age philosophy involves connecting with nature and all its beauty.

The term "New Age" has become a diffuse term applied to anything from New Age travellers to a particular type of book or music. The New Age is primarily a movement which aims to bring about social change by many and diverse means. By its very nature, according to the sociologist of religion Michael York, it is a term of convergence, one that is more than the sum of its parts, or at least is not to be equated with any one of its parts. According to Marilyn Ferguson there is an "Aquarian conspiracy" – without a political doctrine or a manifesto – which aims to bring about a new form of human consciousness. The Aquarian conspiracy, as advocated by Ferguson, is a new world-view, which has arisen as a response to a crisis. In this vision of a different reality, nature's powers are seen as transformative and a powerful ally, not as a force to be subdued. Ferguson sees human beings as stewards of inner and outer resources, and fundamentally embedded in nature. An expansion of consciousness is required to effect a reunion with all living things, she says: "Just as science demonstrates a web of relationship underlying everything in the universe a glittering network of events, so the mystical experience of

A holistic perspective – whereby everything in the cosmos is seen to be interrelated – is an underlying theme of the New Age.

The Edgar Cayce Foundation, Virginia, USA.

A New Age group invoke the Earth Spirit at the Merry Maidens stone circle, Cornwall, England.

James Lovelock, formulater of the Gaia principle.

wholeness encompasses all separation".

More recently, the popularization of New Age ideas has been given an immeasurable boost by the publication of James Redfield's *The Celestine Prophecy* in 1994. Combining a new view of science with a conspiracy adventure drama conducted in the rainforests of Peru, Redfield introduces nine "insights" that teach the perennial wisdom that all religions are concerned with humanity creating a relationship with a higher source of divinity. This is a means of stopping the abuse of power and of finding a positive vision of a way to save this planet.

New Age and Gaia

For New Agers, the earth is entering a new cycle of evolution marked by a new human consciousness. David Spangler, a leading proponent, describes the New Age as a time of abundance and spiritual enlightenment guided by advanced beings, "perhaps angels or spiritual masters or perhaps emissaries from an extraterrestrial civilization whose space-craft were the UFOs, [who] would help to create a new civilization". This new cycle of consciousness concerns the invisible and inner dimensions of all life and is, according to William Bloom, a prominent spokesperson and writer on

the subject, made up of different dynamics that constitute four major fields: ecology, new paradigm science, new psychology and spiritual dynamics.

The ecology field draws on the work of the British scientist James Lovelock who, in 1969, proposed the revolutionary principle known as the Gaia hypothesis – that life shapes and controls the environment rather than the other way around. Every individual life form, from

microbe to human, is involved by its own life processes. Earth's atmosphere is actively maintained and regulated by life on the surface for all the species of living beings. Lovelock's work has helped promote a new scientific understanding of life at all levels, from organisms to social systems and ecosystems. It involves a distinct shift in perception from the mechanistic world-view to an encompassing ecological view.

The New Age is eclectic in its beliefs and practices. Here, a tourist performs the Chinese art of Tai Chi, at the Temple of the Condor, Machu Picchu, Peru. Machu Picchu is said to be the lost city of the Inca, once full of thousands of people as well as various religious shrines and temples.

A ceremony involving group dancing at the Findhorn Centre.

The New Age physicist Fritjof Capra has probably done more than most to popularize New Age science thanks to his critique of mechanistic science, *The Turning Point* (1983), and by his exploration of the parallels between modern physics and eastern religions in *The Tao of Physics* (1976). He calls this change an ecological paradigm. Capra points out that in twentieth-century science a holistic perspective – involving a change in focus from the parts of mechanistic philosophy to the whole, where knowledge is seen as a network of relationships with no firm foundation – has become known as "systems thinking". Systems thinking was pioneered in the early twentieth century by biologists who emphasized the view of living organisms as integrated wholes. It is concerned with context, connections and relationships, and how the essential properties of an organism, or a living system, are properties

Eileen Caddy, of the Findhorn centre.

The meditation room at Findhorn.

of the whole. Living systems are viewed as part of an interactive web or network.

FINDHORN

A New Age community in northern Scotland, Findhorn is run according to messages and guidance received from God through Eileen Caddy, one of its founders. It has become a horticultural mecca for communication with nature spirits, devic presences, fairies and other such beings. Eileen Caddy, her husband Peter, and Dorothy MacLean moved to Findhorn in 1962 and established a community of over a hundred members as a centre of light for the Aquarian age. MacLean communicated with devas, which she felt were part of the myriad forms of thought of the divine potential with a vibrant energy that is the very essence of life.

These ideas are influenced by Theosophy, and have been influential in bringing New Age thinking in line with a Christian interpretation of the divine, largely through a focus on the light and communication with angels. The artist and writer Monica Sjöö has launched an attack on such a view, calling the New Age movment patriarchal and fascistic. She claims that New Age embraces reactionary, anti-life views, which are not in tune with the power of women, symbolized as the Goddess. She argues that by creating a God who is all light and transcendent, the rest of creation is demonized. Consequently, the New Age is concerned with a transformation of nature, both internally as healing and a form of development of a higher consciousness, and externally as a relationship with the wider environment. The interconnectedness between all beings, within a network symbolized as Gaia, is very important, and its spiritual aspect is expressed through harmony and light, often within a Christian interpretation.

Healing is an important aspect of the New Age, and complementary or alternative therapies, such as shiatsu, acupressure, reflexology, reiki and various visualization techniques are very much part of the whole picture.

New Agers see all life as connected. Here, on a Californian beach, musicians prepare to play music for whales in a ceremony to link humanity with the animals.

The Findhorn Foundation, like other New Age groups, communicates with nature spirits, devas, fairies and beings from the otherworld. This painting of a Fairy Tree shows the enchanting world of Faerie.

WESTERN SHAMANISM

The central precept of shamanism in the West is regeneration and a revitalization of earth-based "ways of knowing". Inspired by the idea that shamanism is humanity's most ancient and authentic form of spirituality, many modern Western shamanic practitioners turn to what they see as a primordial means of healing and creating connections to nature. Practices include drumming and journeying, as techniques for self-realization and making contact with an otherworldly realm of spirits. Some emphasize the importance of traditions – such as those practised by the Native American Indians – others place more importance on finding new ways of engaging with the living world.

Many modern Western shamanic practitioners attend drumming classes. Drumming helps to induce a trance state for journeying.

The 1970s saw the emergence of contemporary shamanism, sometimes called neo-shamanism, as a new form of spirituality emanating from the USA. It has been claimed that Mircea Eliade's book *Shamanism: Archaic Techniques of Ecstasy* (1964) was the prototype for the Western shamanism movement, but it took Carlos Castaneda's *The Teachings of Don Juan: A Yaqui Way of Knowledge* (1968), which sold hundreds of thousands of copies, to bring the living experience of an indigenous shamanism to Western culture. This work and nine other books by Castaneda on the same subject are now widely regarded as hoaxes, presenting fiction as fact, but they did popularize shamanism and lead to a fascination with the alternate realities of the shaman.

Shamanism is seen as primordial and authentic by those in the West who are jaded by world religions, particularly Christianity. Native American shamanism, with its circular notion of power and knowledge, symbolized by the medicine wheel, taught about the balance and relationship of all things, and this form of shamanism became particularly fashionble. An alternative to a focus on a particular culture is core shamanism, developed by Michael Harner in his influential book *The Way of the Shaman* (1980). Harner peels off cultural traditions, leaving an essential core, which reveals techniques for changing consciousness during journeying to find power animals, restoring power and healing: the essence is in the technique rather than the specific culture. Harner created the Foundation for Shamanic Studies, which has promoted core shamanism techniques through the widespread use of workshops, and now has a number of accredited teachers.

SHAMANISM IN HISTORY

Traditionally a shaman is a ritual specialist who communicates between different worlds – the ordinary world and the spirit domain – on behalf of his or her people. In the Western, usually urban, context, shamanism may stand for a regeneration and revitalization of ancient Earth-based "ways of knowing" for those who see themselves as dispossessed or alienated from nature as a spiritual source. Westerners can be fascinated with the exotic world of shamanism, but they can also fear it as something that takes them beyond the known.

The West's fascination with shamanism is not new. The historian Gloria Flaherty notes that the curiosity of intellectuals was raised in the fifth century BC when Herodotus reported the death-defying feats of the Scythian soothsaying poets Aristeas and Abaris. She notes that classical scholars throughout the ages have studied Herodotus and have also pointed out numerous other "shamanic" practices of antiquity.

In earlier centuries, as well as today, shamans have been portrayed in ways that reflect Europeans' fascination with the exotic, and rarely in ways that reflect the shaman's own culture. It is an appalling fact that most shamanic societies have been wiped out by European colonialism and imperialism.

During the eighteenth and nineteenth centuries, Western Europeans saw shamans as primitives who worshipped evil spirits.

They have seen in shamanism the origins of theatre, fairy tales and Greek mythology. Flaherty points out that in the eighteenth century there was a good supply of information about shamanism from all over the world, and that by this time certain notions of shamanism had become assimilated into the intellectual mainstream.

Most eighteenth-century observations of shamanism were written from the point of view of interested yet disbelieving western Europeans. Shamanism was viewed in a variety of ways. For some Christian missionaries it was related to native peoples' belief in evil spirits and worship of heathen idols: these "primitives" were thought to have no sense of the true god. For others it concerned a scholarly pursuit of truth into unknown "otherness" and shamanism was subjected to empirical tests and rational analyses. Some attempted to record the activities of vanishing peoples; for others, shamanism epitomized an ageless human activity; while for others there was a fascination with discovering what were seen as the hidden secrets of nature.

The general view of shamanism as an ageless human activity connected with nature has accounted for its rise in popularity in the West. This is the aspect that has led many people to search for a spiritual path in shamanism. According to some Western shamanic practitioners, it is the oldest way in which humanity has sought connection with spirit; it is seen to be an authentic spiritual experience far removed from the dominant religious institutions in the West, which are thought to have lost touch with the experience of spirituality.

THE MEDICINE WHEEL

Modern Western shamanism offers a series of techniques for self-help and self-realization; it is believed to lead to personal empowerment but also teaches that the individual is part of a broader framework that connects with the rest of the cosmos. The Native American medicine wheel teachings offer a framework for understanding what is, for Westerners, a very different way of seeing the world. The medicine wheel has many meanings and manifestations,

A modern shamanistic drum showing symbols of the seasons and the zodiac. The drum is an instrument that the shaman can "ride" to take him or her into the spirit otherworld; the symbols relate the shaman to the cosmos.

Native American "dream catchers" have become part of popular Western shamanism and the New Age. Adopted from Native American Indian traditions, they are believed to hold on to good dreams and dispel the bad ones.

ranging from structuring ceremonies and a means for the expression of dreams and visions, to methods for healing. The path of personal transformation on the medicine wheel is said to take the knower and the known through a spiral of experiences that link the individual, and his or her own course from birth to death, with the seasons and the wider whole.

The teachings of Sun Bear, who is of Chippewa descent, are based on his vision of the medicine wheel and incorporate elements from various Native American cultures. The wheel revolves around a Creator Stone, which is the centre of all life and radiates energy to the rest of the wheel. Seven stones surrounding the Creator form the centre circle, the foundation of all life. They are, in sunwise direction: Earth Mother, Father Sun, Grandmother Moon, Turtle clan, Frog clan, Thunderbird clan and Butterfly clan. Four stones mark the outer circle, and these are the Spirit Keepers: Waboose in the north, Wabun in the east, Shawnodese in the south and

Mudjekeewis in the west. From the Spirit Keeper stones radiate qualities – such as cleansing, renewal, purity, clarity and wisdom – that are necessary to gain the sacred space of the Creator in the centre of the circle. Between the four Spirit Keeper stones are the 12 moon stones of the outer circle.

Issues of cultural appropriation or, in other words, the stealing of an oppressed people's spiritual heritage by the descendents of Western colonialism, are slowly infiltrating popular books and journals aimed at those interested in practising shamanism in the West. There is a move to search for Western "indigenous" versions, and a whole range of shamanisms – from Celtic to Wiccan – are being "rediscovered". Weekend workshops and drumming circles, where participants can journey in trance to find their spirit guides, are becoming more and more popular.

Healing is often a central component of much of this work, and shamanic

Soul journeying is an important part of modern Western shamanic practice.

practitioners journey to retrieve lost soul parts – for themselves and for others – on a regular basis. The essence of shamanic healing concerns the spiritual removal of aspects of a person that should not be

there, and returning those spiritual parts that should. This is often done with the aid of spirit beings sometimes called power animals, or totems.

However, shamanic practitioners are not the same thing as shamans: a shamanic training does not make a shaman. For Gordon MacLellan, who is a contemporary Western shaman working in environmental education, being a shaman is a practical job of mediating between the human world and the world of spirits. Seeing the role of the shaman in modern Britain as one of communicator and "patterner" with nature, he says that a modern shaman has to find new ways of engaging humans with the living world. Shamans work with communities and draw their inspiration from the Otherworld, which is an abode of spirits where we "meet the talking foxes and watch the shapes of the stone people unfold from the rocks on a hillside … This is the shaman's world. The shaman moves through an Otherworld that may

The medicine wheel links the individual into a wider sacred whole. Here a man is meditating at a medicine wheel at Sedona, Arizona, USA.

Shamanic tools

Smudge sticks and smudge fans are used to cleanse the body, mind and surroundings before a spirit journey is commenced, or simply as a way to clear the mind and purify the body. A smudge stick is lit and the fragrant smoke that comes from it is directed to the appropriate place by the fan. Smudge sticks are often made from white sage, but also from other sweet smelling herbs that have particular significance or cleansing qualities. Rattles are sometimes used instead of a drum to help a shaman go into a trance; they can also be used during a healing to call spirits, diagnose illness and open a person to the spirits.

A smudge fan made from feathers.

A rattle made from dried seed pods.

White sage smudge sticks for cleansing.

correspond exactly with the territory she calls home but here is midnight and a world frosted with energy like ice on every leaf, where the mist at dawn is a swirling, pouring cloud of spirals spilling out of damp hollows". The Otherworld is not other at all, it is also this world.

Not tapping directly into an extant tradition, and gaining inspiration from a number of sources, Gordon MacLellan claims that some of the most exciting ceremonies have grown with grass roots environmental action: "Whole rituals take shape through the need of people to draw upon their own energy, to recognize their strength and to acknowledge the land and their feelings for it that can bring them to battle on its behalf." MacLellan feels that these rituals represent a growth that breaks traditions, bridges class, belief and age distinction, and suggests that these eco-warriors are the latest practitioners of a particular magic of the modern age, and the inheritors of shamanic traditions.

Gordon MacLellan, a modern Western shaman.

Western shamanism today is often concerned with healing, and here Jo Crow, a Western shaman, drums herself into a trance during a ceremony.

THE NORTHERN TRADITION

Heathens, or practitioners of the Northern tradition of magic, attempt to recapture an ancient Indo-European way of life through the mythology of Odin and other Scandanavian gods and goddesses. Northern cosmology is focused on the world tree Yggdrasil, the connecting point of nine worlds, at the bottom of which sit the three sister Norns who weave a web of fate called the "wyrd". This is a very specialized tradition and one which, unlike the Western Mysteries, does not take strands of belief from other traditions. The spiritual path that practitioners of the Northern tradition follow looks to the Icelandic Sagas for inspiration in matters concerning human dilemmas and conflicts.

Odin the Norse god with his two crows Huginn (Thought) and Muninn (Memory).

While many modern pagans claim Celtic origins for their practice, some are drawn to the traditions and history of Germanic, Scandinavian or Anglo-Saxon peoples, the spiritual beliefs that are said to be indigenous to northern Europe.

Comprising Germanic, Baltic, Norse and Celtic strands, these beliefs relate to areas of Germany, the Baltic countries of northern Poland and western Russia, Iceland, Scandinavia, Austria, Czechoslovakia, Switzerland, northern France, Ireland and Britain, and are collectively described as the "Northern tradition". Often preferring to call themselves heathens, practitioners of the Northern tradition attempt to recapture and reconstruct what they see as the ancient Nordic tribal religion, mainly through the lore and the sagas as outlined in twelfth- and thirteenth-century literature, especially that of the Icelander Snorri Sturluson (1179–1241). Seeing their beliefs as part of an ancient Indo-European way of life, practitioners of Northern magic create a different spiritual path to those who follow the Western Mystery tradition, with its focus on Egyptian and Judaeo-Christian mythology.

While most practitioners of the Northern tradition see their magical practices as part of a rich variety of spiritual paths and welcome all interested seekers, it is unfortunate that in the past this form of magical organization has

The goddess Freyja, mistress of magic and witchcraft. She is said to own a falcon skin that enables her to fly to the underworld. She is depicted here flying with swans.

attracted a minority who have neo-Nazi sympathies. A tendency to nationalism by some in the Northern tradition in Britain has led to tensions with other pagan or magical groups, but now the general consensus among most heathens is that they will not hold with any form of racism or nationalism.

TROTH TO THE GODS

The main Northern tradition is known as "Odinism" or "¡satr·", meaning "loyalty or troth to the gods", or "allegiance to the deities". The principle god is called Odin in Scandinavian, Wotan in German and Woden in Anglo-Saxon. Odin is associated with inspiration, writing, combat and the dead. He has one eye, wears a wide-brimmed hat and often a blue cloak, and carries a magical spear. Two ravens, Huginn (Thought) and Muninn (Memory) sit on his shoulders, birds of battle and also symbols of flights to find wisdom.

Although the goddesses are equal with the gods in Northern mythology, little is known about them. For example, there is not much information on Odin's partner, the goddess Frigg, who is Queen of the Heavens. There were 12 gods and 13 goddesses in the Norse pantheon, and these included the fertility god Freyr and his sister Freyja, who is associated with war and rides to battle in a chariot drawn by two cats. Freyja is mistress of magic and witch-craft, and owns a falcon skin, which enables her to take falcon form on journeys to the underworld. The god Thor is the son of Odin and the Earth, is second in importance to Odin and represents order, law and stability. Loki, the son of two giants and the foster-brother of Odin, is a trickster figure who embodies all that is dark, unpredictable, and ambiguous. Loki is necessary as a catalyst to create change, without which no movement could take place.

Northern cosmology is centred on the world tree Yggdrasil, which is the connecting point of nine worlds; each world is populated by one race or type of being, such as giants, dwarves, elves, deities and humans. In Norse mythology, the Norns are three sisters who sit

A twelfth-century Viking tapestry depicting Odin on the left carrying an axe, with a representation of the cosmic tree Yggdrasil, from which he hung. In the centre is the god Thor carrying a hammer, and on the right is the fertility god Freyr holding an ear of corn.

at the base of Yggdrasil and spin a web of fate called "wyrd". The past and future are not seen as separate, and the future is seen to be in the present; time is not viewed as a linear progression and wyrd can be changed to some degree. The amount of influence that it is possible to exert on wyrd has been likened to sailing by the psychologist Brian Bates, who is the author of two popular books on the subject. According to him, a skilled magical practitioner is like a sailor who has the ability to trim the sails in order to change or adjust direction but cannot alter the overall course of the

The Norse tradition was depicted in heroic, Romantic terms by a variety of artists, as in this nineteenth-century painting by Hans Gabriel Jentzsch showing a Winter Solstice festival honouring the onset of winter.

current. According to Ronald Hutton, there is not enough information to make comparisons between the cults of the Celts, Romans, Greeks and Eastern peoples and those of the Germanic and Norse peoples, but wyrd, the idea of an overwhelming web of destiny that shapes the whole world, appears to be a significant northern characteristic.

Since 1973, Ásatrú has been one of the officially recognized religions of Iceland, and while it has not reached that status in other countries it is growing in popularity. Northern tradition groups in Britain are the Odinic Rite, Odinshof, Hammarens Ordens Sällskap and the Rune Gild. In America the Ásatrú Alliance, the Ásatrú Folk Assembly, the Odinist Fellowship, the Ring of Troth and the Rune Gild are prominent. Some heathens celebrate the eight pagan seasonal festivals and lunar cycles but others dismiss these as of

A modern heathen celebration of May Day in Navan, Northern Ireland.

recent origin and observe what they see as more authentic Northern European rites of Winternights, Yule and Sigrblot. Winternights is the celebration of the onset of winter, harvest festival and an honouring of the dead; Yule is the observance of the longest night and New Year, a time of oaths and fateful encounters with otherworldly visitors such as the dead and divinities. Sigrblot is a victory celebration of the beginning of summer – of vitality over winter gloom or a celebration of coming victories in trading or raiding.

The runes are used as a divination system in the Northern tradition. Divination was important to the Germanic

peoples, and according to the Roman writer Tacitus, they paid much attention to the "casting of lots":

Their method of casting lots is a simple one: they cut a branch from a fruit-bearing tree and divide it into small pieces, which they mark with certain distinctive signs and scatter at random onto a white cloth. Then the priest of the community, if the lots are consulted publicly, or the father of the family, if it is done privately, after invoking the gods with eyes raised to heaven, picks up three pieces, one at a time, and interprets them according to the signs previously marked upon them.

A modern heathen celebration of midsummer or Sigrblot, the victory of summer over winter. People join hands around a decked pole to celebrate the return of the sun.

A ninth-century casket with runic inscriptions.

Rune stones in Gørlev church, Zealand, Denmark, from the tenth or eleventh century.

The true nature of the runes is said to have been revealed to Odin as he hung upon the world tree Yggdrasil for nine days and nine nights. Odin's account is recorded in the Håvamål:

*I know that I hung on the
windswept tree
For nine days and nine nights,
Wounded by a spear,
And given to Odin,
Myself to myself,
On that tree
Which no man knows
From what roots it grows,
They gave me no bread
Nor drinking horn.
I looked down,
I picked up the runes,
Screaming, I took them.
Then I fell back.*

Heathens, like practitioners of magic in other traditions, seek to live in contact with the "spirit of place", seeing their gods as unique entities and as part of the all-embracing web of wyrd.

Runes are used as signs and symbols of universal mysteries.

Table of Runes:

Today, modern magicians of the Northern tradition use the runes as a system of sacred knowledge and expression of eternal universal laws; like the Tarot, they represent the deeper mysteries in symbolic form. The Elder Futhark is an alphabet of 24 runes or staves, and there are many variations of this basic pattern: some have more characters, like the Anglo-Saxon variant with 29, and others have less, like the Scandinavian version that has 16.

LETTER	SIGN	NAME	MEANING
F	ᚠ	Feoh	Cattle
U	ᚢ	Ur	Auroch
TH	ᚦ	Thorn	Thorn
A	ᚨ	Ansur	A mouth
R	ᚱ	Rad	A cartwheel
K	ᚲ	Ken	A torch
G	ᚷ	Geofu	A gift
W	ᚹ	Wynn	Happiness
H	ᚺ	Hagall	Hail
N	ᚾ	Nied	Need
I	ᛁ	Is	Ice
J	ᛃ	Jara	Harvest
Y	ᛇ	Eoh	A yew tree
P	ᛈ	Peorth	A dice cup
Z	ᛉ	Elhaz	An elk
S	ᛋ	Sigel	The sun
T	ᛏ	Tyr	The god Tyr
B	ᛒ	Beorc	A birch tree
E	ᛖ	Ehwaz	A horse
M	ᛗ	Mann	A human
L	ᛚ	Lagu	Water, sea
NG	ᛜ	Ing	The god Ing
D	ᛞ	Daeg	Day (light)
O	ᛟ	Othel	A possession

SATANISM

For Satanists, Satan or the Devil is symbolic of a hidden force in nature responsible for the workings of earthly affairs and representing the spirit of inspiration and human progress. Revolting against organized religion – which is only suitable for "the herd" – Satanists allegedly seek to harness what have been called dark forces to liberate the will in the advancement of evolution. Claims that Satanists conduct rituals to abuse children are reminiscent of early modern witchcraft accusations, and are vigorously denied. Satanism concerns the self-affirmation and freedom of the individual.

The Christian division of the world into light and dark or good and evil, the battlelines drawn between the God of good against demonic forces of evil headed by the Devil or Satan, has been a positive invitation to some to join the dark side. Anton Szandor La Vey, the founder of the Church of Satan, has taken this position one step further by formulating a religion based on worshipping the dark forces. La Vey was a great showman and played to his audience by dressing up as the Devil but, in his view, the Devil was not a deity that represented the opposite of God but a hidden force in nature responsible for the workings of earthly affairs. The Devil represented the spirit of progress and inspiraton for the advancement of human beings, as well as the spirit of revolt that leads to freedom from organized religions like Christianity, which are only suitable for the "herd".

On Spring Equinox or Walpurgisnacht, 30 April 1966, Anton La Vey shaved his head and declared the beginning of the Age of Satan. This marked the start of a number of Church of Satan workshops, seminars, and rituals that were open to the public and conducted at his home, the "Black House". This was the first church of its type, but it was not the first group that had met to honour Satan. In England in the eighteenth century, Sir Francis Dashwood had formed the Hellfire Club, and Rabelais' fictional utopia, the "Abbey of Thelema", had inspired Aleister Crowley to found his version in

Sicily in 1920, with the motto "Fait ce que voudras" ("Do what thou wilt").

ANTON LA VEY

La Vey was born in Chicago on 11 April 1930, and was allegedly taught legends of vampires and witches by his Gypsy grandmother, who passed on to him the folklore of her native Transylvania. Dropping out of school because it was boring, La Vey joined the Clyde Beatty Circus as a cage boy, watering and feeding lions and tigers. He became an assistant trainer and also played the organ. Later he joined a carnival and it

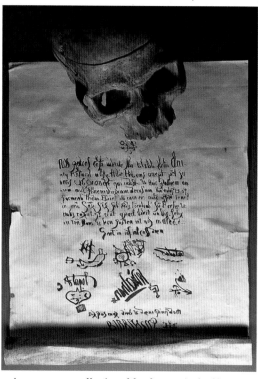

A pact supposedly signed by demons in looking-glass Latin, and used in evidence at the witchcraft trial of Urbain Grandier in 1634. The reversed signatures of Satanas, Beelzebub, Lucifer, Leviathan and Astararoth may be seen.

Sir Francis Dashwood (1708–81), pictured seated, formed a Satanist group called the Hell-Fire Club in the eighteenth century.

was stopped and Church of Satan activities were carried out in Satanic grottos in several countries. La Vey's stated goal was the creation of a police state in which the weak were weeded out and an achievement-oriented leadership was permitted to pursue the mysteries of black magic.

The Satanic Bible is a book that outlines the theory and ritual practice of Satanic magic. Magic is separated into lesser, everyday magic, such as that used for psychological manipulation and tricks to get people to do what the Satanist wants, and greater or ceremonial magic. Satanic rituals, according to La Vey, do not involve the sacrifice of animals or babies; they do not involve a negative reversal of Christian ritual – as in the

Francois Rabelais' (1494–1553) fictional utopia the "Abbey of Thelema" inspired the notorious magician Aleister Crowley to found his own version in the early twentieth century.

Below: Anton Szandor La Vey, the founder of the modern Church of Satan, has followed in the satanic tradition of Dashwood and Crowley in liberating the individual will from the fetters of organized religion. He is shown here on the left with "Satania" lying on an altar and "Hellas" and his wife "Elysia" (on the right) looking on.

Above: Satan is seen as an arch-rebel and individualist by modern Satanists and in Blake's portrayal of him rousing the rebel angels.

was here that he learnt hypnosis and studied the occult as assistant to a magician. During a period when he worked as a photographer for the San Francisco Police Department he saw the worst side of humanity, and came to detest the sanctimonious attitude of people who saw in human violence the work of God's will. He left the Police Department to play the organ in night-clubs and theatres.

In the 1950s La Vey started gaining a reputation for black magic in San Francisco and formed a group called the Order of Trapezoid, which later evolved into the governing body of the Church of Satan. It espoused a down-to-earth philosophy with an emphasis on the "carnal, lustful, natural instincts of man" without guilt or sin. Its methods sought to harness the dark forces to change situations according to will. His publicity stunts included baptizing his own three year-old daughter Zeena in 1967, dedicating her to the Devil. The following year he played the part of the Devil in the film *Rosemary's Baby*. In 1972 the public work at the Black House

The Nine Satanic Principles

1 Satan represents indulgence, instead of abstinence!

2 Satan represents vital existence, instead of spiritual pipe dreams!

3 Satan represents undefiled wisdom, instead of hypocritical self-deceit!

4 Satan represents kindness to those who deserve it, instead of love wasted on ingrates!

5 Satan represents vengeance, instead of turning the other cheek!

6 Satan represents responsibility to the responsible, instead of concern for psychic vampires!

7 Satan represents man as just another animal, sometimes better, more often worse than those that walk on all-fours, who, because of his divine spiritual and intellectual developmenti, has become the most vicious animal of all!

8 Satan represents all of the so-called sins, as they all lead to physical, mental, or emotional gratification!

9 Satan has been the best friend the Church has ever had, as he has kept it in business all these years!

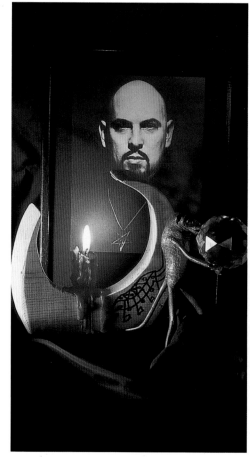

Anton La Vey, the great showman.

popular stereotype of a black mass conducted by a defrocked priest worshipping a naked woman on an altar – but allegedly concern celebration and purges from sin. A Satanic wedding, for example, consecrates the joys of the flesh with a lust rite. La Vey outlines nine Satanic principles (see box above).

The Satanic Church attracted an international following and at its peak it was said to have about 25,000 members (although this claim was probably greatly exaggerated). It also included celebrities among its number; the best-known was the actress Jayne Mansfield, who was killed in a car accident that was allegedly foreseen by La Vey.

THE TEMPLE OF SET

By the mid-1980s another Satanic organization, called the Temple of Set and also based in San Francisco, had attracted several hundred members. It was founded by Michael A. Aquino (a lieutenant-colonel of the US Army Reserve), Lilith Sinclair and Betty Ford (not the First Lady of that name) and is a society based on the worship of the Egyptian god Set or Seth, who is viewed as the forerunner of Satan. The Temple

of Set is an initiatory society that is interested in people of high intelligence and the advancement of genetic evolution. Aquino prophesied an apocalypse in which only the members of the Temple of Set, as the elect, would survive. There are many who are attracted to Satanic activities – the frisson of being a part of an organization that is seen by Christians as the very essence of evil is compelling to some.

SATANIC RITUAL ABUSE

In the late 1980s a moral panic about Satanism that took the form of ritual abuse led to scores of children being taken into care in Britain. The panic started in 1988 in the USA, when allegations of Satanic ritual abuse were made by social workers, and these ideas were passed on to their British counterparts at an international conference. Satanic abuse was seen to involve extreme acts of human sacrifice, cannibalism and the sexual abuse of children in orgiastic rituals, the purpose of which was an act of Devil-worship or witchcraft.

These allegations, which are strikingly similar to those levelled at witches during the early modern witch hunts, were fuelled by evangelical Christian groups.

Jayne Mansfield, the hollywood actress, was a member of La Vey's Satanic Church.

The work of Aleister Crowley has been an inspiration to many Satanists. This seal was designed by him and depicts an inverted pentagram, or five-pointed star, a symbol now used by Satanists.

Satanism and witchcraft bring up people's deepest fears. Here a woman is portrayed as the Devil, and combines femaleness and evil in a manner common to the early modern stereotype of the witch.

"Satanic" activities, from the use of masks and costumes to the invocation of supernatural powers.

In 1994 the British government ordered a report to investigate the abuse. Eighty-four cases of alleged ritual abuse were investigated. Three did show evidence of ritual used to entrap the children by claims of mystical powers, or to prevent them from telling. but none were considered Satanic. In other words, the motivation for the abuse was sexual rather than Satanic. The report was critical of the interviewing techniques of the social services, saying that interviewers had employed leading questions, and used repeated questions, the report said that the children had told the adults what they thought they wanted to hear. This last aspect is reminiscent of the early modern European witch trials in which confessions were extracted to conform to the judge's views of diabolic witchcraft.

Satanism, like witchcraft, tends to bring up peoples' deepest fears. Undoubtedly there are individuals who perform immoral acts – but this does not justify the tendency that society has of branding a whole system of belief on the basis of conjecture and unproven rumour, a lesson that should have been learned from the times of the European witch hunts.

These groups offer counselling to people trying to sever their links with the occult. They claim that an interest in the occult starts people off on the slippery slope towards Satanism, and that people are recruited via New Age fairs and international Satanic organizations. At the time of the allegations, newspaper stories of survivors of Satanic abuse and confessions of former Satanists – who told about young girls being used as "brood mares" by being made pregnant and then forced to have abortions at five months so that the foetus could be used as a sacrifice – added to the panic.

In Britain, the social services and the charity the National Society for the Prevention of Cruelty to Children organized a survey of social workers, and the results reported a wide range of

Charles Manson as he appeared in court in California accused of Satanic murder.

CHAOS MAGIC

Unlike most other magical practices chaos magic is not a spiritual path. Using the maxim "Nothing is true, everything is permitted", chaos magicians emphasize pragmatic techniques and observable results in the world as it is directly experienced as a form of sorcery. The aim is to achieve alternative states of consciousness or "gnosis". Chaos magic has acquired a certain notoriety for being sinister, even Satanic. This is because it rejects spiritual elements in its practices. Above all, it offers an opportunity to explore non-ordinary reality without the hindrance of accepted beliefs, and in the process, its practitioners claim, inspiration, knowledge, power and heightened perception are gained.

Chaos magic was created in the late 1970s with the emergence of punk rock and the theoretical explorations in science that came to be called chaos theory. Influenced by both Aleister Crowley and Austin Osman Spare, chaos magic is above all a practical approach to practising magic. Chaos magicans claim that all the methods of working magic are the same, despite differing symbols and belief systems. Chaos magic is thus a means to an end, rather than an end in itself. It claims to eschew the dogma of other approaches in its emphasis on avoiding the use of any one magical "system", advocating experimentation

The Great Cthulhu, lord of dreams, telepathy and madness, is an entity with octopoid head and wings and is based on the work of the science fiction writer Howard Phillips Lovecraft.

Austin Osman Spare, artist and occultist, and source of inspiration to chaos magicians.

Chaos magic came into being at the same time as punk rock, a movement that was epitomized by the band The Sex Pistols.

with many practices. According to chaos magician Phil Hine, chaos magic is concerned with deconditioning from "the mesh of beliefs, attitudes and fictions about self, society and the world". Through the idea of the "paradigm" (which in chaos magic means the individual taking up a personal, magical role model), the magician can switch into and out of many magical techniques using the maxim. "If it works, use it", while leaving his or her beliefs behind. Chaos is not a religion – its focus is not on what may be termed "spirituality" – it is more specifically the utilization of magical techniques for the attainment of alternate states of consciousness or "gnosis". "Spiritual truth" has no meaning; whatever feels right is important. It glorifies fantasy and is a conscious and deliberate dislocation from any historical and spiritual tradition.

BASIC PRINCIPLES

The basic principles of chaos magic are expressed by the maxim "Nothing is true, everything is permitted". They may be summed up as: an avoidance of any form of dogmatism; a focus on personal experience; technical excellence in development of skills and abilities in the performance of a magical act; deconditioning the self by modifying and discarding beliefs and "ego-fictions"; and an eclectic and diverse approach, choosing from themes as wide apart as science fiction or tantrism, or adopting the beliefs of a spiritual system, if they are thought to serve a useful function. The overall aim is to achieve gnosis as a form of inner knowledge.

Eight forms of magic are represented on the "chaosphere". Octarine is pure or raw magic, representing the development of theories and philosophies. Black magic is death magic and concerns the ritual rehearsal of death. Blue magic is concerned with the control of other people and the creation of wealth. Red magic is associated with war. Yellow magic is involved with the ego or self-image. Green magic is about love. Orange magic concerns thought and living by the wits. Purple or silver is associated with sex magic.

The chaos magician Phil Hine holding a chaosphere-headed staff.

Peter Carroll, in his book *Liber Kaos* (1992), sees magic as a consequence of the structure of the universe, and he visualizes it as five serpents – of space, time, mass, energy and aether – each biting their tails and giving birth to themselves out of their own mouths. Carroll's view of the universe indicates that it is random, as is the individual's relationship with it: he offers no permanent model. His early writings appeared in the magazine *The New Equinox*, and it was here that the magical order the Illuminates of Thanateros (IOT) was first advertised. The IOT was formed in 1978 by Peter Carroll and Ray Sherwin to provide inspiration for chaos magicians. It was not a teaching order with initiated hierarchies but rather an organization where people could come together to practise and publish practical magic. This was not as easy as it sounds, some people expected teaching and leaders, but no rules or instructions were ever given, only suggestions on how to reach "that which could not be taught".

A chaos magic altar demonstrating its eclectic nature: Baphomet sits in the centre surrounded by a skull mala, a glass thunderbolt, a green baboon fetish, a lizard fetish, a crystal with a demon inside, a damaru, and a three-dimensional chaosphere in the bottom right hand corner.

THE THANATEROS RITUAL

Phil Hine, writing in *Condensed Chaos* (1995), describes magic as "a doorway through which we step into mystery, wildness and immanence", and ritual is one way of achieving this. For chaos magicians there is no one shared reality when ritual workings are conducted, but rituals are seen to create opportunities for experiencing a magical state of consciousness. Before any magical work is undertaken a "banishing ritual" is performed. This is a preparation and centring exercise, which allows the magician to focus on the task ahead rather than on more mundane thoughts, and it also is supposed to clear the ritual space from unwanted atmospheres. Banishing rituals typically have three parts. The first section focuses awareness on the magician and is aimed at clearing the mind of unwanted thoughts by the visualization of white light being drawn through the body. The second creates a symbolic universe with the magician at the centre. The following is a suggestion by Phil Hine, and may be done by focusing on the eight rays of magic of the chaosphere and declaring:

These are my weapons
Expressions of my will
I grasp them lightly
I stand poised, at the centre
The Universe dances for my pleasure.

The third section involves an identification of the chosen source of inspiration.

The Thanateros ritual is an example of a "celebration of Chaoist principles" according to Peter Carroll, and it concerns the invocation of the power of chaos. The magician tricks his or her consciousness into an ecstatic magical state by what is called the "neither-neither" effect. By meditating on the death of self in the act of sex, and the birth of self in an encounter with death, the ritual simulates encounters with both sex and death, and then with both of these experiences simultaneously, which is said to force conception beyond its normal limits. After a statement of intent and litanies, Eros and Thanatos are invoked:

The chaos Thanateros ritual is a process that simulates an encounter with sex and death – in the death of self in the act of sex, and the birth of self in an encounter with death. This is a nineteenth-century painting of Thanatos (Greek god of death) depicting aspects of sex and death.

Invocation to Eros:
So come Eros, we invoke thee
You who created us
In the chaotic conjunction
Of genetic roulette
Come create us anew
And kill us again!
Our lovers approach
Our breathing quickens
As they come closer
Our breathing quickens
As we are clasped together
Our breathing quickens
At the thrill of touch
Our breathing quickens
We begin to gasp
We are ready to surrender
Three, Two, One,
(Cry of Climax)!

Invocation to Thanatos
So come Thanatos, we invoke thee
We accept your bargain
Come kill us again
And create us anew
Our nemesis approaches
Grinning skull and upraised scythe

Our breathing quickens
Closer it comes and closer
Our breathing quickens
Death stares us in the face
Our breathing quickens
Upraised terrible scythe
We begin to gasp
When it falls we shall die
Three, Two, One,
(Cry of Death Terror)!

The ritual finishes with ecstatic laughter as an expression of the neither-neither; the energy being raised is either used for itself or to cast a spell.

THE CTHULHU MYTHOS

Another way of working with chaos magic is with what is known as the Cthulhu Mythos. Cthulhu, high priest of the "Great Old Ones", created by science fiction writer Howard Phillips Lovecraft (1890–1937), is a zoomorphic entity with an octopoid head and wings. Contact with him is said to unite the chthonic roots of primeval consciousness to the stellar magicks of the future. Phil Hines writes, in *The Pseudonomicon*, that the Old Ones, who are alien to human civilization and rationality, have a close relationship with wild places – particularly stone circles and "strange manifestations" – and have been cast forth from the earth and forgotten by civilized humanity and its materialistic vision. They are ever-present, "lurking at the frontiers of order, in places where the wild power of nature can be felt". They are chaotic, as Nature is chaotic, and they retain their primal power since they cannot be explained.

The Old Ones manifest into the everyday world through gateways in wild, lonely places entangled with local myth and folklore; associated with "strange lights, subterranean noises, stone circles, ancient ruins, strange angles, tunnels, wells and the gates of dreaming, trance and madness". A core feature of the Cthulhu Mythos is said to be transformation into a new mode of being. After initiation by fear and near madness that shatters the old conception of self, and by dreaming and astral visions, the magician reaches a form of consciousness that is more tenuous and chaotic than ordinary reality.

A statue of Baphomet, who is popular with chaos magicians, displaying hermaphroditic qualities.

Masks are an important part of magical work: they ease the identification with otherworldly beings and the loss of a sense of the self. This is a spirit of Chaos mask.

Tantric Altar

Chaos magic takes an eclectic approach to magic, and may utilize other magicial traditions. Altars are ideal for demonstrating this, as the symbolism and connections can be so diverse. Here, on this Chaos Tantric altar, is a selection of items that takes in several different traditions. It includes a yoni lingam (top right), a small statue of Kali, goddess of death and destruction (top left), a damaru, a thunderbolt (bottom right), and a Tibetan phurba or ritual knife (bottom left) used for "nailing demons". The altar contains eight bowls of water for the eight directions and is surrounded by a skull mala.

A Chaos Tantric altar.

AFTERWORD

We all share a common humanity, as a species we emerged from Africa and spread across all continents of the earth, and we are remarkably similar in having human need to explain and shape the world around us. In this book we have ranged across cultures and time – from informed speculation about humanity's earliest forms of spirituality to specific practices of magic across the globe. We have examined ideas about witchcraft in non-Western and Western societies and, with one eye on the past, we have also looked at present Western magical practices from Western Mysteries, Druidry and the New Age to the most contemporary of all – Chaos magic. One cannot help but be left with a feeling of amazement at the variety of ideas and practices which people all over the world have attempted to communicate and have hoped would explain the realm of spirit. The human ability to create meaning is seemingly inexhaustible and ever-creative.

However, the similarities underlying all the different approaches to magic are also striking: the belief in an interconnecting realm of spirit, often termed the Otherworld in Western cultures, and explained as sympathetic magic by the early anthropologist James Frazer, is a constant thread running through the multiplicities of difference that separate societies and cultures in time and place. This connects us all in terms of physiology – all human beings have the ability to experience sympathetic magic through what have been called alternate forms of consciousness. There is what may be seen as an underlying shamanic dimension to human experience. Shamanism can be viewed very broadly as a form of consciousness which all human beings are capable of sharing but, in order to avoid what anthropologists call Eurocentrism shamanic consciousness must also be viewed according to its specific cultural context. It is also important that Western cultures do not romanticize or "exoticize" the non-Western shamanic cultures that remain – seeing them in ways that deny their full humanity by projecting qualities onto them that have more to do with an imagined way of life than day-to-day reality.

Shamanic consciousness is a source of human creativity and spirituality. Human consciousness has been explained by reference to a two hemisphere model of the brain: the left being concerned with analytical thought processes, the right having an analogical or synthesizing function. Analytical thought and analogical thought have been seen as opposed, as two essentially unconnected modes of operation or as two orientations to reality. More recent work is seeking to overcome this dichotomy of consciousness, seeing the two as biologically intimately connected and as two sides of a unitary process of thinking.

What has been referred to as magic has been divorced from "true" religion; magic has often come to represent the opposite of all that is ordered and good. However, as we have seen, it is hard to maintain a rigid boundary between magic and religion – the one blends into the other, so much so that sometimes the words "magic" and "religion" become almost meaningless when viewed outside a particular situation.

At a time when we as a species are in danger of destroying our planet, it is important to recognize our common humanity, as well as our connection to other forms of life. This does not mean that we must forget our differences or what makes us individuals; neither does it undervalue cultural variation. Magic today offers a view of the world that sees relationships between things – there is a connection shared between mountains, trees, animals, the moon, sun and stars, as well as the person next door. This can be a helpful way of understanding and reassessing our place within the diversity of life on this planet.

I was delighted to accept the offer made by Anness Publishing to write this book because it offered an opportunity to provide an anthropological and historical approach to a subject which has been widely misunderstood and misrepresented. The book encompasses research done over many years and includes material I have taught on courses at Goldsmiths College, University of London, Sussex University and King Alfred's University College, Winchester. I have welcomed the chance to make the material more accessible for a general audience. I would like to thank all those people I have worked with especially Olivia Harris, Brian Morris, Brian Bates and Graham Harvey. This work could not have been completed without the extensive use of other scholars' research, and I am particularly greatly indebted to all the authors mentioned in the bibliography. In the process of discussing ideas and sharing experiences, I have been helped immeasurably by Annie Keeley, Ken Rees, Gordon MacLellan, Jo Crow and Geoffrey Samuel. My thanks to them. This book is dedicated to all those asking questions about spirituality, particularly my son Adrian.

BIBLIOGRAPHY

ANKARLOO, B. and CLARK, S. 1999. Witchcraft and Magic in Europe: Ancient Greece and Rome. Philadelphia University of Pennsylvania Press.

ANKARLOO, B. and HENNINGSEN, G., eds. 1993. Early Modern European Witchcraft: Centres and Peripheries. Oxford: Clarendon.

ARROWSMITH, N., 1977. A Field Guide to the Little People. London: Pan.

ASWYN, F., 1998. Northern Mysteries and Magick: Runes, Gods and Feminine Powers. St Paul, MN: Llewellyn.

BARING, A. and CASHFORD, J., 1993. The Myth of the Goddess. London: Arkana.

BATES, B., 1996. The Way of Wyrd. London: Arrow.

BATES, B., 1996. The Wisdom of Wyrd. London: Rider.

BURTON RUSSELL, G., 1991. The historical Satan. In: J.T. Richardson, J. Best and D. Bromley, eds. The Satanism scare. New York: Aldine de Gruyter.

CAPRA, F., 1976. The Tao of Physics. London: Flamingo.

CAPRA, F., 1983. The Turning Point. London: Flamingo.

CARDOZO, A.R., 1990. A modern American witch-craze. In: M. Marwick, ed. Witchcraft and sorcery. London: Penguin.

CARR-GOMM, P., 1995. The Druid Tradition. Shaftesbury, Dorset: Element.

CARROLL, P., 1987. Liber Null and Psychonaut. York Beach, ME: Samuel Weiser.

CHAMBERLAIN, M., 1981. Old Wives Tales: their History, Remedies and Spells. London: Virago.

CLARK, E.E., 1953. Indian Legends of the Pacific Northwest. Berkeley and Los Angeles: University of California Press.

CLARK, S., 1999. Thinking with Demons. Oxford: Clarendon.

COHN, N., 1993. Europe's Inner Demons: the Demonization of Christians in Medieval Christendom. London: Pimlico.

CROWLEY, V., 1989. Wicca: the Old Religion in the New Age. Wellingborough: Aquarian.

CUNLIFFE, B., 1992. The Celtic World. London: Constable.

CUNLIFFE, B., 1997. Prehistoric Europe: an Illustrated Guide. Oxford: Open University Press.

DOUGLAS, A., 1974. The Tarot. London: Penguin.

ELIADE, M., 1974. Shamanism. Princeton: Princeton University Press.

ELIADE, M., 1975. Some observations on European witchcraft. History of Religions, 14, pp. 149–72.

EVANS-PRITCHARD, E., 1985. Witchcraft, Oracles and Magic Among the Azande. Oxford: Clarendon.

FARRAR, S. and FARRAR, J., 1991. A Witches' Bible Compleat. New York: Magickal Childe.

GARDNER, G., 1988. Witchcraft Today. New York: Magickal Childe.

GIJSWIJT-HOFSTRA, M., LEVACK, B. and PORTER, R., eds. 1999. History of Witchcraft and Magic in Europe: the Eighteenth and Nineteenth Centuries. London: Athlone Press.

GINZBURG, C., 1966. The Night Battles. Baltimore: The John Hopkins University Press.

GINZBURG, C., 1992. Deciphering the Witches' Sabbath. New York: Penguin.

GODBEER, R., 1992. The Devil's Dominion. Cambridge: Syndicate.

GRAVES, R., 1960. The Greek Myths. London: Penguin.

GRAVES, R., 1981. The White Goddess. London: Faber & Faber.

GREENWOOD, S., 2000. Magic, Witchcraft and the Otherworld. Oxford: Berg.

GUILEY, R., 1989. The Encyclopedia of Witches and Witchcraft. New York: Facts on File.

HARVEY, G., 1997. Listening People, Speaking Earth. London: Hurst & Co.

HENNINGSEN, G., 1993. The ladies from outside: an archaic pattern of the witches Sabbath. In: B. Ankarloo and G. Henninsen, eds. Early modern witchcraft. Oxford: Clarendon.

HILL, F., 1996. A Delusion of Satan: the full story of the Salem Witch Trials. London: Hamish Hamilton.

HINE, P., 1995. Condensed Chaos. Arizona: New Falcon Publications.

HINE, P., 1999. Prime Chaos. Arizona: New Falcon Publications.

HUTTON, R., 1991. The Pagan Religions of the Ancient British Isles. London: BCA.

HUTTON, R., 1996. The roots of modern paganism. In: G. Harvey and C. Hardman, eds. Paganism Today. London: Thorsons.

HUTTON, R., 1999. The Triumph of the Moon. Oxford: Oxford University Press.

JAMES, S., 1999. The Atlantic Celts: Ancient People or Modern Invention? London: British Museum Press.

JONES, P. and PENNICK, N., 1995. A History of Pagan Europe. London: Routledge.

KATZ, R., 1982. Boiling Energy: Community Healing among the Kalahari Kung. Cambridge, Ma: Harvard University Press.

KELLY, A., 1991. Crafting the Art of Magic: a History of Modern Witchcraft 1939-1964. St Paul, MN: Llewellyn.

KING, F., 1975. Magic: the Western Tradition. London: Thames & Hudson.

KING, F., 1990. Modern Ritual Magic. Bridport, Dorset: Prism.

KLANICZAY, G., 1993. Hungary: the accusations and the universe of popular magic. In: B. Ankarloo and G. Henningsen, eds. Early modem European witchcraft: centres and peripheries. Oxford: Clarendon.

KNAPPERT, J., 1995. African Mythology. London: Diamond.

La VEY, A., 1969. The Satanic Bible. New York: Avon Books.

LAMER, C., 1981. Enemies of God. London: Chatto & Windus.

LEVACK, B., 1995. The Witch-Hunt in Early Modern Europe. London: Longman.

LÉVI-STRAUSS, C., 1979. The effectiveness of symbols. In: W. Lessa and E. Vogt, eds. Reader in comparative religion: an anthropological approach. New York: Harper & Row.

LOW, M., 1999. Celtic Christianity and Nature: early Irish and Hebridean Traditions. Edinburgh: Polygon.

LUCE, J., 1973. The End of Atlantis. London: Book Club Associates.

LUCIUS APULEIUS, 1960. The Golden Ass. London: Folio Society.

LUHRMANN, T., 1989. Persuasions of the Witch's Craft. Oxford: Blackwell.

MACFARLANE, A., 1999. Witchcraft in Tudor and Stuart England: a Regional and Comparative Study. London: Routledge.

MacLELLAN, G., 1996. Dancing on the edge: shamanism in modern Britain. In: G. Harvey and C. Hardman, eds. Paganism Today. London: Thorsons.

MacLELLAN, G., 1999. Shamanism. London: Piatkus.

MACNULTY, W., 1991. Freemasonry. London: Thames & Hudson.

MAIR, L., 1969. Witchcraft. London: World University Library.

MARWICK, M., ed. 1990. Witchcraft and Sorcery. London: Penguin.

MBITI, J., 1982. African Religions and Philosophy. London: Heinemann.

McKIE, R., 2000. ApeMan: the Story of Human Evolution. London: BBC.

MORGAN, L. H., 1960. The league of the Iroquois. In: M. Mead and R. Bunzel, eds. The golden age of American anthropology. New York: George Braziller.

PENNICK, N., 1994. Practical Magic in the Northern Tradition. Loughborough: Thoth.

PIGGOT, S., 1989. The Druids. London: Thames & Hudson.

RASMUSSEN, K., 1979. A shaman's journey to the sea spirit. In: W. Lessa and E. Vogt, eds. Reader in comparative religion: an anthropological approach. New York: Harper & Row.

ROPER, L., 1994. Oedipus and the Devil: Witchcraft, Sexuality and Religion in Early Modern Europe. London: Routledge.

ROSEN, B., ed. 1969. Witchcraft. London: Edward Arnold.

SHALLCRASS, P., 1996. Druidry today. In: G. Harvey and C. Hardman, eds. Paganism Today. London: Thorsons.

SHARPE, J., 1996. Instruments of Darkness: Witchcraft in England 1550-1750. London: Penguin.

STANFORD, P., 1997. The Devil: a biography. London: Mandarin.

STARHAWK, 1982. Dreaming the Dark. Boston: Beacon.

STARHAWK, 1989. The Spiral Dance. San Francisco: Harper & Row.

STEVENS, A., 1991. On Jung. London: Penguin.

SULLIVAN, L., 1989. Hidden Truths: Magic, Alchemy and the Occult. New York: Macmillan.

SUN BEAR, WABUN WIND and CRYSALIS MULLIGAN, 1992. Dancing with the Wheel: the Medicine Wheel Workbook. New York: Fireside Books.

THOMAS, K., 1973. Religion and the Decline of Magic. London: Penguin.

TYLOR, E., 1970. Religion in Primitive Cultures. Gloucester, Ma: Peter Smith.

VALIENTE, D., 1985. Witchcraft for Tomorrow. London: Robert Hale.

WARNER, M., 1981. Joan of Arc: the Image of Female Heroism. London: Penguin.

WASHINGTON, P., 1993. Madame Blavatsky's Baboon. London: Secker & Warburg.

WILSON, C., 1989. Witches. Limpsfield: Dragon's World.

YORK, M., 1994. The Emerging Network: a Sociology of the New Age and Neo-Pagan Movements. Lanham, MD: Rowman & Littlefield.

SUGGESTED SOURCES FOR FURTHER READING

Human evolution:

C. STRINGER & R. McKIE African Exodus; the origins of modern humanity London: Pimlico 1997

The anthropological study of religion:

W. LESSA & E. VOGT Reader in Comparative Religion: an anthropological approach New York: Harper & Row 1979

B. MORRIS Anthropological Studies of Religion: an introductory text Cambridge: Cambridge University Press 1987

An anthropological study of ritual in Africa:

V. TURNER The Forest of Symbols: aspects of Ndembu ritual London: Cornell University Press 1972

Anthropological studies of spirit healing:

R. KATZ The Straight Path of the Spirit: ancestral wisdom and healing traditions in Fiji Vermont: Park Street Press

B. KAPFERER A Celebration of Demons; exorcism and aesthetics of healing in Sri Lanka 1991

Anthropological study of sorcery:

B. KAPFERER The Feast of the Sorcerer: practices of consciousness and power Chicago: University of Chicago Press 1997

Shamanism:

G. SAMUEL Civilized Shamans: Buddhism in Tibetan societies Washington: Smithsonian 1993

C. HUMPHREY with U. ONON Shamans & Elders: experience, knowledge & power among the Daur Mongols Oxford: Oxford University Press 1996

Psychological approaches to western shamanism:

S. LARSEN The Shaman's Doorway: opening imagination to power and myth Vermont: Inner Traditions International 1998

D. NOEL The Soul of Shamanism: western fantasies, imaginal realities New York: Continuum 1997

History of Western Magic:

C. SNYDER Exploring the World of King Arthur London: Thames & Hudson 2000

F. YATES Giordano Bruno & the hermetic tradition Chicago: University of Chicago Press 1991

Paganism:

S BILLINGTON & M. GREEN [eds] The Concept of the Goddess London: Routledge 1999

C. ALBANESE Nature Religion in America Chicago: University of Chicago Press 1991

S. SUTCLIFFE & M. BOWMAN [eds] Beyond the New Age: exploring alternative spirituality Edinburgh: Edinburgh University Press 2000

S. GREENWOOD Magic, Witchcraft and the Otherworld (from bibliography)

L. HUME Witchcraft and Paganism in Australia Melbourne: Melbourne University Press 1997

PICTURE ACKNOWLEDGEMENTS

AKG: p18T Evening in Aswan, Erich Lessing. p19T Osiris, Erich Lessing. p19B Day and night journey of the sun, Erich Lessing. p21B Hecate, William Blake. p23B Ossian, Francois Baron Gerard. p24T Odin. p25T Das Rheingold, Richard Wagner. p27T Zoroaster. p29BR The Sefirot Tree. p30BR Moghul Prince speaking to a Dervish. p31T Jalal ad-Din ar-Rumi. p31B Whirling Dervish, Lothar Peters. p36BR Agni, Irmgard Wagner. p37BR Pakhandi, Jean-Louis Nou. p38B Dancing Bayadere, VISIOARS. p38M Prince Siddhartha cuts off his hair, Gilles Mermet. p40T Shiva, Jean-Louis Nou. p41TM Indian Buddhist tantrist and magus, 721-c.790, Jean-Louis Nou. p41B Bhairava in the land of burning corpses, Jean-Louis Nou. p43R Figure of a goddess. p50T The Alchemists, Pietro Longhi. p53T Northern and Southern hemispheres. p52T Hipparchus. p53BR Christian-allegorical depiction of the world. Wolfgang Kilian. p54T Paracelsus. p54BL Hermes Trismegistos. Hermann tom Ring. p55TR An alchemist after staying up all night, Thomas Wijck. p61T Hansel and Gretel outside the gingerbread house, Ludwig Richter. p60T nymph, Arnold Böcklin. p62T Persephone and Hecate. p63TL Hecate, William Blake. p63B Sorceress Circe with the Companions of Odysseus that have been transformed into Animals, Alessandro Allori. p63TR Sorceress Circe, Giovanni Battista Luteri Dossi. p65T Medea with the Dagger, Anselm Feuerbach. p67T Hansel and Gretel outside the gingerbread house, Ludwig Richter. p72B Titania and Oberon. p76 The Fairytale Witch, Paula Modersohn-Becker. p77T Hobgoblins, Goya y Lucientes. p74T Persephone and Hecate. p96T. p97B Witches drawing milk from an axe handle. P103T Magic scene, Andrea Locatelli. p105B Three witches at the bedside of a sick woman. p107B Women in herb garden. p109T Witches' Kitchen, Hieronymus Francken the Elder, Erich Lessing. p110T Witch exercising her conjuration rituals. p113 Witches' Gathering, Frans Francken II, Erich Lessing. p118BR Devil conjured up from a magic circle. p119B British Library. p119T. Witches children are initiated into a Sabbath. p122B Burning witches on the market place in Guernsey. p123B A terrible story of three sorceresses of Derneburg. p125BR. p125L Satan and the birth of Sin, Johann Heinrich Füssli. p126TR Persecution of the Turlupins. p129T Knight Templars led into prison, British Library. p134T torture of suspected witch. p135T Jean Bodin. p137BR Essex Witches. p139BR Johann Calvin. p139BL Martin Luther, Lucas Cranach the Elder. p139TR Pope's selling of indulgences, Lucas Cranach the Elder. p140T Caricature of Luther's opponents. p140B Pope Alexander VI as devil. p141T In the Jaws of Hell. p141B Allegory on Luther's thesis against indulgences. p144BR Burning of witches, Paris. p145B Gilles de Rais. p147T Midwife assisting woman in labour. p147BL Affair with the devil, witches' balm…. p149B Catherine Cawches and her daughters, Guernsey. p158 Witches' dancing ground, Harz mountains, Robert Müller. p164B Socrates and disciples. p165T Atlantis. p174T Hypnotic session, Sven Richard Bergh. p180BL Knights of the Round Table. p183B Marching Infantry. p190T Pan. p192BR Artemis Ephesia, Erich Lessing. p193T Diana's Hunt, Luca Giordano. p194T Stag god Cerunnos, Erich Lessing. p234B Freyja. p235B Winter Solstice. **BRIDGEMAN ART LIBRARY:** p16B Medicine mask dance, Paul Kane. p20B The Return of Persephone, Frederic Leighton. p20T Aegeus consulting the Delphic Oracle. p21TL Circe, Wright Barker. p21TR Medea, Anthony Frederick Augustus Sandys. p23T Druid's Ceremony, Noel Halle. p25B Hermod, son of Odin, at the barred gates of Hel, pleading for the return of his brother. p26R The spirit of Samuel appearing to Saul at the house of the Witch of Endor, Salvatore Rosa. p27B Adam and Eve in Paradise, Jan Brueghel. p28T Jewish cabbalist holding a sephiroth. p28L Adam and Eve banished from Paradise, Tommaso Masaccio. p28BR Procession of the Bishop in Front of the Church of S. Ambrogio, Cosimo Rosselli. p29T St Francis of Assisi, Bonaventura Berlinghieri. p33TR Taoist weather manual. p36T Indra, the Aryan God of War seated on an elephant. p36BL Varunani. p38T Padmasana Yoga. p41TR Illustration from 'Theosophica Practica' showing the seven Chakras. p53BL Signs of the Chinese Zodiac surrounding the symbol of Yin and Yang. p52B The God Thoth. p55TL Emblematic diagram of the alchemical processes for the production of the Philosopher's Stone. p59T Three Women and Three Wolves, Eugene Grasset. p59BR Scene of Witches, Salvator Rosa. p62B Medea, Giovanni Benedetto Castiglione. p64T Ulysses and the Sirens, Herbert James Draper. p64B The Golden Fleece, Herbert James Draper. p65T Circe Pouring Poison into a Vase and Awaiting the Arrival of Ulysses, Sir Edward Burne-Jones. p65 Justice and Divine Vengeance pursuing Crime, Pierre-Paul Prud'hon. p66B The Witches in Macbeth, Alexandre Gabriel Decamps. p66T Scene from Midsummer Night's Dream, Francis Danby. p67B Macbeth and the Witches, Theodore Chasseriau. p73T A Dance around the Moon, Charles Altamont Doyle. p73B Diana the Hunter, Orazio Gentileschi. p74L Morgan le Fay, Anthony Frederick Augustus Sandys. p75 Calling shapes and beckoning shadows dire, Arthur Rackham. p77B Dancing Fairies, August Malmstrom. p84T Divination board, Heini Schneebeli. p88B Native American Shaman, Dutch School. p95R Witches' Sabbath, Francisco Jose de Goya y Lucientes. p96B The Sermon, Walter Frederick Roofe Tyndale. p98T Old Cronies, George Henry Boughton. p102B The Sorceress, Lucien Levy-Dhurmer. p104 The Witch gives (advice) as to Sir Tristram's wounds, Walter Crane. p106T Administering medicinal herbs, Polish School. p106B Fennel. p107T Doctor visits patient; an apothecary. P112BL Scene of Sorcery, David Teniers the Elder. p115BL John Dee, English School. p116T Astrological chart with Signs of the Zodiac. p117TR James I and VI of Scotland, John Decritz the Younger. p117B High Commission Court and Star Chamber, English School. p123T Many poor women imprisoned and hanged for witches, English School. p124R The hero Gilgamesh. p125T Satan binds the eyes of the Jews, Ermengald de Bezieres. p126BL Victims tortured to decide on innocence or guilt. p128T Expulsion of Albigenses from Cerlesonne. p129T Looting of Jerusalem, 1099, Jean de Courcy. p130 Judge interrogating prisoners. p131B Mary Sutton, suspected witch, being 'swum', 1612, English School. p132 Good and Evil, Andre Jacques Victor Orsel. p133 The Story of Adam and Eve, Giovanni Boccaccio. p136B Matthew Hopkins, Witchfinder General, English School. p138T John Wycliffe, English School. p138B Wycliffe appearing before the Prelates at St Paul's, English School. p145T Joan of Arc being led to her death, Isidore Patrois. p154T Landing of Pilgrims at Plymouth. p157B The Witches' Sabbath, Francisco Jose de Goya y Lucientes. p157T Magic Circle, John William Waterhouse. p162T Buddha. p162B The Annunciation, Italian School. p163M 'H' in the form of two conjurors. p163TR Alchemy master. p170T Friedrich Anton Mesmer, French School. p192BL Persephone, Anthony Frederick Augustus Sandys. p194B Pan and Psyche, Sir Edward Burne-Jones. p208T Diana, Agostino di Duccio. p218B Days of Creation, Sir Edward Burne-Jones. p218T Annunciation, Fra Angelico. p219B Angel, Sir Edward Burne-Jones. p220R Beguiling of Merlin, Sir Edward Burne-Jones. p220L Bedivere returns Excalibur to the lake, Roman du Saint Graal. p221T Last Supper, Francesco Bassano. p221B King Arthur, Lancelot and the Lady, Roman de Tristan. p222T Stonehenge, Italian School. p222B Wicker Man, Italian School. p229B Fairy Tree, Richard Doyle. p231TL Pehriska-Ruhpa, Karl Bodmer (after). p230BL Mandan Medicine man, George Catlin. p234T Odin. p238B Sir Francis Dashwood, Bartolommeo Nazari. p239TL Francois Rabelais, Eugene Delacroix. p239TR Satan Arousing the Rebel Angels, William Blake. p244 Thanatos, Jacek Malczewski. **CAMERA PRESS:** p202BL Alex Sanders, John Drysdale. p203BL. John Drysdale. p203TL. John Drysdale. p203TR John Hedgecoe. **CHRISTINE OSBORNE PICTURES:** p190B Secret Wicca Ritual. p191T Sacred Goddess Altar. p201TL Goddess. p203BR Artefacts used in Wicca ceremonies. p211B Sacred rites: Goddess Festival, Glastonbury 2000. p212T Starhawk. p212B Sacred spiral dance. p213 'Black madonna'. p230T Drumming class. p231TR Dream rings. **COLLECTIONS:** p22T Castlerigg Stone Circle, Cumbria, Gary Smith. **CORBIS:** p12B Wolfgang Kaehler. p14T David Muench. p15BR The Purcell Team. p17BR Earl and Nazima Kowall. p35BL. p35BR Earl and Nazima Kowall. p39T & 39B Michael Freeman. p50L Sir James George Frazer. p58T Lindsay Hebberd. p58B Paul Almasy. p66T Robert Estall. p80T Peter Johnson. p90T. p159T & 159B Bettmann. p196B Raymond Gehman. p228T People dancing in the Findhorn Foundation, Sandro Vannini. p229T Musicians of the Paul Winter Consort, Roger Ressmeyer. p239B La Vey conducts a devilish service, Bettmann. p241B Charles Manson, Bettmann. **E.T.ARCHIVE:** p16T Aaron's rod as serpent devouring rods or serpents of pharaoh's magicians to release Israelites. p17T Fresco, depicting a traveller and a sorceress. p17BL Fresco of Aztec priest praying. p24B Viking memorial picture stone. p32T Sakgamuni, Confucius and Lao Tzu. p55B The four elements, zodiac signs and alchemical symbols. p60B Centaur Chiron and Hermes, Saverio Altamura. p70T Men transformed into wolves in ferocious flying hunt. p98BL The Witch from Gravenbroch. p101T Magic circle of a witch. p103B Fairies and Elves on their nightly ritual dance. p108B Sorcerers and witches on Sabbath. p112BR Witches Sabbath, Frans Francken. p124BL Gilgamesh between two demi gods. p134B Frontispiece from Compendium Malleficarum, Francesco Guazzo. p163TM Nostradamus. p164T Mosaic of Triumph of Poseidon and wife. p169T Candidate for Master, Freemasonry. p169B Frontispiece to History of Freemasonry.

p178B King Of Woods, Frieda Harris. p181TL Quetzacoatl. p183T Inside the Temple of the Grail, W Hauschild. p208B French Diana Bathing, Francois Boucher. p236BR Rune stone. **FORTEAN PICTURE LIBRARY:** p22B St Beuno's Well, Janet and Colin Ford. p54BR Two alchemists at work. p61B Lucius witnesses a witch rubbing unguent on to her body in order to fly. p127T Torture to obtain a confession. p131T Ducking a Witch. p135B Instruments of torture. p136T Witches create a storm at sea. p143T North Berwick coven. p144T Witch Guillemette being stripped for torture. p147BR Torture of Herr Lirtzen. p148TR Mother Agnes Waterhouse. p149T Judith Philips. p166M Tarot cards: Waite pack. p166BL Eliphas Levi. p171TL Madame Blavatsky. p173R Samuel Liddell MacGregor Mathers. p179TR Blood on the Moon, Austin Osman Spare. p179TL Resurrection of Zoroaster, Austin Osman Spare. p186B White witchcraft altar, Kevin Carlyon. p188T Gerald Gardner, Raymond Buckland. p191BL Drawing down the moon. p196T Winter Solstice ritual, Kevin Carlyon. p197TL Kevin Carlyon binding new initiates, Kevin Carlyon. p201B Wiccan initiation, Raymond Buckland. p204T Raymond Buckland. p204B Priest enters the Temple, Raymond Buckland. p205T Samhain ceremony, Raymond Buckland. p205B Wiccan High Priest and High Priestess, Raymond Buckland. p207BR Title page of Leland's Aradia. p207T Cornish witches invoking the 'owlman', Anthony Shiels. p209T Cornish witch Cait Sidh. p209B Witches dancing at midnight. p223B Emma Restall-Orr, Kevin Carlyon. p225T Arch-Druid at Avebury, Clive Odinson. p225B Druids at Winter Solstice, Stonehenge, Clive Odinson. p226BR Edgar Cayce Foundation, Klaus Aarsleff. p227T Fountain International members, Paul Broadhurst. p227B Tourist doing Tai Chi, Klaus Aarsleff. p226BL Celtic music at Roughtor, Paul Broadhurst. p228BL Eileen Caddy, Dr Elmar R Gruber. p228BR Findhorn meditation room, Tony Healy. p232B Man meditating at Medicine Wheel, Arizona, Klaus Aarsleff. p237TL Rune stones, Klaus Aarsleff. **SUSAN GREENWOOD:** p195(all) owl mask, plaque and Bubo made by Maria Strutz, p233TR, p245(all). **HULTON PICTURE LIBRARY:** p90B Lewis H Morgan. p111B Mother Shipton's favourite mode of travelling. p166TR AE Waite. p170BL Helena Petrovna Blavatsky. p170BR Henry Steel Olcott. p171TR Anne Besant. p171B Krishnamurti with Annie Besant. p172BR Miss Horniman. p175TR Garb of the Golden Dawn, A Crowley. p175BL Alan Bennett. p176BM Aleister Crowley in robes of Golden Dawn. p176TR Aleister Crowley. p177BL Self-portrait-Aleister Crowley. p177TR Certificate acknowledging Crowley as member of High Order of Freemasons. p178T Aleister Crowley, Fosco Maraini. p189B Margaret Murray. p210T Jules Michelet. p240B Jayne Mansfield, Keystone Press Agency. p242BR Sex pistols. p242BL Austin Spare, Bert Hardy. **HUTCHISON LIBRARY:** p13T Shaman, Andrey Zvoznikov. p34T Shinto Priest, R Ian Lloyd. p37TL Holy Man Chanting a Mantra, Michael MacIntyre. p37TM Ancient Indian Coin depicting Goddess Kali, Goycoolea. p42BL Traditional Zulu diviner. p43L Witch doctor, Victoria Falls, Zimbabwe, Mary Jelliffe. p44BR Witch doctor with juju fetishes, Harvey. p45TR Casting out devils. P46B Ancestor worship ceremony, Michael MacIntyre. p47BR Fetishes for sale, Mary Jelliffe. p79TL Potent juju symbols. p81 Ritual cleansing by smoking of baby after birth, John Ryle. p82T Shaman diviner, John Ryle. p82B Tribal chief. p83T Shilluk people making thatched roof for mud hut. p83B Pende festival dancers, Michael MacIntyre. p84B Storytelling, Dinka tribe, Sarah Errington. p85B Dodoth women, Sarah Errington. p86T Traditional healer, Ingrid Hudson. p87T xylophone players, John Ryle. Images: p33L The Tai Chi symbol. p97T Curse doll. p107M Zodiac with plants and herbs. p110BR Mother Shipton casting a horoscope. p114T Hermaphrodite. p114B Macrocosmus Schema of Great World. p165ML Ya-uli. p165BR Atlantean Mystery Pyramid. p167B Tree of Life. p167TR Cabbala, Great Countenance. p174T Rosicrucian – reincarnation. p174B Rosicrucian Rosy Cross. p174BL Order of Pectoral. p174BM Pectoral Cross. p174BR Symbol used in Hermes Lodge of Stella Matutina. p206T Drawing down the moon. p231B Shamanistic drum. p238T Devils pact. p240T Anton La Vey. p241TR Woman devil. James Wood: p233BR Modern shaman. **MARK FIENNES:** p192T Diana, Frans Floris. **MARY EVANS PICTURE LIBRARY:** p42BR Female witch doctor of the Usumbura religion, of East Africa. p50BR Kaffir witch doctor discovers unfavourable signs. p51T Bronislaw Malinowski in the Trobriand Islands. p51B Swaziland witch-doctor goes round the village 'smelling' for the sorceror. p61T The Golden Ass. p68T Witches dine with the devil, dance round the gallows… . p68B Witches with their familiars. p69T A sabbat in the Basque country. p69B Mother Chattox rides to Pendle Hill. p100 Witch, accompanied by beggar and fool. p101B La sorciere des Vosges. p102T Jennet urges her cat, Tib, to attack her victim. p105T French village wise woman. p110BL Mother Shipton with familiar. p111T Mother Shipton admonishes Cardinal Wolsey. p112T Isobel Gowdie tells how she and her companions were visited by 'Black John'. p142B La Murqui, witchfinder, indicates marks that prove a pact with Satan. p143B Justice Chamber, Valenciennes. p146BL The 'Malefitz Haus'. p146T Konrad von Marburg sends another victim to the torture chamber and stake. p150T Norwegian 'huldre'. p150B Scandinavian witches call up monsters. p151T Swedish witches. p151B Finnish witches sell favourable winds to sailors. p172T William Butler Yeats. p172BL Maud Gonne. p179B Symbolic painting for Crowley's Temple of the A.A, JFC Fuller. p181M Carl Gustav Jung. p180BR The Passing of Arthur. p210B Witchcraft in flight. p211T Susan B Anthony. p224T Druid priestess. p224B Druids of Anglesey. p241TL Ceremonial seal designed by A Crowley. **MICK SHARP PHOTOGRAPHY:** p186T Modern offerings at prehistoric rock carvings. p187T Tintagel Castle. p187B Madron Well. p199T Bethesda Woods. p226T Sunset from Snowdon summit. **NORMAN BANCROFT HUNT:** p88TR Portrait of Black Elk, Oglala Sioux. **PANOS PICTURES:** p10B Sunrise at Xakanaxa, inside Moremi Game Reserve on the Okavango Delta, Botswana, Pietro Cenini. p10T Victoria Falls, Zimbabwe, Neil Cooper. p11 South eastern wall of Cho-Oyu (8201m) Kumbu, Nepal, JC Callow. p15BL Tashiparkhel Tibetan camp, Wangchuck, Tibetan shaman wearing special ringer hat for trances, Alison Wright. p30T Faith healer tapes up toes and fingers to 'lock in' a djin which possesses the patient. JC Tordai. p30BL Herbalist's souq in the old Medina. Jeremy Horner. p32B Pilgrims burning spirit money at the temple of the Spirits' retreat, Hangzhou, Sandrine Rousseau. p34B Shamanic ritual on a boat, Jean-Léo Dugast. p35T wooden good luck charms at a Shinto in Kyoto, J Holmes. p42T Ritual killing of a cow, Betty Press. p44BL Kikuyu witch doctor, Kenya. Stuart Hollis. p45TL Traditional healer's medicines, David Reed. p45B Traditional cure for migraine in Mali, Neil Cooper. p47T Zangbeto (village guardian) at voodoo festival, Caroline Penn. p47BL Voodoo initiates in 'kapame', Caroline Penn. p78L Traditional medicines, Giacomo Pirozzi. p78T Akodessewa market in Lome, Anders Gunnartz. p86B Circumcision dance, Ray Wood. p87B Fetish priest with attendants, Caroline Penn. **PAPILIO PHOTOGRAPHIC:** p15TR Arctic Wolf. **PETER NEWARK'S AMERICAN PICTURES:** p89TL Native American Shaman of the Assiniboin tribe, Edward Curtis. p91B Shaman blows pollen over pueblo shrine. p154B Arresting a suspected witch, Howard Pyle. p155L Cotton Mather. p155T Salem. p155BR Girl 'bewitched' at trial. **PETER NEWARK'S HISTORICAL PICTURES:** p59L Witches brewing up a hailstorm, Ulrich Molitor. p70B Witches, cats and rats. p94L Sorcery, AB Frost. p94R Witches concocting flying ointment, Hans Baldung Grien. p108T Devil rides off with Witch. p109B Demon carrying off child. p115TR Queen Elizabeth I, Isaac Oliver. p124M Satan gives images to witches to use as charms. p142T Bamberg witch trials, Bavaria. p148B Christian Bowman burned at the stake. p148TL English Witch Anne Turner. p153B Vlad the Impaler. p156B Faustus. Peter Newark's Military Pictures: p128B Expedition embarking for a crusade. p144BL Joan of Arc. p152 Maria Theresa. p153T Dracula. **PETER NEWARK'S PICTURES:** p118T Page of symbols. p118BL Page of symbols 'the seales of the earth'. p119TL Trick bodkins. p122T Man suspected of sorcery. p127BL Waldenses fleeing from their burning village. p127BR Early Papal Crusade against the Waldenses. p137TL Witch sits with devils. p156T Jane Wenham. RA Gilbert: W Wynn Westcott. p175BM Samuel and Mina Mathers. **REX FEATURES:** p184. p189T Wicker Man, Lesley Smith. p227TR James Lovelock. p236T May Day, N Ireland, Lesley Smith. **ROBERT ESTALL PHOTO LIBRARY:** p13B Bushman dancing, David Coulson. p85T Himba women, Namibia, Angela Fisher/Carol Beckwith. **SALLY GRIFFYN:** p200T Doreen Valiente. p217B. **SCALA:** p89B Interior view of the Medicine Lodge, George Catlin. p99 Rissa di giocatori, Pieter il Giovane Bruegel. **SOCIETY OF THE INNER LIGHT:** p180T Dion Fortune. p182B Dion Fortune. **TONY STONE IMAGES:** p198T Water droplet on pink heather, Charles Krebs. **WELLCOME LIBRARY:** p48B A shaman or medicine man with extensive body painting. **WERNER FORMAN ARCHIVE:** p12T. p14BL. p14BR. p18B Detail from coffin of Nespawershepi. p26L Darius I hunts lions from his chariot in a conventional southern Mesopotamian landscape. p33BR An 'immortal' playing a flute in the Tao paradise. P40BR Shiva and Shakti. p40BL Linga, a phallus, symbol of the god Lord Shiva. p44T Senufo kunugbaha mask used in anti-witchcraft rites. p46T A Fon bocio figure. p48TL Bark painting depicting a Wandjina. p48TR A churinga. p49T Petroglyph incised in the rock at an Aboriginal sacred site. p49BL Bark painting depicting three spirit figures. p49BR Aboriginal bark painting of two crocodiles. p79B Shrine of an Ashanti spirit medium. p79TR Stool shrine associated with the spirit of the tree. p80B Western Pende divination instrument, 'Gulukoshi'. p88M Medicine pipe. p89TR Sun Dance effigi doll. p91T Chest lid. p116BL Crystal ball of Dr John Dee. p116BM Obsidian mirror once belonging to Dr Dee. p198-199B Ring Of Brodgar. p235T Tapestry detail.

NOTES

These references give the sources for direct and indirect quotes within the text.

p 23 CUNLIFFE, B., 1992. The Celtic World. London: Constable.

p 29 SORRELL, R., 1988. St Francis of Assisi and Nature. Oxford: OUP.

p 31 HUXLEY, A., 1994. The Perennial Philosophy. London: Flamingo.

p 33 PALMER, M., 1996. The Book of Chuang Tzu. London: Penguin.

pp 34–35 KENDALL, L., 1988. The Life and Hard Times of a Korean Shaman. Honolulu: University of Hawaii Press.

p 43 KNAPPERT, J., 1995. African Mythology. London: Diamond.

p 49 BOURKE, JOHNSON and WHITE, 1980. Before the Invasion: Aboriginal Life to 1788. Oxford: OUP.

p 54 GOODRICK-CLARKE, N., 1990. Paracelsus: essential readings. Wellingborough: Aquarian.

p 65 COHN, N., 1993. Europe's Inner Demons: the Demonization of Christians in Medieval Christendom. London: Pimlico.

pp 68–69 ARROWSMITH, N., 1977. A Field Guide to the Little People. London: Pan.

p 70 HENNINGSEN, G., 1993. The ladies from outside: an archaic pattern of the witches Sabbath. In: B. Ankarloo and G. Henningsen, eds. Early Modern European Witchcraft: Oxford: Clarendon.

p 73 LUCIUS APULEIUS, 1960. The Golden Ass. London: Folio Society.

p 77 BARING, A. and CASHFORD, J., 1993. The Myth of the Goddess. London: Arkana.

p 85 EVANS-PRITCHARD, E., 1985. Witchcraft, Oracles and Magic Among the Azande. Oxford: Clarendon.

p 88 NEIHARDT, J.G., 1995. Black Elk Speaks: being the Life Story of a Holy Man of the Oglala Sioux. Lincoln, NE: University of Nebraska Press.

p 97 MACFARLANE, A., 1999. Witchcraft in Tudor and Stuart England: a Regional and Comparative Study. London: Routledge.

p 99 MACFARLANE, A., 1999. Witchcraft in Tudor and Stuart England: a Regional and Comparative Study. London: Routledge.

p 105 CHAMBERLAIN, M., 1981. Old Wives Tales: their History, Remedies and Spells. London: Virago.

p 106 CHAMBERLAIN, M., 1981. Old Wives Tales: their History, Remedies and Spells. London: Virago.

p 107 CHAMBERLAIN, M., 1981. Old Wives Tales: their History, Remedies and Spells. London: Virago.

pp 116–117 ROSEN, B., ed. 1969. Witchcraft. London: Edward Arnold.

pp 118–119 ROSEN, B., ed. 1969. Witchcraft. London: Edward Arnold.

p 124 SANDARS, N.K., ed. 1960. The Epic of Gilgamesh. London: Penguin.

p 126 COHN, N., 1993. Europe's Inner Demons: the Demonization of Christians in Medieval Christendom. London: Pimlico.

p 130 CLARK, S., 1999. Thinking with Demons. Oxford: Clarendon.

p 133 KRAMER, H. and SPRENGER, J., 1971. Malleus Maleficarum. Transl. by Montague Summers c.1486. New York: Dover.

p 147 ROPER, L., 1994. Oedipus and the Devil: Witchcraft, Sexuality and Religion in Early Modern Europe. London: Routledge.

p 149 ROSEN, B., ed. 1969. Witchcraft. London: Edward Arnold.

p 149 LAMER, C., 1981. Enemies of God. London: Chatto & Windus.

p 153 ANKARLOO, B. and HENNINGSEN, G., eds. 1993. Early Modern European Witchcraft: Centres and Peripheries. Oxford: Clarendon.

pp 154–155 GODBEER, R., 1992. The Devil's Dominion. Cambridge: Syndicate.

p 165 LUCE, J., 1973. The End of Atlantis. London: Book Club Associates.

p 167 WANG, R., 1983. The Qabalistic Tarot. York Beach, Maine: Samuel Weiser.

p 168 KING, F., 1990. Modern Ritual Magic. Bridport, Dorset: Prism.

p 178 CROWLEY, A., 1991. Magick in Theory and Practice. Secaucus, NJ: Castle.

p 183 FORTUNE, D., 1989. The Sea Priestess. Wellingborough: Aquarian.

p 190 GARDNER, G., 1988. Witchcraft Today. New York: Magickal Childe.

p 194 GADON, E., 1990. The Once and Future Goddess. Wellingborough: Aquarian.

p 201 KELLY, A., 1991. Crafting the Art of Magic: a History of Modern Witchcraft 1939–1964. St Paul, MN: Llewellyn.

p 205 BUCKLAND, R., 1989. The Complete Book of Saxon Witchcraft. York Beach, Maine: Samuel Weiser.

p 236 WILLIS, T., 1986. Discover Runes. London: Harper Collins.

p 237 PENNICK, N., 1994. Practical Magic in the Northern Tradition. Loughborough: Thoth.

p 240 La VEY, A., 1969. The Satanic Bible. New York: Avon Books.

p 244 HINE, P., 1995. Condensed Chaos. Arizona: New Falcon Publications.

p 244 CARROLL, P., 1987. Liber Null and Psychonaut. York Beach, ME: Samuel Weiser.

INDEX

Italics refer to picture captions.